Engage: Exploring Nonviolent Living is a revision and expansion
of Pace e Bene's *From Violence To Wholeness* program.
Here is what people have said about this process·

I'm very fired up after the one-day nonviolence workshop…and hope to do more with Pace e Bene.…I've been telling everyone I know about it and have surely become either a crushing bore or a bearer of hope.

LIA OLSON

First, it is inclusive. Because it is multi-disciplined, it recognizes that people learn in different ways. In this way, the curriculum has a way to reach everyone. Second, it provides a safe environment where relationships can be discovered. In safety, people are accepted and therefore are more willing to accept the differences between themselves and others. Third, *FVTW* asks that participants move from the philosophical to the practical, providing both tools and experiences that participants can use outside of the classroom environment.

DENISE TORRES

My weekend at the Pace e Bene retreat was rich and intimate. In a short period of time, I got to know a diverse group of people committed to healing themselves, their communities, and the world. Analytically, I knew I left the weekend with new tools and skills. When I co-facilitated a workshop one week later, however, I was struck by how much the training had helped me mature my perspectives about facilitation and deepened my confidence. In my opinion, there were three components of the training that I most drew from: sharing, diversity, and teamwork. …The retreat was only a few days. And I know I will draw from it for years to come.

BRYAN NEUBERG

In one short year since a few of us met the workbook on a retreat and determined to "bring it home" to others, the essential insights and opportunities of the program have become our own. Not only does *"From Violence to Wholeness"* enrich the vital small group of us who have become "sisters and brothers," it also has led to events and plans for worship and mission that will shape our congregation and reach our larger community.

REV. JOHN AUER

The process has become integrated into my life and my understanding of relationships. It has helped me deepen my practice and being of who I am. It helped me begin a more articulated journey of what has always been in my consciousness. I always had certain values but not practiced ways of living those values out and being intentional about them.

EMILY LIN

This training helped me see and recognize the piece of truth that we all possess.

JOI MORTON-WILEY

The Pace e Bene facilitator retreat was a wonderful opportunity to gather together and discuss practical ways of healing the violence that plagues our communities, relationships, ecosystem and earth. Pace e Bene presents the most comprehensive approach to peace I have ever encountered, as it embraces the physical, spiritual and emotional elements of humanity torn in division. It further seeks to reconcile this division …This weekend revealed that while our world faces brokenness on many levels, it also holds the capacity to heal.

SHAHLA MOUSAVI

Continuing the Journey From Violence to Wholeness …

Engage:

Exploring
Nonviolent Living

*a study program
for learning, practicing, and experimenting
with the power of creative nonviolence
to transform our lives and our world*

Laura Slattery, Ken Butigan, Veronica Pelicaric, and Ken Preston-Pile

Pace e Bene Press • Oakland, California, USA • 2005

For information, address Pace e Bene, 1420 W. Bartlett Ave., Las Vegas, NV 89106, USA.

ISBN: 0-9669783-1-5

Library of Congress Cataloging-in-Publication Data

Engage: Exploring Nonviolent Living: a study program for learning, practicing, and experimenting with the power of creative nonviolence to transform ourselves and our world / by Laura Slattery, Ken Butigan, Veronica Pelicaric, and Ken Preston-Pile.
Includes bibliographical references.
ISBN 0-9669783-1-5
1. Exploring Nonviolent Power. 2. Structural Violence and Nonviolent Power. 3. Putting Nonviolent Power into Action. 4. Resources.

Design and layout: Chris McGee, Barking Dog Design, *barkingdogdesign@cox.net*

Notice: The materials presented in this book are resources for exploring nonviolent living. How these resources are employed is the responsibility of the readers and program participants. Pace e Bene Nonviolence Service does not accept responsibility for the way these materials are presented and used.

Pace e Bene Nonviolence Service

Pace e Bene (pronounced *pah-chay bay-nay*) means "peace and all good" in Italian. St. Francis of Assisi used this expression as a greeting and as a means of proclaiming the way of peace in the midst of a violent world.

Pace e Bene Nonviolence Service is based in Las Vegas, Nevada, with offices and program staff in Oakland, California; Chicago, Illinois; Montreal, Quebec, Canada; Perth, Western Australia, Australia; and a growing network of collaborators in North and South America. Pace e Bene offers resources to assist in the journey of personal and social transformation, such as retreats, workshops, presentations, classes, and a variety of publications, including *The Wolf*, its quarterly newsletter.

Pace e Bene's staff and animating group engage in nonviolent action and work with a wide range of nonviolent movements for justice and peace. We are available to lead one-day and weekend *Engage: Exploring Nonviolent Living* Workshops and the weekend *Engage: Exploring Nonviolent Living* Facilitator's Workshop in local communities.

Nevada Office
1420 W. Bartlett Ave., Las Vegas, NV 89106
Phone & Fax: (702) 648-2281
www.paceebene.org; paceebene@paceebene.org

California Office
2501 Harrison St., Oakland, CA 94612
Phone: (510) 268-8765 Fax: (510) 268-8799
pbcal@paceebene.org

We are grateful for permission to use copyrighted materials from the following publishing companies and individuals:

Jo Clare Hartsig, "Shine on in Montana." Reprinted by permission of the Fellowship of Reconciliation. Alexandr Solzhenitzyn, "If only it were so simple…" from the *Gulag Archipelago 1918-1956*, Abridged, by Aleksandr I. Solzhenitsyn. Parts I-IV translated by Thomas P. Whitney. Parts V-VII translated by

Harry Willetts. Abridged by Edward E. Ericson, Jr. Copyright © 1985 by the Russian Social Fund. Reprinted by permission of HarperCollins.

Sue Monk Kidd, "That's How I Like to See a Woman," excerpted from *The Dance of the Dissident Daughter* (Harper Collins, 1996). Reprinted by permission of HarperCollins Publishers, Inc.

Jerry Large, "The Costs of a Violent Society" *Seattle Times*, (Thu, 15 April, 2004 – Fourth edition ROP Northwest Life – Page C1). Reprinted with the permission of the *Seattle Times*.

Catherine Ingram, "There is so much focus on the distinction …" by Thich Nhat Hanh – Reprinted from *In the Footsteps of Gandhi: Conversations with Spiritual Social Activists* (Berkeley: Parallax Press, 1990) with permission of Parallax Press, Berkeley, California.

Alice Walker, "I believe war is a weapon of persons...", excerpt from *Sent by Earth: A Message from the Grandmother Spirit After the Bombing of the World Trade Center and the Pentagon* (Canada: Seven Stories Press, 2001) pg. 17. Reprinted with permission of the publisher.

Miki Kashtan of Bay Area Nonviolent Communication, Definition of Nonviolence. Printed with permission of author.

John Dear, "Definition of Nonviolence" from *Forgetting Who We Are, Disarming the Heart: Toward a Vow of Nonviolence* (Paulist Press, 1987). Permission granted by the author.

Cynthia Stateman, "Soul Force." Permission granted by the author.

UNESCO's "The Seville Statement" – UNESCO Culture of Peace: Programme 7, Place de Fontenoy, 75352 PARIS 07 SP FRANCE. Adopted by the UNESCO General Conference at its 25 session, Copyright UNESCO 1989, reproduced with permission.

Walter Wink, "Popeye and the Violence System" excerpted from *Engaging the Powers: Discernment and Resistance in a World of Domination* (Minneapolis, MN: Fortress Press, 1992). Reprinted by permission from *Engaging the Powers* by Walter Wink copyright © 1992 Augsburg Fortress.

Sam Keen, "The Enemy Maker" from *Faces of the Enemy* (Olympic Marketing Corporation, 1986). Permission granted by the author.

Shelley Douglass, "The Power of Non-cooperation." Permission granted by author.

Michael Nagler, "Story of Karen Ridd" in *The Search for a Nonviolent Future: A Promise of Peace for Ourselves, Our Families, and Our World* (Inner Ocean, Maui, 2004). Permission granted by publisher. Definition of Nonviolence, from class notes. Permission granted by author.

Sharon Ellison "Communication: An Introduction to a Historical Model and to the New Powerful, Non-Defensive Communication Model." Permission granted by author.

Martin Luther King, Jr., Various quotes reprinted by arrangement with the Estate of Martin Luther King, JR, c/o Writers House as agent for the proprietor, New York, NY.

Angie O'Gorman, "Love your enemies…wanting wholeness and well-being for those who may be broken…" in "Defense Through Disarmament" in *The Universe Bends Toward Justice: A Reader on Christian Nonviolence in the U.S.* (Philadelphia: New Society Publishers, 1990), pg. 242. Reprinted by permission of the author.

Pierre Marchand, "The essence of nonviolence is understanding and compassion, so when you cultivate understanding and compassion…" in an article "Cultivating the Flower of Nonviolence: An Interview with Thich Nhat Hanh" for F*ellowship Magazine* (*Ja*n/Feb. 1999). Reprinted with permission of *Fellowship*.

Thich Nhat Hanh, "Compassion" excerpted from *Peace is Every Step* (New York: Bantam Books, 1991). Used by permission of Bantam Books, a division of Random House, Inc.

Veronica Pelicaric and Leonor Andrade, "Learning a New Dance – A story from Venezuela." Permission granted by authors.

Askari Mohammad, "Romaine Patterson's Angel's Wings," by for Time Classroom, *http://www.time.com/time/classroom/laramie/qa_patterson.html; The Bear Facts*, Alief-Hastings High School, Alief, Texas; For TIME Classroom. Permission pending

Heidi Kiran Mehta, adaptation of "Anti-Racist Glossary." Used with permission of the author.

Bahia Asante Cabral, Margo Adair, and William Aal, Definition of "Internalized Privilege," from *Tools for Change*. Used with permission of the authors.

Antonia Darder, " Dominant Culture, " exerpted from Cultlure and Power in the classroom: A Critical Foundation for Bicultural Education, 1991. Reprinted with permission of Greenwood Publishing.

Starhawk, "Three Forms of Power," excerpted from *Truth or Dare: Encounters with Power, Authority and Mystery* (HarperSanFrancisco, 1989). Reprinted by permission of HarperCollins Publishers, Inc.

Cynthia Kaufman, "What's a Doll to You." An excerpt from *Ideas for Action – Relevant Theory for Radical Change* (South End Press, 2003) pp. 121,129. Reprinted with permission of South End Press.

The Exchange Project, Peace Development Fund, Definition of "Privileges." Reprinted with permission of the Peace Development Fund.

Cesar Chavez, "Letter from Delano" Copyright 1969 *Christian Century*. Reprinted by permission from the April 23, 1969, issue of the *Christian Century*. Subscriptions: $49/yr. from P.O. Box 378, Mt Morris, IL 61054. 1-800-208-2097.

Cynthia Stateman, "Townies vs. Outsiders." Used with permission of the author.

Scott Peck, "Stages of Community Building," from *A Different Drum: Community Making and Peace* (New York: Adult Publishing Group, 1978). Reprinted with the permission of Simon and Schuster.

Leonard Desroches, excerpt from *Allow the Water: Anger, Fear, Power, Work, Sexuality, Community and the Spirituality and Practice of Nonviolence*. Used with permission of the author.

Christian Smith, "The Birth of Sanctuary" excerpted from *Resisting Reagan: The U.S. Central America Peace Movement* (Chicago: University. of Chicago Press; 1996) Reprinted with permission of The University of Chicago Press.

Robert J. Burrowes, "The Political Objective and Strategic Goal of Nonviolent Actions" excerpted from *Nonviolence Today* 48, Jan/Feb 1996, Fellowship of Reconciliation. Permission granted by Fellowship of Reconciliation.

Rosemary Lynch and Alain Richard, "The Decalogue for a Spirituality of Nonviolence." Reprinted with permission of the authors.

Christian Smith, "History is made by people…" in *Resisting Reagan: The U.S. Central America Peace Movement* (Chicago: Univ. of Chicago Press; 1996), pg. 87. Reprinted with permission of the University of Chicago Press.

Rainer Maria Rilke, "I would like to beg you to have patience with everything…" in *Letters to a Young Poet*, 1903 (translated: Stephen Mitchell. New York: Random House, 1984). Reprinted by permission of Random House, Inc.

Alice Walker, "There is always a moment in any kind of struggle…." From *Anything We Love Can be Saved: A writer's Activism*, Reprinted by permission of by Random House, Inc.

John Evaristo Flores, "The Story of Roberto Morales." Reprinted with permission of author.

Bill Moyer, "Eight Stages of Successful Social Movements", "Principles of Successful Social Movements." Reprinted by permission of the author.

WETA, *Freedom in Our Lifetime: South Africa, 1984-1986*. This is a segment of *A Force More Powerful*, a six-part series broadcast on Public Broadcasting System. For more information: *www.pbs.org/weta/forcemorepowerful/series/*. Reprinted with permission of WETA.

Bob Irwin and Gordon Faison, "The Dynamics of Nonviolent Action" excerpted from "Why Nonviolence"; edited by David H. Albert in 1978; Revised December 1983 by Bob Irwin; Scanned and adapted in 2001 by Peter Woodrow; Prepared for and posted on the Web by Randy Schutt, September 2002. Permission granted by author.

Cesar Chavez, "Farmer Workers' Prayer." Permission granted by the Cesar E. Chavez Foundation.

Starhawk, "On Being Community" excerpted from *Dreaming the Dark: Magic, Sex, and Politics* (Boston: Beacon Press; 1997) permission pending

El Grupo Affinity Group, "Loving the Police Out of the Intersection." Permission granted by the group to use their story.

Robert Fulghum, "The Story of Vedran Smailovic" Excerpted from *Maybe (Maybe Not): Second Thoughts From a Secret Life* (New York: Villard Books, 1993). Used by permission of Villard Books, a division of Random House.

Bill Cane, "Circles." Adapted from *Universal Church: Circles of Faith, Circles of Hope* (Orbis Books). Permission granted by author.

Bill Moyer, "Seven Strategic Assumptions of Successful Social Movements." Permission granted by author.

Servicio, Paz y Justicia, "Preparing for Nonviolence" excerpted from *Relentless Persistence: Nonviolent Action in Latin America* (New Society Publishers, 1991). Translated from the Portuguese by Phil McManus. Used with permission of the author.

David Albert, "Rice Bags Defeat Nukes" in *People Power: Applying Nonviolence Theory*, pg. 43 from War Resisters League (WRL) 2002 calendar (end of Apr, May). Used with permission of WRL.

Mulford Q. Sibley, ed. "2000 Year Old Example of Nonviolent Resistance" in *The Quiet Battle: Writings on the Theory and Practice of Non-Violent Resistance*, War Resisters League Calendar. Used with permission of WRL.

Barbara Deming, "Two Hands" and quote: "can put more pressure on the antagonist for whom we show human concern…." *On Revolution and Equilibrium* (War Resisters League, 1990). Used with permission of WRL.

Jonathan Schell, "Before a Drop of Blood Was Shed," excerpted from *The Unconquerable World: Power, Nonviolence, and the Will of the People* (Metropolitan Books, 2003).

After considerable effort, the publisher has been unable to contact the copyright holder of the items listed below to see if any permissions are required. No infringements whatsoever are intended, and the use of these texts is gratefully acknowledged.

Mzwakhe Mbuli, "Now is the Time." From album *Change is Pain* (Rounder Select, 1987).

Usman Farman, "Brother Grab my Hand." Found on internet.

Lilla Watson, "If you have come to help me . . ." quote.

Sara Marand, "The Spirit of the Redwoods" interview with Julia Butterfly Hill, excerpted from *Spirit of the Redwoods: An Interview with Julia "Butterfly" Hill*, with thanks to Maerian Morris and Luna Media Services.

"Working Women" excerpted from *http://www.amazoncastle.com/feminism/myths.shtml*.

Pam McAllister, "What has drawn me most strongly …" excerpted from *You Can't Kill the Spirit: Stories of Women and Nonviolence* (New Society Publishers, 1988).

Arnold Mindell, Ph.D., Definition of "Rank," from *Sitting in the Fire: Large Group Transformation Using Conflict and Diversity* (Lao Tse Press, Portland, OR, 1995).

Johan Galtung, adaptation of "Structural violence" definition.

Studs Terkel, "Why I Quit the Klan: An Interview with CP Ellis." in *American Dreams: Lost and Found* (New York: New Press, 1999).

Ron Chisom & Michad Washington, Definition of "Power" in *Undoing Racism: A Philosophy of International Social Change* (People's Institute Press, 2nd ed, 1997).

TABLE OF CONTENTS

The *Engage* Study Program is dedicated to the
many women and men throughout the world whose
examples of faith, love, and nonviolent commitment have
illuminated the journey of becoming more deeply human.

Introduction:

Exploring
Nonviolent Living:
The Engage Study Program

INTRODUCTION: **Exploring Nonviolent Living**

Welcome to the *Engage* Study Program. This twelve-part study and action program offers participants a wide variety of principles, stories, exercises, and readings for learning, practicing, and experimenting with the power of creative nonviolence for personal and social transformation. We invite you to join with others and embark on this exploration of, and experimentation with, nonviolence.

THE NEED FOR SKILLS FOR PERSONAL AND SOCIAL CHANGE

Every day, throughout the world people face the daunting challenge and consequences of violence and injustice. Some people confront this violence with violence. Others remain passive in the face of this destructiveness. Neither of these approaches, in our estimation, lead to long-term solutions because they often fail to address the root causes of violence or stop the cycle of destruction, resentment, and retaliation that violence and injustice create.

There are a growing number of people around the world, however, who are using the more effective approach of creative nonviolence, the subject of our study program, to bring about change in their societies. Some current examples include the bringing down of Serbian president Slobodan Milosevic in 2000, the frustrated electoral fraud and restored democracy in the Republic of Georgia in 2003, and the Orange Revolution in Ukraine in 2004, which cleared the way for the rightful installation of the popularly elected president.

People are also using nonviolence to challenge personal, interpersonal, and social patterns of violence in their own lives. The more we are equipped with the vision and skills of nonviolence, the greater the chance for the emergence of effective nonviolent solutions in our lives and in the world. *Engage* has been created for this purpose.

We have chosen to name this program *Engage* because it indicates action, response, involvement, and an effort to address and solve problems. We seek to re-frame how nonviolence is perceived. If we see it differently, we can tap its power. This is especially urgent because, despite the growing success of nonviolence, nonviolent people power is often ignored, misunderstood, and under-utilized. Assumptions based on selective readings of history and a set of persistent stereotypes (which assert that nonviolence is passive, weak, and ineffective, in spite of growing evidence to the contrary) block access to this power and hinder its deployment. The understanding of nonviolence that we have and that is used throughout this book is that nonviolence is a creative and active power for justice and the well-being of all that uses neither violence nor passivity.

FROM VIOLENCE TO WHOLENESS

Engage is a thorough revision and expansion of *From Violence To Wholeness*, Pace e Bene's nonviolence education and training program. Since 1997, twenty thousand people have participated in 400 *From Violence To Wholeness* workshops, trainings, courses, and study groups in the U.S. and around the world. This programming has provided participants with a vision, method, and skills to challenge and transform patterns and policies of violence in their lives and in the larger world. *From Violence To Wholeness* has helped thousands of people in a variety of contexts discover powerful alternatives to violence in their lives and in society, including:

- the residents of a housing project in a Midwestern city in the United States who used this process for a year to constructively transform the despair, rage, injustice, and violence they faced in their interpersonal relationships and in the midst of dehumanizing conditions. After this yearlong program, a pattern of suicide and physical violence ended.

- a *From Violence To Wholeness* facilitator who survived the genocide in Rwanda used *FVTW* with other Rwandan refugees living in southern France.
- a statewide coalition that used the *From Violence To Wholeness* process for training and strategizing in mounting a long-term campaign to stop state budget cuts.
- communities who have used this process in areas of war and intense social conflict, including hundreds of Colombians who traveled through numerous militarized zones to take part in seven *From Violence To Wholeness* trainings.

These are just a few of many ways that this program has been used to help in the creation of nonviolent transformation.

Building on the success of this project, the new *Engage* Study Program is designed for use in a wide variety of religious and non-religious settings to bring the power and tools of nonviolent living to people throughout society.

THE ENGAGE STUDY PROGRAM

Engage offers participants an orientation and process for introducing you to the ongoing spiritual journey of the nonviolent life. It recognizes that this journey is life-long. It does not pretend that one "achieves" this in twelve weeks or even twelve years. Pace e Bene regards this training as a modest introduction to some tools and techniques with which to experiment. It offers a vision and toolbox that may be handy in applying grounded nonviolence to the challenges of our lives and to the cry for change and healing in our world.

Guided by four commitments to relationship building, diversity, spiritual practice, and nonviolent action, *Engage* seeks to support the deep, slow work of becoming more whole human beings. It seeks to do this by:

- Cultivating the integration of the whole person: mind, heart, body, and spirit;
- Connecting personal transformation and social change;
- Offering spiritual grounding for the nonviolent life;
- Exploring the history and practice of active nonviolence;
- Providing concrete skills for putting nonviolent power into practice;
- Creating safe space for transforming personal and social violence;
- Helping people make connections with many different movements for change;
- Encouraging the development of nonviolence support groups to help make a difference in our lives and our world; and
- Offering a leadership training program for those interested in facilitating and supporting workshops, retreats, and study groups.

THE STRUCTURE OF THE ENGAGE STUDY PROGRAM

This program is designed to be a small-group learning process in personal and social transformation appropriate for a wide range of settings. It can be led by people with a minimum of facilitation experience, not only by those with significant background in leading group process.

The more experienced a facilitator is, the more effective she or he will likely be, and it is for this reason Pace e Bene offers the three-day *Engage* Facilitation Training. For those who wish to gain more in-depth skill in facilitation, we encourage you to take this training.

At the same time, the curriculum has been organized so that people with little formal facilitation training can carry it out.

The Study Program is composed of twelve 2.5-hour small-group sessions.

Part I (Sessions 1-5) familiarizes the participants with how violence and nonviolence work.

Part II (Sessions 6-8) explores nonviolent responses to structural violence.

Finally, Part III (Sessions 9-12) guides participants through the process of developing and carrying out nonviolent action.

Each session uses a multiplicity of learning styles and methods to explore nonviolence: story telling; role-plays; small and large group discussions; creative imagination exercises; journaling; and action. A "Wall of Learning and Growing" is put up each session for participants to write or draw whatever insights or awareness they are having; this will indicate the cumulative learning going on through the process. At the end of each session in this book, several blank pages are provided for participants to write about the process, their actions, and their reflections on the readings.

For more details on facilitating this twelve-part process, please see the Engage *Study Program Facilitation Guidelines in Part Four.*

A WORD ABOUT THIS BOOK

The *Engage* Study Program represents a substantially revised and expanded version of the *From Violence to Wholeness* curriculum that Pace e Bene Nonviolence Service first published in 1996. It reflects the feedback that we have received after leading hundreds of workshops based on this material and after hearing from many people who have used this book in study programs, classes, and trainings.

More significantly, the current book has been broadened to be useful and accessible to people from all walks of life. The original format, emerging as it did from a Franciscan nonviolence project, had been designed primarily as an exploration of Christian nonviolence for people in churches and faith-based organizations. The response in the intervening years has been very robust from many churches and denominations, and we are passionately committed to continuing strong and vital nonviolence education programming in many religious settings.

Several reasons, however, persuaded us to develop a second version of *From Violence To Wholeness*, a format that people from any religious tradition (or no religious tradition) could make use of.

The primary reason is simple: we were asked to do it. An increasing number of people began coming to the *From Violence To Wholeness* workshops and study groups who did not identify as either Christian or religious. They told us that this was a powerful process, and it would be even more powerful for them if it were framed more broadly and inclusively. They urged us to develop a "general audience" format.

Their prompting gradually helped us see a second reason to do this. Not only might we be able to create a program that people with no explicit religious stance would find comfortable and fruitful, but perhaps this process could also be one where people *from many different religious traditions* would be similarly comfortable. We set out to craft a framework that in either case would create room for this flexibility and contextualization.

Finally, this line of thinking brought us to yet another, but related, reason: to help encourage the process of *mainstreaming nonviolence and peacemaking*. Such a "civil society" format could be used in an endless array of public- and private-sector settings — social service agencies, schools, nonprofit organizations, police departments, corporations, and any number of groups and voluntary associations.

The more people from all walks of life can participate — and *participate together* — in a nonviolence formation process, the more widely the tools of nonviolence will be distributed. Even more significantly, the more people gain this vision and toolbox, the more widespread will be the growing awareness that the *conventional* default positions of responding to violence (either passivity or more violence) can be trumped by the creative and audacious nonviolent alternative.

Interestingly, there was near-universal assent from all who asked us to create this new book that the program continue to be grounded in an inclusive spirituality that takes seriously the deep transformation that nonviolence implies. In light of this, we have again sought to offer a process that roots the nonviolent journey in the profound mystery of encountering and engaging with the woundedness and sacredness of all beings.

AN INCLUSIVE SPIRITUALITY

The development of this Study Program has been guided by a desire to offer a nonviolence education process that is inclusive and accessible to people from many contexts and orientations. At the same time, we did not want to purchase this accessibility at the price of spiritual depth. If nonviolence is regarded or approached only as a political, economic, cultural, or sociological phenomenon, it loses its heart. Nonviolence is rooted in the depths that make alternatives to cruelty and injustice possible: love, compassion, hope, possibility, self-transcendence. These are powerful forces and energies that draw human beings to our inmost, elemental foundations, even as they urge us to change the world.

These depths are central to nonviolence, and therefore it is not inappropriate to term the nonviolent life a kind of "spiritual journey." But to take this approach does not mean that a spiritually grounded nonviolence must only reflect a particular religious tradition.

There is great richness and depth in specific theologies and practices of nonviolence, peacemaking, and justice in many religious traditions, and there is enormous power in the members of each tradition understanding, claiming, and deepening its particular visions and practices designed for personal and social transformation. It is for this reason that Pace e Bene has worked for nearly two decades in Christian churches and communities. At the same time, though, there is power in recognizing how the spirituality of nonviolence is a legacy of all humanity in many settings, and in creating a program where people from all — or no — explicit religious orientations can explore these depths.

We therefore set out to instill in this book an "inclusive general-audience spirituality" that seeks to open space for people from many different social locations to reflect on a spirituality and practice of transformative nonviolence. This inclusive spirituality is the living, unfolding experience of our journey toward wholeness in relationship to our ultimate value and meaning as persons, communities, and humanity. Put simply, inclusive spirituality is life creatively and compassionately seeking the wholeness and well-being of all.

ACKNOWLEDGMENTS

First and foremost we acknowledge all the known and unknown cultures, peoples, or communities throughout the world who have experienced enormous violence and have experimented creatively throughout history with the possibilities of active and powerful nonviolence. We especially acknowledge communities of color and all communities who have faced the searing violence of racism, poverty, and cultural destruction. Without their experiments in truth and relentless persistence there would be no body of nonviolent theory or practice of nonviolence as we know it.

The book in your hands is rooted in this powerful tradition, and we gratefully honor this reality.

This *Engage* Study Program represents a substantially revised and expanded version of the *From Violence To Wholeness* text that was first written by Ken Butigan and published in 1996. (Sr. Patricia Bruno, O.P., contributed to the original book's editing; she also gathered four of the readings used in the original text.)

The new edition reflects the feedback that we have received after leading hundreds of workshops based on this material and after hearing from many people who have used this book in study programs, classes, and trainings. It is designed for general audiences and was written by Ken Butigan, Veronica Pelicaric, Ken Preston-Pile, and Laura Slattery. Christina Leaño, Joi Morton-Wiley, and Jonathan Relucio began work with us on a book project in which some of the material is incorporated here. We are grateful for their significant contribution. We would also like to especially thank Denise Torres who has written portions of the first couple of chapters.

In addition, this process represents the thought and work of many past and present members of the Pace e Bene community, including Alain Richard, OFM, Rosemary Lynch, OSF, Louis Vitale, OFM, Michele Fischer, SC, Mary Litell, OSF, Peter Ediger, Julia Occhiogrosso, Patricia Bruno, OP, Joan Brown, OSF, Mary Morton, Brendan McKeague, Moira Finley, Graciela Martinez, Cynthia Stateman, and Linda Jaramillo. A special thanks to our readers and copyeditors, including L. R. Berger, Peter Ediger, Lyn Fine, Cynthia Okayama Dopke, and Robert A. Irwin; to our graphic designer, Chris McGee and Barking Dog Design; and to our pilot groups: Bay Area Nonviolent Peaceforce; Tidewater/Hampton Roads Network for Nonviolence in Virginia; and Tuolumne County Citizens for Peace.

We have adapted and used exercises and readings from many communities and individuals, and have tried to credit them faithfully in the Credit and Citation portion following the last session. For more information on any of the readings or exercises, please refer to those pages.

DEEPENING YOUR EXPERIENCE OF ENGAGE:
KEY VIDEOS AND BOOKS ON NONVIOLENCE

To deepen and reinforce the *Engage* Study Program we recommend that participants draw on some of the following videos and books on nonviolence. For a much more extensive listing, see Part Four.

We encourage all participants to watch the video series, *A Force More Powerful* (2000). This series (produced for and broadcast on the Public Broadcasting System in the U.S.A.) features six half-hour segments on successful nonviolent struggles around the world. We also recommend *Bringing Down a Dictator* (2002), a video about the nonviolent campaign that ended Serbian President Slobodan Milosevic's tyrannical regime in 2000, created by the same film producers. (See *www.aforcemorepowerful.org*.) Richard Attenborough's full-length motion picture *Gandhi* is also a powerful complement to the *Engage* Study Program.

Any of the following books will also deepen and broaden your experience of *Engage*.

Ackerman, Peter, and Jack DuVall. *A Force More Powerful: A Century of Nonviolent Conflict* (New York: St. Martin's Press, 2000).

Chernus, Ira. *American Nonviolence: The History of an Idea* (Maryknoll, NY: Orbis Books, 2004).

Desroches, Leonard. *Allow the Water: Anger, Fear, Power, Work, Sexuality, and the Spirituality and Practice of Active Nonviolence* (Toronto, Ontario: Dunamis Publishers). Contact: 407 Bleeker St., Toronto, Ontario, Canada M4X 1W2.

Egan, Eileen. *Peace Be With You: Justified Warfare or the Way of Nonviolence* (Maryknoll, NY: Orbis Books, 1999).

Gandhi, Mohandas K. *My Experiments with Truth [Gandhi: An Autobiography]* (Boston: Beacon Press, 1957).

Glassman, Bernie. *Bearing Witness* (New York: Bell Tower, 1998).

Juergensmeyer, Mark. *Gandhi's Way: A Handbook of Conflict Resolution* (Berkeley: University of California Press, 1984 [2002]).

King, Jr., Martin Luther. *Stride Toward Freedom* (New York: Harper & Brothers, 1958).
_____. *The Trumpet of Conscience* (New York: Harper and Row, 1967).

King, Mary. *Mahatma Gandhi and Martin Luther King, Jr.: The Power of Nonviolent Action* (Paris: UNESCO Publishing, 1999).

Lanza del Vasto, Jospeh Jean. *Warriors of Peace: Writings on the Techniques of Nonviolence* (New York: Alfred A. Knopf, 1974).

McAllister, Pam, ed. *Reweaving the Web of Life: Feminism ad Nonviolence* (Philadelphia: New Society Publishers, 1983).
_____. *You Can't Kill the Spirit: Stories of Women and Nonviolent Action* (Philadelphia: New Society Publishers, 1988).

McManus, Philip, and Gerald Schlabach, eds. *Relentless Persistence: Nonviolent Action in Latin America* (Philadelphia: New Society Publishers, 1991).

Moyer, Bill. *Doing Democracy: The MAP Model for Organizing Social Movements* (Gabriola Island, British Columbia: New Society Publishers, 2001).

Nagler, Michael. *Is There No Other Way? The Search for a Nonviolent Future* (Berkeley, CA: Berkeley Hills Books, 2001).

Powers, Roger S., and William B. Vogele, eds. *Protest, Power, and Change: An Encyclopedia of Nonviolent Action from ACT-UP to Women's Suffrage* (New York: Garland Publishing, 1997).

Schell, Jonathan. *The Unconquerable World: Power, Nonviolence and the Will of the People* (New York: Metropolitan Books, 2003).

Sharp, Gene. *The Politics of Nonviolent Action* (Boston: Porter Sargent, 1973).

_____. *Waging Nonviolent Struggle: 20th Century Practice and 21st Century Potential* (Boston: Porter Sargent, 2005).

Wink, Walter. *Engaging the Powers: Discernment and Resistance in a World of Domination* (Minneapolis: Fortress, 1992).

_____, ed. *Peace is the Way: Writings on Nonviolence from the Fellowship of Reconciliation* (Maryknoll, NY: Orbis Books, 2000).

Zinn, Howard, ed. *The Power of Nonviolence: Writings by Advocates of Peace* (Boston: Beacon Press, 2002).

PART ONE:

Exploring Nonviolent Power

Session 1:
The First Step

SESSION 1: **The First Step**

OBJECTIVES:
- To become familiar with the goals and methods of the *Engage* Study Program
- To begin to explore the meaning and dimensions of active nonviolence
- To begin getting to know each other

AGENDA:
- Welcome [2 min.]
- Opening [20 min.]
- Sharing Our Names [20 min.]
- Introducing the *Engage* Study Program [5 min.]
- Making Agreements [10 min.]
- Beginning to Explore Nonviolence [20 min.]
- Break [10 min.]
- Nonviolence Partners [15 min.]
- Conclusion [30 min.]
    - Nonviolence Journal
    - Nonviolent Action
    - Next Session's Reading
    - Evaluation
    - Closing

READINGS:
- Reading #1: Usman Farman, "Brother, if you don't mind, there is a cloud of glass coming at us. Grab my hand, let's get the hell out of here!"
- Reading #2: Sue Monk Kidd, "That's How I Like to See a Woman"
- Reading #3: Jerry Large, "The Costs of a Violent Society"

NOTES FOR THE FACILITATOR

PREPARATION: TWO WEEKS BEFORE
- Review the Facilitation Guidelines found in Part Four.
- Review the entire session in depth. Role-play or practice setting up and facilitating exercises beforehand. Wherever possible, put material into your own words. Feel free to make notes for this purpose on 3x5 cards or in the book next to the written instructions.
- Always attempt to put the material into your own words.
- Find a site for the study program, or at least Sessions 1 & 2. Make sure the site is accessible if that is a concern of one or more of the participants. Provide the participants with directions to the meeting site.
- Establish a meeting time that will work for everyone. Arrange carpools or rides if necessary. Consider providing (or organizing) refreshments.
- Gather everyone's contact information. Make sure that everyone has yours.
- If possible, send copies of the Starting Points and the Commitments (found in Session 1) to the participants. These can be downloaded from our website.

NOTES FOR THE FACILITATOR

PREPARATION: ON THE DAY OF THE SESSION
- Write the following items (found in Session 1) on separate pieces of easel paper:
  - The Goals of the program
  - The Agreements
  - The Description of Nonviolence
  - The three questions under the *Nonviolence Partners* exercise
- Arrange the chairs, including yours, in a circle, with a small table in the center. Place candle, holder, and matches on table.
- As people arrive, ask them to sign in with their contact information.
- Play some appropriate background music on a CD player as people enter. Play music at a low volume during the Sharing of Names exercise.
- For a variation on the Opening, see *www.paceebene.org*
- Make sure everyone has the *Engage* Study Program Book.
- *Needed Materials:* Name badges; felt pens for writing names; compact disk or audiotape player; recorded music; small table; a candle, candleholder or plate, and matches; easel; easel paper pads (also known as "flip chart" paper); a bell; art supplies (this could include crayons, color markers, pastels, white 8 1/2 X 11" paper, colored construction paper, clay, wire, aluminum foil, etc).

SESSION 1: **The First Step**

WELCOME — 2 MIN.

Review the Facilitation Guidelines (found in Part Four) ahead of time as you prepare to begin Engage.

After people have arrived and have settled in, present the following in your own words:

> Welcome to the first session of the *Engage* Study Program. *Engage* is an exploration of the power and potential of nonviolence in our lives and in the world. My name is _____ and I will be facilitating this program.
>
> In this opening session, we will begin to explore the power of active nonviolence, and we will also be introduced to the goals and process of *Engage*.

OPENING — 20 MIN.

Convey the following in your own words:

> As a way to start our process, I invite you to come to the table one at a time and light a candle in honor of a person who has been an example of peace for you. Maybe this is someone you know personally. Or maybe this is someone you've heard or read about.
>
> Feel free to share this person's name out loud if you feel comfortable doing so, and to say a sentence or two about how she or he has influenced you.

Model this by going first. After the last person has finished, offer the following in your own words:

> Let's take a moment of silence to honor and thank the spirit of all those who, in the past or the present, have worked to make the world a better place. May their work support and encourage us on our journey to explore and experiment with the power of nonviolence for personal and social change. Thank you!
>
> Before we start looking at the material, let me share a few housekeeping items.

Share any necessary housekeeping or logistical information.

> A human being is a part of the whole that we call the universe, a part limited in time and space. [We] experience [our]selves, [our] thoughts and feelings, as something separated from the rest — a kind of optical illusion of [our] consciousness. This illusion is a prison for us, restricting us to our personal desires and to affection for only the few people nearest us. Our task must be to … widen our circle of compassion to embrace all living beings and all of nature.
>
> — ALBERT EINSTEIN

SHARING OUR NAMES — 20 MIN.

The following exercise uses an easel, easel paper and non-toxic felt markers. If an easel is not available, distribute a sheet of paper to each person to write his or her full name on. Distribute felt markers for this purpose. To introduce this exercise, put the following into your own words:

> As we begin this study program, let's take a moment to get better acquainted. I'd

like to invite each of you, one at a time, to write your name on the easel. This can include middle names, nicknames, or names you (or your family) no longer use.

Then take a minute or less to share with the group something about your names. (This could include where they come from; why your parents named you what they did; what your names mean; or anything else you'd like to share about them.) I'll begin.

Model this process by going first. As you are about to finish, share with the group the name you prefer to be called. When you are finished, ask the person to your right to go. When she or he is finished, ask the person what she or he prefers to be called. Welcome the person using her or his name and clapping. Then invite the next person to the right. Continue this process around the circle until everyone has shared. Then share in your own words the following sentiment:

Sharing our names, and where they come from, can help call to mind the web of relationships that has made us who we are: our families, our ancestors, our cultures, and the societies we have emerged from. This study program explores the importance of relationship and the ways we are connected to one another. Relationship and connectedness are at the heart of active nonviolence.

FOUR STARTING POINTS OF THE STUDY PROGRAM

- *We begin by acknowledging the roots of nonviolence.* The *Engage* Study Program acknowledges the many rich sources of active nonviolence, especially movements of poor people, communities of color, and all who have faced fierce oppression and who have long histories of nonviolent struggle.

- *Nonviolence does not mean perfection!* Alain Richard, a former Pace e Bene staff member who has been engaged in nonviolent activities for much of his life, often says, "Just because I talk about nonviolence doesn't mean that *I am* nonviolent. I will probably not be really nonviolent until fifteen minutes after I am dead!" Nonviolence is not a state of idealistic perfection. It is something we construct and grow into. As Gandhi stressed, nonviolence is a continual series of "experiments with truth" through which we gradually learn how to be nonviolent.

- *Nonviolence does not assume that the world is nonviolent.* Sometimes we think that for nonviolence to be effective, the whole world has to somehow become nonviolent. Active nonviolence does not hold to this illusion. In fact, it assumes that the world is often violent and unjust. But it also recognizes that there is a path that can heal.
  Nonviolence does not attempt to create a world where there is no conflict. It recognizes that we face conflict all through our lives. This program explores the ways in which nonviolence is a more effective means of addressing and resolving conflict than violence.

- *The* Engage *Study Program is only a first step.* The path of nonviolence is a lifelong journey. Much experimentation, learning, and action are needed. Therefore, we are modest about this twelve-part study program. Typically, one will not fully understand, much less integrate, the power of nonviolence in such a short time. Nevertheless, this process has an important goal: to offer an orientation to nonviolent living and to begin the process of grounding oneself in that life. *Engage* introduces a vision and a toolbox of methods and techniques for nonviolent living.

INTRODUCING THE *ENGAGE* STUDY PROGRAM — 5 MIN.

Share the following in your own words:

> Before we continue, let's take a look at the goals of the *Engage* Program. These goals include:

- To explore and experiment with nonviolence as a way of life.
- To examine our current beliefs and practices with regard to violence and nonviolence.
- To obtain practical skills for responding to violence.
- To promote the formation, or deepening, of groups whose members have a commitment to continue the study of and experimentation with active nonviolence in their own lives and in the world.

MAKING AGREEMENTS — 10 MIN.

Present the following in your own words:

> Engage depends on creating safe space for sharing and learning. Safe space helps create an environment where we are free to reflect deeply on our own experience of violence and nonviolence. Based on past experience and the work of other groups, we invite the group to agree to use the following four guidelines. A fuller version of each of these agreements is found in the nearby sidebar.
>
> I invite a participant to read these four agreements aloud to the group.

Ask for a volunteer to read the following:

> During our time together:

- I agree to share and participate at whatever level feels safe and comfortable.
- I agree to maintain confidentiality about personal stories or experiences shared in my small group or in the large group, unless I have been given permission to share them with others.
- I agree to listen with my full and complete attention, and to wait until a person has completed his or her thoughts before I speak.
- I will strive to appreciate and honor our differences.

Then ask:

- Are there any questions?
- Are there any modifications or additions?
- Do we agree to use these guidelines during this program?

When agreement is reached, post the list on a nearby wall for this and all subsequent sessions. Explain that, since the convener may not always notice if one of these agreements has been broken, all participants should feel empowered to interrupt the process if they notice this has happened and ask that the situation be addressed.

GROUP AGREEMENTS

I agree to share and participate at whatever level feels safe and comfortable.

- I will share what I want to share. If I choose not to share, that's fine. If I want to share a little, that's fine. If I want to share more, that's fine. Together we will create an environment where our feelings and thoughts are respected.
- While I have the opportunity to always share at whatever level I feel safe and comfortable, I may be open to voluntarily take opportunities as they arise to feel uncomfortable when that might aid my growth. In every case, this is up to me.
- The facilitators are not acting in the capacity of professional psychotherapists or counselors. They are ordinary people helping us explore alternatives to the violence in our lives and the larger world. If something comes up for me during our time together I know I am encouraged to seek assistance from an appropriate health professional.

I agree to maintain confidentiality about personal stories or experiences shared in my small group or in the large group, unless I have been given permission to share them with others.

- In the Engage process we work in small and large groups. I will not share a story or experience that someone else has shared in either small or large groups unless she or he has given their permission. When in doubt I will err on the side of caution and not share the story or experience. I will feel free, however, to share any insights that this story or experience may have stimulated.

I agree to listen with my full and complete attention, and to wait until a person has completed his or her thoughts before I speak.

During our time together I will strive to appreciate and honor our differences.

- Diversity is an opportunity for me to grow and learn in a new way. I will try to be open to and celebrate persons, approaches, and ways of being that are different from mine.
- As part of this, I recognize that there are power dynamics in every group, including this one. I will do my best to be sensitive to the use of power based on race, gender, ability, sexual orientation, money, or class. If someone uses power over someone else in this group (for example, if someone discounts another person's experience), I will try to respond to this situation in a clear and loving way.

BEGINNING TO EXPLORE NONVIOLENCE — 20 MIN.

Brainstorm and write on the easel (in a column down the left side of the paper) responses to the following question:

> What are some typical beliefs, societal views or stereotypes about nonviolence? What might be some of your own concerns about nonviolence?

Some of the examples may include: Nonviolence is passive, ineffective, utopian; nonviolent people are wimpy, unpatriotic, unemployed, unrealistic, doormats. Develop a long list. Then reflect with the group on this list. For example, ask people to reflect on "passivity" – what does this mean? Why do they think people draw this conclusion? Explore several of these terms and help the participants explore the reasoning behind these views and attitudes. Then ask:

What are some of the "actual" qualities or attributes of people who practice nonviolence?

Write down the words people suggest in a column on the right side of the easel paper (opposite the list of "typical beliefs").

This list may include qualities like courage, creativity, spiritual centeredness, passion, a disarming spirit, compassion, and determination. Reflect with the group on this list. Then ask:

When we contrast these two lists, what do we see?

Then ask participants:

Where do you think the "typical beliefs" about nonviolence come from? Do we hold some of these beliefs? What impact do we think they have?

After the group reflects on this, share the following in your own words:

It is crucial that we explore the typical beliefs – what we might call "stereotypes" -- of nonviolence.

This is important because many people in our society hold these views. This is also important because it is quite possible that *we ourselves* hold these views. Our views about nonviolence can sometimes reinforce the rationale for "acceptable violence." This rationale can sound like this:

If nonviolence is ineffective, then the only recourse must be violence. When these attitudes and assumptions lead people to dismiss nonviolence, they prevent us from claiming and making use of one of the most important forms of power at our disposal.

This study program will be an opportunity to explore this power and see if it offers ways to create alternatives in our lives and in the world. As we begin our nonviolent journey, we are all invited to test these "stereotypes" and "qualities and attributes" of nonviolence throughout our time together.

I also invite you to explore and test the following understanding of nonviolence that we will be using:

Tape the definition of nonviolence to the wall, then read it aloud:

Nonviolence is a creative power for justice and the well-being of all that uses neither passivity nor violence.

BREAK — 10 MIN.

If the group is ahead of time after the break, consider inviting the participants to read the story "Shine On in Montana" aloud as an example of nonviolence.

Shine On in Montana

by Jo Clare Hartsig

In the early 1990's a spate of hate crimes were perpetrated in five states in the Northwest region of the United States by an organization, known as the Aryan Nation, against Jews, people of color, and gays and lesbians, among others. Here is how the community of Billings, Montana, responded.

On December 2, 1993, a brick was thrown through the window of five-year-old Isaac Schnitzer's bedroom window. The brick and shards of glass were strewn all over the child's bed. The reason? A menorah and other symbols of Jewish faith were stenciled on the glass as part of the family's Hanukkah celebration. The account of the incident in the *Billings Gazette* the next day described Isaac's mother, Tammie Schnitzer, as being troubled by the advice she got from the investigating officer. He suggested she remove the symbols. How would she explain this to her son?

Another mother in Billings was deeply touched by that question. She tried to imagine explaining to her children that they couldn't have a Christmas tree in the window or a wreath on the door because it wasn't safe. She remembered what happened when Hitler ordered the king of Denmark to force all Danish Jews to wear Stars of David. The order was never carried out because the king himself and many other Danes chose to wear the yellow stars. The Nazis lost the ability to find their "enemies."

There are several dozen Jewish families in Billings. This kind of [solidarity] tactic could effectively deter violence if enough people got involved. So Margaret McDonald phoned her pastor, Rev. Keith Torney of First Congregational United Church of Christ, and asked what he thought of having Sunday School children make paper cut-out menorahs for their own windows. He got on the phone with his clergy colleagues around town, and the following week hundreds of menorahs appeared in the windows of Christian homes. When asked about the danger of this action, Police Chief Wayne Inman told callers, "There's greater risk in not doing it."

Five days after the brick was thrown at the Schnitzer home, the local newspaper, the *Gazette*, published a full-page drawing of a menorah, along with a general invitation for people to put it up in their windows. By the end of the week at least six thousand homes (some accounts estimated up to ten thousand) were decorated with menorahs.

A sporting-goods store got involved by displaying "Not in Our Town! No Hate. No Violence. Peace on Earth" on its large billboard. Someone shot at it. Townspeople organized a vigil outside the synagogue during Sabbath services. That same night bricks and bullets shattered windows at Central Catholic High School, where an electric marquee read "Happy Hanukkah to our Jewish Friends." The cat of a family with a menorah was killed with an arrow. A United Methodist Church had windows broken because of its menorah display. Six non-Jewish families had their car and house windows shattered. One car had a note that said "Jew lover."

Eventually these incidents waned, but people continued in their efforts to support one another against hate crimes. After being visited at home and threatened by one of the local skinhead leaders, Tammie Schnitzer is now always accompanied by friends when she goes on her morning run. During the Passover holiday last spring, 250 Christians joined their Jewish brothers and sisters in a traditional Seder meal. New friendships have formed, new traditions have started, and greater mutual understanding and respect have been achieved.

This winter families all over Billings took out their menorahs to reaffirm their commitment to peace and religious tolerance. The light they shared in their community must be continuously rekindled until hatred has been overcome.

Although there is no historical evidence to support the story of the Danish king, it continues to inspire countless number of people to risk their well-being for the sake of others.

NONVIOLENCE PARTNERS — 10 MIN.

Please convey the following in your own words:

> In this program we invite each participant to form a "nonviolence partnership" with one other member. A nonviolence partner is someone you can reflect with about the issues and material of this program on an ongoing basis. This partnership will offer one another mutual support and encouragement in the nonviolence journey.
>
> Specifically, at the beginning of each session we will check in with our nonviolence partner on our "homework" and on what has come up for us in the intervening time. If partners wish, they can also check in between sessions.
>
> To form our "nonviolence partnerships," I invite everyone to get up from your seats and to come out into the center of the room.
>
> Pretend that we are in New York City during the 5 p.m. rush hour on a Friday afternoon. It is crowded on the street, and everyone is walking every direction to the subway, the bus, and the parking garages.
>
> We are part of this rush of commuters, going in every direction.

Direct people to start moving in circles, and zigzagging through the crowd, encouraging them to get into the spirit of rush hour. After a minute, call out "Stop!" and have them pair up with the person nearest them. Ensure everyone has someone. If there is an odd number, ask three people to form the final group. Share the following in your own words:

> Please turn to the person you are with and meet your Nonviolence Partner for this study program. I invite you to pull two chairs together, reintroduce yourselves, and reflect together on the following questions, with each person taking one minute for each question:

Post the questions for partners to discuss.

- "Some wishes I have for this study program are…"
- "Some fears or reservations I have about this study program are…"
- "Some support I could use might be…"

After four minutes, sound the bell and invite the other person to share on the questions. Then, after the pairs have finished sharing, state the following:

> As we travel together, do not hesitate to talk over your experiences with each other. And if you have questions, bring them in. They are often the most intriguing part of this path.

> "If only it were all so simple! If only there were evil people somewhere insidiously committing evil deeds and it were necessary to separate them from the rest of us and destroy them. But the line dividing good and evil cuts through the heart of every human being. And who is willing to destroy a piece of his [or her] own heart?"
>
> — ALEKSANDR SOLZHENITSYN
> 1970 NOBEL LAUREATE

> "Nonviolence is not primarily a tactic. It is a way of living and being and expressing the truth of your soul in the world."
>
> — DANIEL BERRIGAN

CONCLUSION — 10 MIN.

State the following in your own way:

At the end of each session, we will conclude by offering suggestions for reflection and action between now and the next session. This includes ideas and questions for nonviolent journaling; nonviolent action; readings for the next session; what this program calls "The Wall of Learning and Growing"; and evaluating this session. This is then followed by a closing.

Present the following components one at a time:

⊙ Nonviolence Journal

Please use the blank page entitled "Nonviolence Journal" following this section to describe any feelings, thoughts, images, or issues sparked by this session, and during the week as you reflect back or as you complete your homework and readings. These journals are confidential. It is up to you if you would like to share from it with your partner or in the larger group.

Suggested Topic or Questions:
1) What do you want to learn in the next 11 sessions? Is there a particular skill you want to improve by the end of the course?
2) What is one thing that was said in class that surprised you, or seemed unusual to your way of thinking? What was your initial reaction to it?

⊙ Nonviolent Action

Take one or more of the following actions between now and the next session:
1) Ask one or two people what they think of when they hear the word: "nonviolence;"
2) Ask one or two people what they think of when they hear the words: "nonviolent power";
3) Take some time to reflect on specific people who have modeled what might be considered nonviolent living. Pick one or two of these people and express your gratitude for their presence in your life and how they have influenced you. Then, on the second blank page, write down any reflections you have after completing one or more of these actions.

⊙ Questionnaire

Please fill out the first questionnaire at the back of the book and hand it in at next session.

Please assign a number to each of the participants at this time so that their questionnaires will be confidential. Ask them to put the number on both copies of the questionnaire. Please collect them at the beginning of the second session.

⊙ Next Session's Reading

To prepare for the next session, please read the readings found at the end of this session between now and the next gathering and write any thoughts or insights that come from the readings on the blank page entitled "Reading Reflections." (Please do *not* read the material in the *body* of Session 2, except the sidebars and quotes, because some of the exercises are better experienced than read.)

ENGAGE STUDY PROGRAM COMMITMENTS

Weekly components of the *Engage: Exploring Nonviolent Living* program include:
- ☐ Attending each session
- ☐ Journaling (at least one page)
- ☐ Nonviolent action (as described at the end of each session)
- ☐ Reading the 2 or 3 readings of each session
- ☐ Reflecting with my Nonviolence Partner

Please indicate your willingness to participate fully in this program by making the commitment to yourself **before the beginning of the third session.** You are invited to symbolize your commitment by signing below. If you can't attend a particular session, please let the facilitator know.

Understanding that the more I put into something, the more I get out of it, I commit myself to completing each of the components of the *Engage* Study Program.

Signature _____

⊙ Commitments

Review the commitments found in the box on the next page with participants. Ask if there are any questions or concerns.

⊙ Evaluation

What were the positive things from this session – what worked for you? *(List these items on easel paper.)* What could be improved? *(List them on easel paper.)*

CLOSING — 15 MIN.

Sharing Our Hopes and Goals

As our closing, I'd like to ask for a moment of silence for each of us to consider what our hopes are in learning about nonviolence for ourselves, our community, and our planet. If you want, feel free to open your book and write them in the space provided.

My hope or goal for this process: _____

_____

_____

Invite the participants to close their books and join in a circle holding hands.

I invite each person, one at a time, to again share your name, where you are from, and, at whatever level you feel comfortable, a hope or goal for your participation in this process.

After everyone is finished ask people to take a moment of silence, then convey:

> Let us affirm and embrace both the hopes and dreams that have been shared and those that still remain deep within our hearts. (Pause) In closing I would like to read the following poem by Mzwakhe Mbuli, a South African performance artist and activist:

Now is the time
To climb up the mountain
And reason against habit.
Now is the time.

Now is the time
To renew the barren soil of nature
Ruined by the winds of tyranny.
Now is the time.

Now is the time
To commence the litany of hope.
Now is the time.

Now is the time
To give me roses, not to keep them
For my grave to come.

Give them to me while my heart beats,
Give them today
While my heart yearns for jubilee.
Now is the time...

Close the session by thanking the participants for attending this first gathering of Engage.

KEY ORGANIZATIONS: NONVIOLENCE TRAINING

Pace e Bene Nonviolence Service. *www.paceebene.org;* Engage: *www.EngageNonviolence.org;* 1420 W. Bartlett Ave., Las Vegas, NV 89106; 702-648-2281; *paceebene@paceebene.org.* Launched in 1989, Pace e Bene cultivates nonviolent living and the emergence of nonviolent cultures through training, publishing, advocacy, and spiritual practice. Pace e Bene has led hundreds of nonviolence trainings, workshops, retreats and classes for thousands of people throughout the world.

Alternatives to Violence Project (AVP/USA). *www.avpusa.org;* 1050 Selby Ave., St. Paul, MN 55104; 877-926-8287; *avp@avpusa.org.* AVP empowers people to lead nonviolent lives through affirmation, respect for all, community building, cooperation, and trust. AVP/USA is an association of community-based groups and prison-based groups offering experiential workshops in personal growth and creative conflict management. The national organization provides support for the work of these local groups.

Fellowship of Reconciliation (FOR/USA). *www.forusa.org;* 521 N. Broadway, Nyack, NY 10960; 845-358-4601. FOR seeks to replace violence, war, racism, and economic injustice with nonviolence, peace, and justice. It is an interfaith organization committed to active nonviolence as a transforming way of life and as a means of radical change. They educate, train, build coalitions, and engage in nonviolent and compassionate actions locally, nationally, and globally.

Training for Change, 1501 Cherry St., Philadelphia, PA 19102; 215-241-7035; *peacelearn@igc.org; www.trainingforchange.org.* Training for Change offers workshops teaching skills and tools to individuals and groups working for nonviolent social change.

HOMEWORK

NONVIOLENCE JOURNAL

Suggested Topic or Question:

1) What do you want to learn or get out of the next 11 sessions? Is there a particular skill you want to improve by the end of the course?

2) What is one thing that was said in class that surprised you, or seemed unusual to your way of thinking? What was your initial reaction to it?

HOMEWORK

NONVIOLENT ACTION

Take one or more of the following actions between now and the next session:

1) Ask one or two people what they think of when they hear the word: "nonviolence;"
2) Ask one or two people what they think of when they hear the words: "nonviolent power";
3) Take some time to reflect on specific people who have modeled what might be considered nonviolent living. Pick one or two of these people and express your gratitude for their presence in your life and how they have influenced you.

Write down any reflections you have after completing one or more of these actions.

"Brother, if you don't mind, there is a cloud of glass coming at us. Grab my hand, let's get the hell out of here!"

by Usman Farman

The following is an excerpt from a speech delivered two weeks after the attack on the World Trade Center in September 2001.

My name is Usman Farman and I graduated from Bentley with a Finance degree last May. I am 21 years old, turning 22 in October; I am Pakistani, and I am Muslim. Until September 11th, 2001, I used to work at the World Trade Center in building #7. I had friends and acquaintances who worked in tower #1 right across from me. Some made it out, and some are still unaccounted for. I survived this horrible event.

I'd like to share with you what I went through that awful day, with the hopes that we can all stay strong together through this tragedy of yet untold proportions. As I found out, regardless of who we are, and where we come from, we only have each other.

I commute into the city every morning on the train from New Jersey. Rather, I used to. I still can't believe what is happening. That morning I woke up and crawled out of bed. I was thinking about flaking out on the train and catching the late one, I remember telling myself that I just had to get to work on time. I ended up catching the 7:48 train, which put me in Hoboken at 8:20 a.m. When I got there I thought about getting something to eat; I decided against it and took the PATH train to the World Trade Center.

I arrived at the World Trade Center at 8:40 in the morning. I walked into the lobby of building 7 at 8:45 — that's when the first plane hit. Had I taken the late train, or gotten a bite to eat, I would have been 5 minutes late and walking over the crosswalk. Had that

happened, I would have been caught under a rain of fire and debris, I wouldn't be here talking to you. I'd be dead. I was in the lobby, and I heard the first explosion; it didn't register.

They were doing construction outside and I thought some scaffolding had fallen. I took the elevators up to my office on the 27th floor. When I walked in, the whole place was empty. There were no alarms, no sprinklers, nothing. Our offices are, or rather, were, on the south side of building seven. We were close enough to the North and South Towers, that I could literally throw a stone from my window and hit the North tower with it. My phone rang and I spoke with my mother and told her that I was leaving. At that moment I saw an explosion rip out of the second building. I called my friend in Boston, waking her up, and told her to tell everyone I'm okay, and that I was leaving. I looked down one last time and saw that the square and fountain that I eat lunch in was covered in smoldering debris.

Apparently, I was one of the last to leave my building. When I was on the way up in the elevator, my coworkers from the office were in the stairwells coming down. When I evacuated, there was no panic. People were calm and helping each other; a pregnant woman was being carried down the stairwell.

I'll spare the more gruesome details of what I saw — those are things that no one should ever have to see, and beyond human decency to describe. Those are things that will haunt me for the rest of my life; my heart goes out to everyone who lost their lives that day, and those who survived with the painful reminders of what once was. Acquaintances of mine who made it out of the towers only did so because 1000 people formed a human chain to find their way out of the smoke. Everyone was a hero that day.

We were evacuated to the north side of building 7, still only 1 block from the towers. The security people told us to go north and not to look back. Five city blocks later I stopped and turned around to watch. With a thousand people staring, we saw in shock as the first tower collapsed. No one could believe it was happening; it is still all too surreal to imagine. The next thing I remember is that a dark cloud of glass and debris about 50 stories high came tumbling towards us. I turned around and ran as fast as possible.

I didn't realize until yesterday that the reason I'm still feeling so sore was that I fell down trying to get away. What happened next is why I came here to give this speech.

I was on my back, facing this massive cloud that was approaching. It must have been 600 feet high; everything was already dark. I normally wear a pendant around my neck, inscribed with an Arabic prayer for safety, similar to the cross. A Hasidic Jewish man came up to me and held the pendant in his hand, and looked at it. He read the Arabic out loud. What he said next, I will never forget. With a deep Brooklyn accent he said, "Brother, if you don't mind, there is a cloud of glass coming at us. Grab my hand, let's get the hell out of here!" He helped me stand up, and we ran for what seemed like forever without looking back. He was the last person I would ever have thought who would help me. If it weren't for him, I probably would have been engulfed in shattered glass and debris.

I finally stopped about 20 blocks away, and looked in horror as tower #2 came crashing down. Fear came over me as I realized that some people were evacuated to the streets below the towers. Like I said before, no one could have thought those buildings could collapse. We turned around and in shock and disbelief, began the trek to midtown. It took me 3 hours to get to my sister's office at 3rd Avenue and 47th Street. Some streets were completely deserted, completely quiet, no cars, no nothing — just the distant wail of sirens. I managed to call home and say I was okay, and get in touch with coworkers and friends whom I feared were lost.

> *He helped me stand up, and we ran for what seemed like forever without looking back. He was the last person I would ever have thought who would help me. If it weren't for him, I probably would have been engulfed in shattered glass and debris.*

We managed to get a ride to New Jersey. Looking back as I crossed the George Washington Bridge, I could not see the towers. It had really happened.

As the world continues to reel from this tragedy, people in the streets are lashing out. Not far from my home, a Pakistani woman was run over on purpose as she was crossing the parking lot to put groceries in her car. Her only fault? That she had her head covered and was wearing the traditional clothing of my homeland. I am afraid for my family's well-being within our community. My older sister is too scared to take the subway into work now. My 8-year-old sister's school is under lockdown and armed watch by police.

Violence only begets violence, and by lashing out at each other in fear and hatred, we will become no better than the faceless cowards who committed this atrocity. If it weren't for that man who helped me get up, I would most likely be in the hospital right now, if not dead. Help came from the least expected place, and it goes only to show that we are all in this together regardless of race, religion, or ethnicity. Those are principles that this country was founded on.

Please take a moment to look at the people sitting around you. Friends or strangers, in a time of crisis, you would want the nearest person to help you if you needed it. My help came from a man who I would never have thought would normally even speak to me. …

The one thing that won't help, is if we fight amongst ourselves, because it is then that we are doing exactly what they want us to do, and I know that nobody here wants to do that. Again, my name is Usman Farman and I graduated from Bentley with a Finance degree last May. I am 21 years old, turning 22 in October; I am Pakistani, and I am Muslim, and I too have been victimized by this awful tragedy. The next time you feel angry about this, and perhaps want to retaliate in your own way, please remember these words: "Brother, if you don't mind, there is a cloud of glass coming at us. Grab my hand, let's get the hell out of here."

SESSION 2: READING 2

That's How I Like To See a Woman

by Sue Monk Kidd

It was autumn, and everything was turning loose. I was running errands that afternoon. Rain had fallen earlier, but now the sun was out, shining on the tiny beads of water that clung to trees and sidewalks. The whole world seemed red and yellow and rinsed with light. I parked in front of the drugstore where my daughter, Ann, fourteen, had an after-school job. Leaping a puddle, I went inside.

I spotted her right away kneeling on the floor in the toothpaste section, stocking a bottom shelf. I was about to walk over and say hello when I noticed two middle-aged men walking along the aisle toward her. They looked like everybody's father. They had moussed hair, and they wore knit sportshirts the color of Easter eggs, the kind of shirts with tiny alligators sewn at the chest. It was a detail I would remember later as having ironic symbolism.

My daughter did not see them coming. Kneeling on the floor, she was intent on getting the boxes of Crest lined up evenly. The men stopped, peering down at her. One man nudged the other. He said, "Now that's how I like to see a woman—on her knees."

The other man laughed.

Standing in the next aisle, I froze. I watched the expression that crept into my daughter's eyes as she looked up. I watched her chin drop and her hair fall across her face.

Seeing her kneel at these men's feet while they laughed at her subordinate posture pierced me through.

For the previous couple of years I had been in the midst of a tumultuous awakening. I had been struggling to come to terms with my life as a woman—in my culture, my marriage, my faith, my church, and deep inside myself. It was a process not unlike the experience of conception and labor. There had been a moment, many moments really, when truth seized me and I "conceived" myself as woman. Or maybe I reconceived myself. At any rate, it had been extraordinary and surprising to find myself—a conventionally religious woman in my late thirties—suddenly struck pregnant with a new consciousness, with an unfolding new awareness of what it means to be a woman and what it means to be spiritual *as a woman*.

Hard labor had followed. For months I'd inched along, but lately I'd been stuck. I'd awakened enough to know that I couldn't go back to my old way of being a woman, but the fear of going forward was paralyzing. So I'd plodded along, trying to make room for the new consciousness that was unfolding in my life but without really risking change.

I have a friend, a nurse on the obstetrical floor at a hospital, who says that sometimes a woman's labor simply stalls. The contractions grow weak, and the new life, now quite distressed, hangs precariously. The day I walked into the drugstore, I was experiencing something like that. A stalled awakening.

Who knows, I may have stalled interminably

if I had not seen my daughter on her knees before those laughing men. I cannot to this day explain why the sight of it hit me so forcibly. But to borrow Kafka's image, it came like an ice ax upon a frozen sea, and suddenly all my hesitancy was shattered. Just like that.

The men's laughter seemed to go on and on. I felt like a small animal in the road, blinded by the light of a truck, knowing some terrible collision is coming but unable to move. I stared at my daughter on her knees before these men and could not look away. Somehow she seemed more than my daughter; she was my mother, my grandmother, and myself. She was every woman ever born, bent and contained in a small, ageless cameo that bore the truth about "a woman's place."

In the profile of my daughter I saw the suffering of women, the confining of the feminine to places of inferiority, and I experienced a collision of love and pain so great I had to reach for the counter to brace myself.

This posture will not perpetuate itself in her life, I thought.

Still, I didn't know what to do. When I was growing up, if my mother had told me once, she'd told me a thousand times, "If you can't say something nice, don't say anything at all." I'd heard this from nearly everybody. It was the kind of thing that got cross-stitched and hung in kitchens all over my native South.

I'd grown up to be a soft-voiced, sweet-mouthed woman who, no matter how assailing the behavior before me or how much I disagreed with it, responded nicely or else zip-locked my mouth shut. I had swallowed enough defiant, disputatious words in my life to fill a shelf of books.

But it occurred to me that if I abandoned my daughter at that moment, if I simply walked away and was silent, the feminine spirit unfolding inside her might also become crouched and silent. Perhaps she would learn the *internal* posture of being on her knees.

> It occurred to me that if I abandoned my daughter at that moment, if I simply walked away and was silent, the feminine spirit unfolding inside her might also become crouched and silent. Perhaps she would learn the internal posture of being on her knees.

The men with their blithe joke had no idea they had tapped a reservoir of pain and defiance in me. It was rising now, unstoppable by any earthly force.

I walked toward them. "I have something to say to you, and I want you to hear it," I said. They stopped laughing. Ann looked up.

"This is my daughter," I said, pointing to her, my finger shaking with anger. "You may like to see her and other women on their knees, but we don't belong there. *We don't belong there!*"

Ann rose to her feet. She glanced sideways at me, sheer amazement spread over her face, then turned and faced the men. I could hear her breath rise and fall with her chest as we stood there shoulder to shoulder, staring at their faces.

"Women," one of them said. They walked away, leaving Ann and me staring at each other among the toothpaste and dental floss.

I smiled at her. She smiled back. And though we didn't say a word, more was spoken between us in that moment than perhaps in our whole lives.

I left the drugstore that day so internally jolted by the experience that everything in me began to shift. I sat in the car feeling like a newborn, dangled upside down and slapped.

Throughout my awakening, I'd grown increasingly aware of certain attitudes that existed in our culture, a culture long dominated by men. The men in the drugstore had mirrored one attitude in particular, that of seeking power over another, of staying up by keeping others down.

Sitting in my car replaying my statement back to those men—that women did not belong on their knees—I knew I had uttered my declaration of intent.

That night Ann came to my room. I was sitting in bed reading. She climbed up beside me and said, "Mama, about this afternoon in the drugstore..."

"Yeah?"

"I just wanted to say, thanks."

The Costs of a Violent Society

by Jerry Large

If someone punched you in the nose and took your money, we could all agree that you'd been the victim of violence.

But what if someone polluted the air you breathe, or denied you health insurance? Would that constitute violence? What if the schools near your home offered a lower-quality education than those just a few miles away in a wealthier neighborhood — would that hurt as much as that punch? Would it cost your family as much as a robbery?

Neil Wollman thinks so.

Wollman is a professor of psychology at Manchester College in Indiana and a senior fellow in the Peace Studies Institute there. He thinks that while we are worried about individual violence, many more people are being hurt by institutional and structural harm.

"We are a society that talks about equality and the value of equality," he says, "but our institutions and social structures don't always serve that ideal. Sometimes they do the opposite."

A few years ago he and some other professors and students started combing through census data and other studies to get a sense of how much harm is done by the way our society is organized.

"We were trying to look at violence in a more comprehensive way. Hunger, homelessness. It's a little different way of looking at harm."

All of the data they collected are reported elsewhere, but they wanted to draw the statistics together and see whether it told them something about the nature of our society.

They looked at data beginning in 1995 and found that rates of most kinds of face-to-face, interpersonal violence have declined. Rates for murders, sexual offenses, and robbery were down.

But many structural problems, what Wollman calls "social negligence," worsened.

Emergency food requests rose 20-fold from 1984 to 2002, including a 17 percent rise from 2002 to 2003.

In 2003, a record 84 percent of cities turned people away from overflowing homeless shelters.

In 2002, 43.6 million Americans lacked health insurance, a 5.7 percent increase from 2001.

The school dropout rate has gone down a bit but is still troubling, as are disparities in educational outcome between some minority groups and white students.

> *What if someone polluted the air you breathe, or denied you health insurance? Would that constitute violence? What if the schools near your home offered a lower-quality education than those just a few miles away in a wealthier neighborhood — would that hurt as much as that punch? Would it cost your family as much as a robbery?*

In a summary of the report, Wollman says, "Given the basic nature of these long unfulfilled needs — and the fact that a number of other countries see fit to provide (assistance) in these areas — we may need to look more closely at ourselves and our self-image of being a compassionate people."

But, wait a minute, aren't we the most advanced country on the planet? We have it pretty darned good. And some things are getting better.

In fact, Wollman called me because he'd read a column I wrote about the status of black Americans. He wanted me to see his group's analysis of census data on the poverty gap, which shows a narrowing of the gap between white Americans and other groups of Americans.

The gap closed by 19 percent over the past seven years. Of course, people who aren't white are still 162 percent more likely to be below the poverty line than white people, but the narrowing gap is good news.

However, even as some gaps are closing, one troubling gap widened. The income gap between the top 5 percent of the population and the bottom 10 percent grew, and is the widest it has been since the government started tracking it in 1967.

"These income gaps are not good for a society (that) holds equality as a primary value," Wollman said.

Other studies have shown a significant correlation between economic gaps and health.

We may be ahead of most nations in wealth and achievement, but we are also ahead in stress. People measure themselves not against other societies, but against their fellow citizens.

Americans struggle to rise up the ladder or to stay at the top. People up and down the food chain are stressed.

The Population Health Forum lists the United States in 26th place for life expectancy among developed nations and says life expectancy rates match economic inequality. The higher the inequality in a society, the worse everyone's health is.

A burglar may hurt one family at a time, but a system that supports inequality damages millions of lives at once and ultimately harms everyone.

REFLECTIONS ON THE READING

Session 2:
The Situation
We Often Face

SESSION 2: **The Situation We Often Face**

OBJECTIVES:
- To explore the experience of violence
- To consider some of the ways violence works, and
- To analyze violence in preparation for studying and understanding nonviolence

AGENDA:
- Welcome [2 min.]
- Opening [5 min.]
- Reflecting on Homework [10 min.]
- Zones of Learning [10 min.]
- The Violence Spectrum [35 min.]
- Break [10 min.]
- What is Violence? [20 min.]
- Reflecting Creatively on the Experience of Violence [15 min.]
- Small Group Reflection on the Experience of Violence [15 min.]
- Conclusion [20 min.]
      Nonviolence Journal
      Nonviolent Action
      Next Session's Reading
      Putting up the Wall of Learning and Growing
      Closing

READINGS:
- Reading #1: Sue Monk Kidd, "That's How I Like to See a Woman"
- Reading #2: Jerry Large, "The Costs of a Violent Society"

NOTES FOR THE FACILITATOR

SESSION PREPARATION: BEFORE

- Review the entire session in depth. Role-play or practice setting up and facilitating exercises beforehand. Wherever possible, put material into your own words. Feel free to make notes for this purpose on 3x5 cards or in the book next to the written instructions.
- *Needed Materials:* Name badges; felt pens for writing names; compact disk or audiotape player; recorded music; small table; a candle, candleholder or plate, and matches; easel; easel paper pads (also known as "flip chart" paper); a bell; artistic supplies (could include: crayons, color markers, pastels, white 8 1/2 x 11" paper, colored construction paper, clay, wire, aluminum foil, etc).
- On easel paper:
  - Write the general description of violence found in the "What is Violence" section.
  - Write up questions for "What is Violence" small group discussion.
  - Draw the graphic of concentric circles.
- For alternatives on the Nonviolence Spectrum and the Small Group Reflection see *www.paceebene.org*

PREPARATION: ON THE DAY OF THE SESSION

- Set a table in the center of the room with a candle and matches. Have a compact disk or audiotape of reflective music in a nearby audio-player.
- *Assemble and Put Up "The Wall of Learning and Growing."* To create the wall, tape 4-8 pieces of easel paper together on an available wall (or floor). Write "The Wall of Learning and Growing" in large letters at the top. Write the following headings: *Insights (or Aha's)*, *Tools*, and *Applications*. (Ideally, the Wall will be left in place between sessions; if this is not possible, store the Wall between the sessions and assemble it each session).

SESSION 2: **The Situation We Often Face**

WELCOME — 2 MIN.

Present the following in your own words:

> Hello and welcome back. In Session 2 we are going to consider some of the ways that violence works and explore how analyzing violence can help us understand more about nonviolence.

OPENING — 5 MIN.

> Before we get started however, let's take a few moments of silence to disconnect from the busy-ness of the day. *(Light candle)*
>
> Start by taking a few deep breaths — deep enough so that your belly goes out. Refresh your mind by imagining yourself doing something refreshing — whatever that means to you. Standing in a cool breeze, taking a cold drink of water, whatever it is to feel refreshed, imagine yourself doing it right now. *(Pause for two or three minutes.)*

REFLECTING ON HOMEWORK — 10 MIN.

Share the following:

> Now, I invite you to get together with your Nonviolence Partner to reflect for a few minutes on your experiences or insights since the last session, as well as to reflect on your readings, journaling, or nonviolent action.

Sound the bell and let the participants know when there is a minute left.

ZONES OF LEARNING — 10 MIN.

> Thank you all for sharing. This program is about education, learning, and growing. We have found the Zones of Learning to be a useful tool to help us maximize our learning. Let's look at the diagram on the following page:

Point to circles and read/explain diagram. Then share in your own words:

> When we have positive experiences that we're used to and we've had many times before, we are in our comfort zone. This can mean anything from reading a good book, to spending time with friends, to doing a familiar job task. Even though we're comfortable with this experience, we can learn and grow from it.
>
> Sometimes we have experiences that are newer, that make us a little nervous; we may be in our discomfort zone. It may be a brand new job assignment or a new stage in a relationship. It's an event that's not too far outside your experience, but makes you

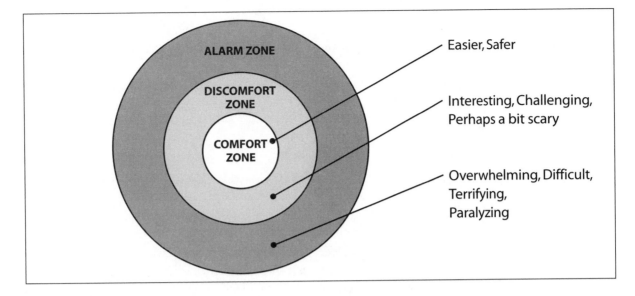

uneasy. It provides you with a good opportunity to grow and learn.

Sometimes things happen to us that really scare us. It's so sudden or so unfamiliar that you find yourself feeling afraid, stuck, lost, confused, and generally wanting to hide in bed. Perhaps it may be an emergency you witness on the street or an extremely short deadline on a very tough job assignment.

As we consider these we can see that personal transformation can take place when we are in our *comfort zone*. It is more likely to occur when we step out of our *comfort zone* into our *discomfort zone*.

But experiences that are too challenging can move us into our *alarm zone*, where fear and distress shut down our learning, growth, and transformation.

Our comfort zone can offer us a center and a base for learning — and for action. Our discomfort zone can offer us new ways to grow and change. The alarm zone can overwhelm us. In practicing nonviolence, we will see how our transformation — as persons and as societies — depends on the importance of comfort and voluntary discomfort, and also being aware of and cautious of the paralyzing impact of the alarm zone.

Ask for questions. If you are unsure of the answer don't hesitate to say so or to ask the rest of the group for their thoughts. Then:

As we begin to explore the nature of violence, I encourage you to begin practicing becoming aware of what zone you are in and to explore going into the discomfort zone.

This exercise has been adapted from a handout "Using Discomfort Zones For Learning," by Future Now: A Training Collective, which incorporated ideas first developed by Training for Change.

THE VIOLENCE SPECTRUM — 35 MIN.

Clear a large space. (If necessary, move chairs and other objects to the side.) Write "Violent" on one piece of paper, and "Not Violent" on another piece of paper. Place the piece of paper with "Violent" on the wall on one side of the room; place the paper with "Not Violent" on the wall on the other side of the room. Place some masking tape on the floor in a line from the "Violent" to the "Not Violent" side. Ask people to get up and move into this open space. Then share:

Now we are going to explore our understanding of violence with an exercise called the "Violence Spectrum." We will reflect on a variety of situations and think about to what degree the actions of the people in these situations are "violent."

To help us, we are designating one side of the room as violent (*point to it*) and the other side (*indicate it*) as "not violent."

The closer you position yourself to the "Violent" side of the room along the line, the more violent you think the person is being in this situation.

The closer you position yourself to the "Not Violent" side of the room along the line, the less violent you think the person is being in this situation.

If you are undecided, stand in the middle of the room off the line.

I will now give you a situation, and then ask you to decide if the person in the situation is being violent or not violent. When you hear this, please move to a place relative to the center line that indicates what you think or feel. Then I'll ask you why you are located where you are. If you hear a point from someone else that you have not considered but that makes you change your point of view, you can move from your position.

Let me be clear from the beginning: everyone's decision or position is equally valid! Please respect everyone else's opinion!

Read one of the situations from the list below:

- Gloria spray-paints "this insults women" on a sexist billboard. From your point of view, is Gloria's action violent or not violent?
- Hank drains the oil from his car and pours it into the gutter. From your point of view, is his action violent or not?
- A person does nothing as a man on a nearby street repeatedly slaps a woman who appears to be his wife or girlfriend. From your point of view, is the onlooker's action violent or not violent?
- Alice has greatly insulted John. In turn, John refuses to talk to Alice. Is John's action violent or not violent? (After the initial discussion you might change it a bit by saying "John has shut Alice out of his life. From your point of view, is John's action violent or not violent?")
- A bartender serves a customer another drink even though she knows the customer is an alcoholic and is drunk. From your point of view, is the bartender's action violent or not?
- A waste incinerator is releasing toxic waste into the air in a low-income neighborhood. An environmental rights group protests at the incinerator, eventually causing it to shut down. From your point of view, are the group's actions violent or not violent?
- Beverly shoots a burglar who comes into her house. From your point of view, is her action violent or not violent?
- A character on a TV police show is murdering other people. From your point of view, is the police show violent or not?
- A junior high teacher shows a tape of the beheading of a person in Iraq to his class. From your point of view, was his action violent or not violent?
- During the Summer Olympics of 2004 the U.S. media often showed and interviewed spouses of competing athletes. No U.S. media covering the Olympics ever showed or interviewed a partner of a homosexual athlete. From your point of view, is the media's lack of coverage violent or not violent?

- David puts mouse poison out in his house. From your point of view, is David's action violent or not violent?
- A company decides to move to Mexico to save labor costs. This costs a small town in the United States 200 jobs, while creating 250 jobs for Mexicans. From your point of view, are the company's actions violent or not violent?
- Greg spanks his child who is misbehaving. From your point of view, is his action violent or not violent?

Ask participants whether the actions of the person or group are "violent" or "not violent." Invite participants to move to a space in the room that represents their thinking. Then:

Why have you located yourself where you did?

Call on people by alternating between participants on opposite ends of the line. Because participants are given limited information in the scenario, they will often make certain assumptions about it. During the discussion, ask people to pay attention to their assumptions. As the energy starts to wane for a particular scenario, ask the following:

What could have been a different response by the person acting in this situation that would have resulted in a "win-win" situation, where both parties benefit and get their needs met?

Do two or more other scenarios in the same way.

Debriefing the Violence Spectrum

After you have finished with all the scenarios you wanted to present, invite participants to return to their chairs. Debrief this exercise by asking the following question. Write the responses on a piece of easel paper.

What did you learn in this exercise?

In concluding this exercise and transitioning to the break, sum up briefly (in a sentence or two) the learnings of the group. If the following points were not made, consider making them at this time:

This exercise often:
- Reveals the wide range of opinions people hold about violence;
- Highlights that we often bring our assumptions and biases to the decisions we make; and
- Allows us to begin thinking about how to respond more nonviolently in different situations.

* For a variation on this exercise, see *www.paceebene.org*

> *I believe war is a weapon of persons without personal power, that is to say, the power to reason, the power to persuade, from a position of morality and integrity; and that to go to war with an enemy who is weaker than you is to admit you possess no resources within yourself to bring to bear on your fate.*
>
> — ALICE WALKER

BREAK — 10 MIN.

ENGAGE IN ACTION

The spike in violence had been horrifyingly dramatic.

Over a few short weeks, a public housing project for the mentally ill in a large Midwestern U.S. city had experienced five suicides, two questionable deaths, and numerous fist-fights. In spite of this growing, violent wave, the housing case manager couldn't persuade mental health agencies to provide the long-term support she knew was needed. Because of the chronic nature of mental illness, with its often slow response to behavioral interventions, she believed that what was required was ongoing mental health outreach to form a support group with the residents. But the assistance for this just wasn't there.

"I felt a deep compassion for the suffering of these wounded sisters and brothers," the case manager later wrote. Aware of the way that, for all people, our woundedness lies at the root of violence in ourselves, toward others, and in our culture, she wondered, "Can I help them face their wounds with active nonviolence?"

She decided to try. To do this, she turned to Pace e Bene Nonviolence Service's study program, *From Violence To Wholeness*, (now entitled *Engage: Exploring Nonviolent Living*) and adapted it to the special circumstances of the housing project.

Though the program was designed for ten weekly sessions, she expanded it to a 30-week process. She then began gathering with the residents who wanted to explore nonviolence as a creative and effective process to resolve the violence in their lives and in the world. Each session, they reflected together on the previous week's experiences of violence and possible nonviolent responses. They discussed basic readings and viewed videos on Gandhi, Dorothy Day, Martin Luther King, Jr., and Cesar Chavez, highlighting the principles they had lived by, and how their very lives had demonstrated an alternative to the cycle of violence. In each session the group did role-playing, skits, and group activities to experience the toolbox of techniques to become nonviolent peacemakers.

"I have been humbled by many of the behavioral changes and testimonies of the residents," wrote the case manager (who prefers to remain anonymous to protect the privacy of the persons involved). "By about the twelfth week, physical fights and verbally abusive behavior were greatly reduced and at some sessions were not present at all. Some residents made statements that their psychiatrist or their community support worker commented on how they were changing.

"The residents themselves expressed statements of 'feeling peace,' 'feeling less angry,' 'more in control.' You could also hear a sense of pride in their conversations with one another and with other residents in the building who had chosen not to participate. They were not in a support group for the mentally ill because they were 'crazy'; rather, they were in a 'nonviolence group' learning to be peacemakers with themselves and others in the building, working to make it a better place to live."

WHAT IS VIOLENCE? — 20 MIN.

Sound the bell to let participants know it is time to return. Then present in your own words:

As we look further into the nature of violence, it would be helpful to have a working definition. The one adopted for use here is this:

> Violence is any physical, emotional, verbal, institutional, structural, or spiritual behavior, attitude, policy, or condition that diminishes, dominates, or destroys ourselves or others.

As we can see, this is very far-reaching. It includes many of the definitions we all carry with us, but it includes a great deal more. With this in mind, let's look at some assumptions that are commonly made when a person is deciding what is violent and what is not violent, some that perhaps were made during the last exercise:

1. An act is violent only when someone is physically harmed.
2. A violent act is always intentional.
3. Some kinds of violence are acceptable.
4. Violence is something done to someone else.
5. Violence is only done to people or animals.

Ask the group:

How does any one of these assumptions affect our actions? *(Write answers on easel.)*

Let's break up into small groups, and consider one of the following questions. To choose which one, write each down on a piece of paper and have someone select the one your group will use. *(Post questions.)*

There is so much focus on the distinction between nonviolence and violence, between nonviolent people and violent people. But in reality it's not that easy to take sides like that. One can never be sure that one is completely on the side of nonviolence or that the other person is completely on the side of violence. Nonviolence is a direction, not a separating line. It has no boundaries.

— THICH NHAT HANH

1. Do you think that intention plays a role in defining an action as violent or not violent? If so, in what way?
2. What if an intention is good, but clearly the act is violent — say, physically hurting someone. Does that make a difference? Does it make it a different kind of violence?
3. Are some types of violence acceptable where others are not? If so, how do we decide which is which?

Add any question that will invite participants to explore the deeper questions on the nature of violence per the assumptions already stated.) Then bring participants back to large group.

STATEMENTS ABOUT VIOLENCE

Engage:

Violence is any physical, emotional, verbal, institutional, structural, or spiritual behavior, attitude, policy, or condition that diminishes, dominates, or destroys ourselves or others.

Violence crosses boundaries without permission, disrupts authentic relationships, and separates us from other beings.

Violence is often motivated by fear, unrestrained anger, or greed to increase domination or power over others. It can also be motivated by a desire for justice in the face of injustice: a longing to put things right, to overcome an imbalance of power, to end victimization or oppression.

Often, those who perpetrate violence do so with the conviction that they are overcoming a prior violence or injustice. Violence often provokes new violence. This spiral of retaliatory violence is often propelled by social or personal scripts that are enacted in situations of conflict.

Miki Kashtan:

Violence comes out of fear or desperation when people do not see any other options for meeting their needs. Under such circumstances, the likelihood increases that people will act in ways that compromise the emotional, physical, social, or spiritual safety of others. Violence involves losing one's awareness of other people's humanity, and thus leads people to act in ways that they would otherwise not choose.

John Dear:

Violence is best defined as that act of forgetting or ignoring who we are: brothers and sisters of one another. …Violence is any behavior that dehumanizes us, from thoughts of self-hatred to intentional harm or physical injury done to another. Our apathy and indifference in the face of relievable suffering and our willingness to defend our possessions and self-interests have harmful effects on others and are a participation in violence. The lack of love and the anxiety in our hearts, the unwillingness to suffer with others and to forgive others, and the insecurity, the fears and untruth in which we frame our lives are all participations in violence because their consequences are harmful to others.

Johan Galtung:

There are three types of violence: direct violence, structural violence, and cultural violence.

Direct violence refers to physical acts of violence.

Structural violence is the violence built into the very social, political, and economic systems that govern societies, states, and the world. It is the different allocations of goods, resources, opportunities, between different groups, classes, genders, nationalities, etc. Its relationship to direct violence is similar to that of the bottom nine-tenths of an iceberg, hidden from view.

Cultural violence includes those aspects of a culture that legitimize violence and make violence seem like an acceptable means of responding to conflict. It is a way a community or individuals view themselves in relation to themselves, to "others," and the world. It often supports a sense of superiority over, and dehumanization of, other cultures.

SHARING AN EXPERIENCE OF VIOLENCE — 30 MIN.

Creative Reflection [15 min.]

Invite participants to use the creative supplies to reflect on an experience of violence.

> The Violent Spectrum exercise gave us an opportunity to reflect on some examples of violence. We will now have the opportunity to personalize our exploration of violence a little to deepen our understanding of our own small and large experiences of violence. We will take about 10 minutes to reflect on a personal experience of violence using a creative medium, for example, crayons, markers, clay, and so forth.
>
> Please reflect on a time, that you'd feel comfortable sharing in a small group, when you either were violent to someone or someone was violent to you. Violence occurs every day of our lives. In our culture it can feel like we are basically enrolled in Violence 101. Choose one of those experiences and reflect on it using the creative supplies. You may want to focus on an experience or situation that has been resolved, at least in a very basic sense. After you reflect on this experience you will have the opportunity to share with two other people.
>
> Again, please reflect at whatever level you feel comfortable. As we've said before, this process is not psychotherapy or counseling but a process for exploring how we can bring the vision and method of nonviolence into our lives and the larger world. I invite you to focus on an experience in light of this.

Small Group Reflection [15 min.]

Call people back into the large group and divide the total number of participants by three, and have participants count around the circle up to that number. Then have the 1's gather in one part of the room, the 2's in another place, and so on. It is okay if not all the groups have the same number of participants.

Then, again in your own words:

> I invite you to relax and be aware of the presence of those in your circle. I want to ask you, one at a time, to share (again at whatever level you feel comfortable) either the personal experience of violence that you drew or wrote about or about the reflection you had as you were drawing or journaling. We will each have five minutes.

After 10 minutes tell the groups they have 5 minutes left, so they should be shifting to the last person. Call the groups back into the large group after 15 minutes. Once seated, share:

> I invite you to come to the center of the room and place your artwork on the communal table.

After participants have finished, invite them to take a moment of silence to honor the sharing of their experiences of violence.

CONCLUSION — 20 MIN.

Review the homework for next session:

If you have not made the commitment to yourself that was found at the end of Session 1, I encourage you to think about doing that in the next week.

⊙ Nonviolence Journal

Suggested Topic:
We've all had the experience of having a bad day and then expressing our frustration at a relatively minor situation at home. Think of a time when this went badly. Here is an example: Jane has had a very bad day at work. When she comes home, she finds that the dishes her partner promised he (or she) would do are still dirty. Jane starts yelling, "You are so irresponsible! I can't count on you for anything. Why am I the one who always has to do everything around here? You are such a slob!"

You are invited to remember a situation like this in which you reacted like Jane. Then ask yourself the following questions:
1) What is happening in your body just before you start reacting? Where do you feel the sensation? In your head, your stomach, your hands? What does it feel like?
2) At the moment you react, what is it you're reacting to? What do you really need right at that moment? Is it for the dishes to be done, or is it really something else? What is that something else?
3) At the moment you react does your partner (family member, whoever) seem like a person (human being) to you, or does he or she feel like something else which isn't exactly a person but maybe more of a thing — like a slob, for example? If so, when did that happen? How did it happen?

⊙ Nonviolent Action

1) Read the Statements on Violence and reflect on which of the statements most connects with your experience and how they might broaden your understanding of violence. Using one of them, count the number of "violent instances or expressions" in a half-hour of television or radio, or on the front page of a newspaper. OR:
2) Using the idea of the three comfort zones, pick a day when you try to be observant about which zone you're in at any particular time. Notice what the sensations are that are going on as you may move from one zone to another, or any other thoughts that accompany your experience.

⊙ Next Session's Reading

Please read the readings located at the end of this session.

⊙ Introduce the Wall of Learning and Growing

The Wall of Learning and Growing is a way to gather and accumulate individual and group learnings and insights throughout the Engage program. At the end of each session (and throughout the session, as appropriate), you are invited to add any insights or aha moments, any tools for acting more nonviolently that you might have learned, or any ways you are going to apply these learnings in your everyday life. If you've had any insights or learnings this session or in the last session, we'll take a couple of minutes right now to write or draw your insights on the "Wall."

⊙ Commitment

If you have not yet made the commitment found at the end of the first session, please consider doing so before the next session.

⊙ Closing

The following exercise is used in Indonesian cultures to release and balance the energy of strong emotions. The exercise consists of holding each finger for a minute, wrapping the opposite hand around that finger. The finger-hold does not change the situation or reality, but helps you to be more centered, not to be controlled by the emotion, and able to make clearer decisions.

You can do these holds with either hand. The theory is that through each finger runs a channel or meridian of energy connected with different organs of the body. By holding each finger you are able to drain and balance the energy flow. As you hold a finger, usually within a minute or two you will feel an energy pulse or throbbing sensation. This indicates that the energy is flowing and balanced, and usually the strong feeling or emotion passes.

Share with the group that each of the fingers is associated with an emotion in the following way:

- Thumb: Sadness
- First finger: Fear
- Middle finger: Anger
- Ring Finger: Anxiety
- Pinky: Self-esteem

Review it once or twice.

If you are feeling a certain emotion and holding the finger corresponding to that emotion with the other hand for a minute or two, the emotion may start to decrease. Let's try it now.

After a couple of minutes, ask if anyone noticed a change in their feeling state. Encourage the participants to use this tool anytime they are feeling strong emotions.

Thank you for coming tonight and for your willingness to look at the violence in our world and in our lives.

KEY ORGANIZATIONS: TRANSFORMING VIOLENCE

TRANSCEND. *www.transcend.org;* Tel: +40 742 079 716; Fax: +40 2 64 420 298. TRANSCEND is a peace and development organization for conflict transformation by peaceful means. Its mission is to bring about a more peaceful world by using action, education/training, dissemination, and research to handle conflicts creatively and nonviolently. Members of its network include about 150 invited scholars and practitioners from 50 countries, working on 20 programs.

Victim-Offender Reconciliation Program (VORP). *www.vorp.com;* 1007 NE 118th Avenue, Portland, OR 97220; 503-255-8677; *martyprice@vorp.com.* VORP works to bring restorative justice reform to our criminal and juvenile justice systems, to empower victims, offenders, and communities to heal the effects of crime, to curb recidivism, and to offer our society a more effective and humanistic alternative to the growing outcry for more prisons and more punishment.

HOMEWORK

NONVIOLENCE JOURNAL

Suggested Topic or Question:

Most of us have had a bad day and then expressed our frustration over a relatively minor situation at home. Think of a time when this went badly. Here is an example: Jane has had a very bad day at work. When she comes home, she finds that the dishes her partner promised he (or she) would do are still dirty. Jane starts yelling, "You are so irresponsible! I can't count on you for anything. Why am I the one who always has to do everything around here? You are such a slob!"

You are invited to remember a situation like this in which you reacted like Jane. Then ask yourself the following questions:

1) What is happening in your body just before you start reacting? Where do you feel the sensation? In your head, your stomach, your hands? What does it feel like?

2) At the moment you react, what is it you're reacting to? What do you really need right at that moment? Is it for the dishes to be done, or is it really something else? What is that something else?

3) At the moment you react does your partner (family member, whoever) seem like a person (human being) to you, or does he or she feel like something else which isn't exactly a person but maybe more of a thing — like a slob, for example? If so, when did that happen? How did it happen?

NONVIOLENT ACTION

Take one or more of the following actions between now and the next session:

1) Read the Statements on Violence and reflect on which of the statements most connects with your experience and how they might broaden your understanding of violence. Using one of them, count the number of "violent instances or expressions" in a half-hour of television or radio, or on the front page of a newspaper. OR:

2) Using the idea of the three comfort zones, pick a day when you try to be observant about which zone you're in at any particular time. Notice what the sensations are that are going on as you may move from one zone to another, or any other thoughts that accompany your experience.

Soul Force

by Cynthia Stateman

The phone call came just after dinner. It was my cousin Philip. He said, "We need you to come home. Daddy has been killed."

I had just been to Kingston the previous summer for the fabulous celebration my hometown had put on to honor Uncle John on his 75th birthday. He had been Kingston's first black physician, and had served that town for 50 years.

How could Uncle John have been killed?

When I was a little girl, I liked to ride with him on Saturday mornings as he made his rounds in his big red Edsel station wagon. We would start off with visits to his patients in town, and then head out on dusty tobacco roads to the shacks and trailers where the sharecroppers and mill workers lived. Folks would pay him whatever they could — money if they had it, a handful of eggs, firewood, a handshake, a prayer. Who would kill my Uncle John? He built a clinic on Reed Street. It was the very first, and for many years it had been the only clinic or hospital where Black folks could go without having to wait until last to be seen by a doctor. Why would anyone kill my Uncle John?

Some punk kid, poor white trash, had broken into the clinic with a gun in his pocket, looking for something to steal. Uncle John caught him by surprise, and was shoved hard against the wall. He fell to the floor, gasping for breath. Yeah, the kid dialed 911, and then he tried to run for it. But it was too late — Uncle John was dead and the cops were at the door.

My cousins were arguing with one another when I arrived. Shock, fatigue, heartbreak, anger, and grief. Visitors had been stopping by to let them know that the whole town was outraged by the crime. My cousins had been assured by one and all that the DA would do as he had promised — send that good-for-nothing poor white cracker punk kid straight to death row.

But the public defender had come by, too. He confirmed that the DA was planning to charge the kid with a capital offense, and said that the kid had made up his mind to plead guilty. He said, "The charge doesn't fit the crime. That boy committed a crime for sure, and it is a terrible tragedy, but it would be a real stretch of the law to call it a capital offense." He had a question and a favor to ask. Did our family want justice or did we want vengeance? Shock, fatigue, heartbreak, anger and grief. Would the family be willing, he asked, to speak to the DA on behalf of justice? Would we be willing to ask the DA to file charges that were truly commensurate with the crime? My cousin Donny threw him out the house.

Donny shouted, "What a lot of nerve!" Rhonda asked, "What do you think Daddy would have wanted?" Philip asked, "But, it would hurt to talk to the DA?" Donny bellowed, "Over my dead body!" Frank said, "It's not fair. It's not our job to tell the DA what to do." Ellen insisted, "I think the public defender is right, and you know it too!" "I don't care!" Donny cried, "A punk like that is going to end up on death row sooner or later anyway. Our father is dead because of him. Don't talk to me about justice. Where was the justice in Daddy dying like that?" Rhonda said, "I don't know. All I know is how awful all of this is. I don't know what the right thing to do is." I asked, "Has anybody considered the possibility of talking to the kid?"

We piled into the van and headed for the jailhouse. Donny stayed behind. We bullied, badgered, threatened, and made a whole lot of noise before the attorneys would agree to set up the visit. It was awkward it first. The punk sat on one side of the table, staring down at his hands. We sat on the other side, taking in every detail: blue eyes, thin lips, pointed nose, dimpled chin, brown hair, crooked teeth, high forehead, ragged fingernails bitten down to the quick. Rhonda broke the silence. "You know, the DA is calling for your life. And your lawyer said you're going to plead guilty." He nodded. "I need to know what happened. We need to know why. We need to understand this thing." He was silent. "Tell me!" He raised his eyes, "I'm sorry about your father." "It's too late for sorry." Rhonda said. "How old are you?"

His name is David. He had just turned 19. He'd grown up in the trailer park known as "The Bottoms," down by the river, just outside of town. Squalid. Ignorant. Dangerous. Crackerville. We asked questions, and he talked for more than an hour. He told us what happened. He said he owed a guy some money; money he didn't have; money he had no legitimate way of getting; money the guy was willing to kill him for. "Look. I'm sorry about your daddy. I really am. He was a good man. I remember him coming down to the Bottoms a long time ago, knocking on doors, letting everybody know that us kids could come to the clinic and get shots and such. My mama took all of us. Said there wasn't too many people around like him that cared anything about Bottom folks."

He said that he wasn't scared of prison. No, he hadn't been "inside" before; had never been caught. "I been in the wrong place, doing the wrong thing, for the wrong reason plenty times." He said that prison didn't seem like it was would be too bad; he'd lived a lot worse. He said his daddy was inside, and so was an uncle and one of his brothers; maybe they'd hook up. Death row? "I ain't never expected to live to no ripe old age anyway." He had quit school in the 9th grade. He said that, if he had it to do all over again, he would join the military. He had tried to enlist, but had failed the test. He said, "you got to have your reading up to be in the Army nowadays."

We sat in the van and talked. "Jeez, what a loser." "Uh huh." "He's only 19." "Face it, David doesn't have a snowball's chance in Hell of turning his life around." "He's illiterate." "Yep." "Pathetic." "Uh huh." "I hate to say this, but prison just may be a step up for him." "He could learn to read in there." "Right, Rhonda. What are you doing?" "I'm making a list of books. What if we suggested that he had to learn to read, and finish a long list of books, and had to get his GED as conditions for parole? And what if, as a condition for probation, he had to learn a trade, and keep a job, and do some serious community service work for 5 or 10 years after he was released?" "Well, he is only 19." "Add the Autobiography of Malcolm X to your list." "If David could make good somehow, then maybe Daddy's death would have some meaning." "This is crazy." "Yep." "Do we talk to the DA?" "Uh huh." The DA was incredulous. But we stood our ground and made our case. He agreed to reduce the charges against David and to submit our recommendations to the court.

Donny was so angry at us all that he had threatened to boycott the memorial service. His wife had only been able to talk him into coming at the very last minute. To make matters even worse for Donny, the court had, with the family's consent, granted David's request to attend the service. It had been agreed that David and his mother would join us in the opening procession, and would sit with us during the service. There were hundreds of people in attendance. The aisles were filled, and every seat was taken. One after another, Uncle John's family and friends stood and came forward, to tell a story, to share a song, to recite a poem, to remember him, to speak of loss, and to say good-bye. When David stood, I was confused at first, and I had thought that perhaps he was preparing to leave. But no, he turned to the congregation and began to speak. "A good man is dead because

> *Did our family want justice or did we want vengeance? Shock, fatigue, heartbreak, anger and grief. Would the family be willing, he asked, to speak to the DA on behalf of justice?*

of what I did. I'm sorry." He gestured towards my cousins. "They spared my life. I didn't deserve that. I'm going to be in prison for a very long time, but I'm not being sent there to die. What I want to ask all of you here is: Is there any way you can forgive me?"

The pastor reached out to David and asked him to kneel. He called for a laying on of hands, placed his right hand on David's head, and began to pray. The pastor prayed for forgiveness. Ellen was the first to rise and place her hands upon David's back. The pastor prayed for mercy. Philip and Rhonda rose and joined them. The pastor prayed for reconciliation. Donny stood and added his hands. He prayed for young people like David whose lives we've given up on. The rest of the family rose together, and we added our hands. Before too long, the entire gathering had come forward; laying hands on one another until we were all connected as one. The pastor prayed, and we prayed with him. We prayed for David to be healed, and we prayed for ourselves to be healed; and when it was done, we sang "Amazing Grace."

I conducted a workshop on active nonviolence, what Gandhi called "Soul Force," a few months ago. My audience was a wonderful group of Christian activists, fully committed to working for social justice.

When I asked them how they had applied the principles of active nonviolence, and what effect it has had on their lives, they spoke of sit-ins, marches, leafleting, demonstrations, petitions, civil disobedience, boycotts, and arrests. They spoke of civil rights, women's rights, human rights, peace, and justice. I asked, "What about your personal lives?" They were puzzled by the question. I tried to clarify. "What are the ways in which the principles of active nonviolence have affected your relationships at work, in church, in school, with family, with personal friends and enemies?" After a moment of silence, one of the participants said, "I'm not sure I understand what you mean." We spent the rest of the time we had together discussing the principles of active nonviolence, and the implications of Soul Force with regard to disarming our hearts. It didn't occur to me to share this story until after the workshop had ended. That's why I am sharing it now. Let us not ever forget that the whole point of active nonviolence is to open up the possibility to heal and to be healed.

These events took place when Cynthia Stateman was an intern with Pace e Bene. She is currently a United Methodist Church minister pastoring a church in California.

SESSION 3: READING 2

The Seville Statement
The United Nations Educational, Scientific and Cultural Organization

---

The following statement challenging many conventional assumptions about violence was developed and signed by a large international group of scientists under the auspices of UNESCO, the United Nations Educational, Scientific and Cultural Organization. It was published in 1986.

Introduction

Believing that it is our responsibility to address from our particular disciplines the most dangerous and destructive activities of our species, violence and war; recognizing that science is a human cultural product which cannot be definitive or all encompassing; and gratefully acknowledging the support of the authorities of Seville and representatives of the Spanish UNESCO, we, the undersigned scholars from around the world and from relevant sciences, have met and arrived at the following Statement on Violence. In it, we challenge a number of alleged biological findings that have been used, even by some in our disciplines, to justify violence and war. Because the alleged findings have contributed to an atmosphere of pessimism in our time, we submit that the open, considered rejection of these misstatements can contribute significantly to the International Year of Peace.

Misuse of scientific theories and data to justify violence and war is not new but has been made since the advent of modern science. For example, the theory of evolution has been used to justify not only war, but also genocide, colonialism, and suppression of the weak.

We state our position in the form of five propositions. We are aware that there are many other issues about violence and war that could be fruitfully addressed from the standpoint of our disciplines, but we restrict ourselves here to what we consider a most important first step.

We, the undersigned scholars from around the world and from relevant sciences, have met and arrived at the following Statement on Violence. In it, we challenge a number of alleged biological findings that have been used, even by some in our disciplines, to justify violence and war.

First Proposition

IT IS SCIENTIFICALLY INCORRECT to say that we have inherited a tendency to make war from our animal ancestors. Although fighting occurs widely throughout animal species, only a few cases of destructive intraspecies fighting between organized groups have ever been reported among naturally living species, and none of these involve the use of tools designed to be weapons. Normal predatory feeding upon other species cannot be equated with intraspecies violence. Warfare is a peculiarly human phenomenon and does not occur in other animals.

The fact that warfare has changed so radically over time indicates that it is a product of culture. Its biological connection is primarily through language which makes possible the coordination of groups, the transmission of technology, and the use of tools. War is biologically possible, but it is not inevitable, as evidenced by its variation in occurrence and nature over time and space. There are cultures which have not engaged in war for centuries, and there are cultures which have engaged in war frequently at some times and not at others.

Second Proposition

IT IS SCIENTIFICALLY INCORRECT to say that war or any other violent behavior is genetically programmed into our human nature. While genes are involved at all levels of nervous system function, they provide a developmental potential that can be actualized only in conjunction with the ecological and social environment. While individuals vary in their predispositions to be affected by their experience, it is the interaction between their genetic endowment and conditions of nurturance that determines their personalities. Except for rare pathologies, the genes do not produce individuals necessarily predisposed to violence. Neither do they determine the opposite. While genes are co-involved in establishing our behavioral capacities, they do not by themselves specify the outcome.

Third Proposition

IT IS SCIENTIFICALLY INCORRECT to say that in the course of human evolution there has been a selection for aggressive behavior more than for other kinds of behavior. In all well-studied species, status within the group is achieved by the ability to cooperate and to fulfill social functions relevant to the structure of that group. 'Dominance' involves social bondings and affiliations; it is not simply a matter of the possession and use of superior physical power, although it does involve aggressive behaviors. Where genetic selection for aggressive behavior has been artificially instituted in animals, it has rapidly succeeded in producing hyper-aggressive individuals; this indicates that aggression was not maximally selected under natural conditions. When such experimentally-created hyper-aggressive animals are present in a social group, they either disrupt its social structure or are driven out. Violence is neither in our evolutionary legacy nor in our genes.

Fourth Proposition

IT IS SCIENTIFICALLY INCORRECT to say that humans have a "violent brain." While we do have the neural apparatus to act violently, it is not automatically activated by internal or external stimuli. Like higher primates and unlike other animals, our higher neural processes filter such stimuli before they can be acted upon. How we act is shaped by how we have been conditioned and socialized. There is nothing in our neurophysiology that compels us to react violently.

Fifth Proposition

IT IS SCIENTIFICALLY INCORRECT to say that war is caused by 'instinct' or any single motivation. The emergence of modern warfare has been a journey from the primacy of emotional and motivational factors, sometimes called "instincts," to the primacy of cognitive factors. Modern war involves institutional use of personal characteristics such as obedience, suggestibility, and idealism, social skills such as language, and rational considerations such as cost-calculation, planning, and information processing. The technology of modern war has exaggerated traits associated with violence both in the training of actual combatants and in the preparation of support for war in the general population. As a result of this exaggeration, such traits are often mistaken to be the causes rather than the consequences of the process.

Conclusion

We conclude that biology does not condemn humanity to war, and that humanity can be freed from the bondage of biological pessimism and empowered with confidence to undertake the transformative tasks needed in this International Year of Peace and in the years to come. Although these tasks are mainly institutional and collective, they also rest upon the consciousness of individual participants for whom pessimism and optimism are crucial factors. Just as 'wars begin in the minds of men,' peace also begins in our minds. The same species who invented war is capable of inventing peace. The responsibility lies with each of us.

Source: UNESCO Culture of Peace Programme 7, Place de Fontenoy, 75352 PARIS 07 SP France.

REFLECTIONS ON THE READINGS

Session 3:
Ways We Often React

SESSION 3: **Ways We Often React**

OBJECTIVES

- To explore our beliefs and attitudes about violence
- To explore a range of responses to violence and conflict

AGENDA

- Welcome [1 min.]
- Opening [5 min.]
- Reflection on Homework [10 min.]
- Cultural Beliefs and Attitudes about Violence [50 min.]
- Break [10 min.]
- Some Ways of Reacting to Violence [20 min.]
- Our Own Ways of Reacting to Violence [15 min.]
- "Two Hands of Nonviolence" Posture [20 min.]
- Conclusion [15 min.]
    Nonviolence Journal
    Nonviolent Action
    Next Session's Reading
    Adding to the Wall of Learning and Growing
    Identifying a Nonviolence Principle
    Evaluation
    Closing

READINGS

- Reading #1: Cynthia Stateman, "Soul Force"
- Reading #2: The United Nations Educational, Scientific and Cultural Organization, "The Seville Statement"

NOTES FOR THE FACILITATOR

SESSION PREPARATION: BEFORE

- Review the entire session in depth. Role-play or practice setting up and facilitating exercises beforehand. Wherever possible, put material into your own words. Feel free to make notes for this purpose on 3x5 cards or in the book next to the written instructions.
- Play close attention to time in the session. You don't need to call on everyone with a hand raised when doing debriefs.
- Materials needed:
  - Three 3x5 cards for each person; pen or pencil for everyone; tape dispenser; large bowl
  - Easel pad, pens
- Write out on small strips of paper the five questions under the section on "Cultural Beliefs and Attitudes about Violence."
- Write out on easel paper:
  - Johan Galtung's description of cultural violence
  - Possible Cultural Beliefs and Attitudes about Violence
  - Three small group reflection questions on the Popeye reading
  - Optional: The descriptions (the main ideas) of the Ways of Responding to Violence (Avoiding, Accommodating, and Using Counter-Violence)
- If the Popeye story is not familiar in your cultural or social context, try to find a story, film, etc. that resonates with your setting.
- For a more interactive option for facilitating "The Two Hands of Nonviolence Posture" see website: *www.engagenonviolence.org*.

SESSION 3: **Ways We Often React**

WELCOME — 1 MIN.

Share in your own words:

Welcome back for our third session of the *Engage* Study Program. In this session, we will continue our exploration of the experience and dynamics of violence. We will take a look at some of the cultural beliefs and attitudes about violence and how they are supported. We will explore some different responses or "scripts" that are typically used to deal with violence and conflict, and we will consider an alternative way of responding.

OPENING — 5 MIN.

Ask the participants to gather and sit in their seats. Read the following slowly:

I invite you to close your eyes,
sit quietly,
feeling the rhythm of your breathing,
allowing yourself to become calm and receptive.
Think of a difficulty that you face in your life.
As you sense this difficulty, notice how it affects your body,
heart,
and mind.
Feeling it carefully, begin to ask yourself a few questions,
listening inwardly for their answers.

How have I treated this difficulty so far? *(Pause a while)*
How have I suffered by my own response and reaction to it? *(Pause a while)*
What does this problem ask me to let go of? *(Pause a while)*

In using this reflection to consider your difficulties,
the understanding and openings may come slowly.

After a couple of minutes, invite the participants to open their eyes. If it seems appropriate, repeat this reflection. Ask participants to "listen for deeper answers from your body, heart, and spirit."

REFLECTING ON HOMEWORK — 10 MIN.

I again invite you to get together with your Nonviolence Partner to take a few minutes to reflect on your experiences or insights since the last session, as well as to reflect on the readings, journaling, or nonviolent action.

CULTURAL ATTITUDES AND BELIEFS ABOUT VIOLENCE — 50 MIN.

Introduction [5 Min.]

Say the following in your own words:

In the last session we explored the complexity of violence in the Violence Spectrum and also looked at some of our assumptions about what is or isn't violence.

Now we will look at some of the prevailing cultural attitudes and beliefs (ones that we have been taught since childhood and that surround us in our daily lives) about the power and necessity of violence.

One way to do that is to look at the stories of our culture. To introduce this concept, let's read a short piece from scholar Walter Wink on the Popeye cartoon.

Invite a few people to share in reading the reflection aloud.

POPEYE AND THE MYTH OF REDEMPTIVE VIOLENCE
Adapted from Walter Wink

Walter Wink has studied what he terms the "myth of redemptive violence." In this myth, the world is created and maintained through justified violence overcoming the forces of chaos. Wink asserts that this myth has existed throughout the course of history and is alive and well in our world today. While the following adaptation uses the Popeye cartoon as a contemporary example of this myth, the same pattern can be seen throughout our world, from innumerable movie plots to government policies to interpersonal relationships.

Few cartoon shows have run longer or been more influential in U.S. culture than Popeye and Bluto. In a typical segment, Bluto abducts a screaming and kicking Olive Oyl, Popeye's girlfriend. When Popeye attempts to rescue her, the massive Bluto beats his diminutive opponent to a pulp, while Olive Oyl helplessly wrings her hands. At the last moment, as Bluto is trying, in effect, to rape Olive Oyl, a can of spinach pops from Popeye's pocket and spills into his mouth. Transformed by this infusion of power, Popeye easily demolishes the villain and rescues his beloved.

The format never varies. Neither party ever gains any insight or learns from these encounters. Violence does not teach Bluto to honor Olive Oyl's humanity, and repeated pummelings do not teach Popeye to swallow his spinach *before* the fight.

The structure of this combat myth is thus faithfully repeated on television every week: a superior force representing chaos attacks aggressively; the champion fights back, defensively, only to be humiliated in apparent defeat; the evil power satisfies its lust while the hero is incapacitated; the hero escapes, defeats the evil power decisively, and reaffirms order over chaos.

The psychodynamics of the television cartoon or comic book are marvelously simple: children identify with the good guy so that they can think of themselves as good. This enables them to project onto the bad guy their own repressed anger, violence, rebelliousness, or lust, and then vicariously to enjoy their own evil by watching the bad guy initially prevail. When the good guy finally wins, viewers are then able to reassert control over their own inner tendencies, repress them, and reestablish a sense of goodness.

This structure cannot be altered. Bluto does not simply lose more often — he must *always* lose. Otherwise this entire view of reality would collapse. The good guys must always win. In order to suppress the fear of erupting chaos the same mythic pattern must be endlessly repeated in a myriad of variations that *never in any way alter the basic structure*. No premium is put on reasoning, persuasion, negotiation, or diplomacy. There can be no compromise with an absolute evil.

Small Group Reflection [10 Min.]

Share the following in your own words:

As Walter Wink explains, these beliefs, endlessly repeated, condition our minds to accept without question the propriety of violence in any situation in which our safety (whether it is physical, psycho-emotional, or spiritual safety) is in jeopardy, or when asserting power will create an advantage for us. For this reason it is important to take a closer look at them.

Invite the group to break into groups of three and discuss the following questions. Allow about 4-5 minutes for sharing.

- Can you think of movies or stories that follow this structure?
- Can you think of situations — personal or social, contemporary or historical — that are examples of this?
- What are the possible consequences of this pattern?

Large Group Reflection [20 Min.]

Call the group back together and take about 2 or 3 responses for each question.

Then share the following in your own words:

We have looked at an example of one of the ways that our beliefs and attitudes about the power and necessity of violence get shaped. Johan Galtung, a long-time researcher and author of many books on violence and nonviolence, describes these cultural attitudes that support the use of violence as Cultural Violence.

Read, or invite a participant to read.

Cultural violence includes those aspects of a culture (the beliefs, values, and ways of being) that give legitimacy to violence and make violence seem like an acceptable means of responding to conflict. It is also a way a community or individuals view themselves in relation to themselves, to "others," and to the world. It often supports a sense of superiority over, and dehumanization of, other cultures.

We will explore the first part of Galtung's definition in our time together here. We will explore the second part as part of our homework.

Some possible cultural beliefs about violence may include:

Read, or invite a participant to read, the following that you have printed on the easel paper.

- Violence is the most direct and effective way to confront conflict.
- Violence is necessary to protect ourselves and others.
- Violence is justified to restore justice in the face of injustice.

- Violence is the bottom line. It is the way things are. It cannot be changed.
- Violence is necessary to help establish order and restore stability.
- Though violence separates and disconnects us from each other, it is a price that must be paid for our safety.

Ask the group:

- Were any of these beliefs present in the Popeye story?
- Are any of these beliefs found in or promoted by our culture? If so, which ones?
- Are there other beliefs about violence in our culture?

Let's take a moment to explore more deeply some of the implications of these cultural attitudes and beliefs.

Now break up into small groups. Have a member from each group come to the center and pick a topic question from a bowl. Each group should choose a secretary to take notes.

Small Group Sharing [10 Min.]

Take about 5 minutes in the small groups.

- Choose one of the beliefs listed and discuss the role this belief plays (or doesn't play) in our culture.
- How are these beliefs reinforced in society?
- What might be some ways to test these beliefs?
- Are beliefs changeable?
- What is the relationship between violence and separation?

Large Group Debrief [10 Min.]

Bring the small groups back together. Ask for a volunteer to share the question their group was answering and the main ideas from their conversation.

After all have shared, thank the participants and convey the following:

When we return we will look at typical ways of responding to violence.

> *"Think of what a world we could build if the power unleashed in war were applied to constructive tasks."*
> — ALBERT EINSTEIN

BREAK — 10 MIN.

SOME WAYS OF RESPONDING TO VIOLENCE — 20 MIN.

Share the following in your own words:

Now that we have examined societal beliefs about violence we are going to look at some ways of responding to violence. To better assess how we as individuals might react to violence, let's look at some of the common responses people have to it.

There are three common ways to respond to personal and interpersonal violence. These strategies or "scripts" (habitual ways of responding) include:

- Avoiding violence
- Accommodating violence
- Responding to violence with violence

Let's look at each one of these.

Hand out three 3x5 cards and pens or pencils to everyone. Then present the following ideas:

I. Avoiding Violence

When we use the strategy or script of avoidance or passivity to deal with violence, we:
- Steer clear of getting involved.
- Decide that it is "not my problem."
- Get someone else to deal with it (say, the police or the military).
- Look the other way.
- Feel powerless to do anything.
- Don't know what to do.
- Think to ourselves, "We're not the problem makers. Why do we have to do something?"
- Deny that the violence exists.

Ask the group if they have any questions, and then:

Can you think of a time when you have responded to violence (done to you, to another, or to the planet) by avoiding the violence? If so, please write a word or two or draw a picture that describes the incident on one of the cards I handed out.

THE ENEMY MAKER

To Create an Enemy …
Start with an empty canvas.
Sketch in broad outline the forms of
Men, women, and children.

Dip into the unconscious well of your own
Disowned darkness
With a wide brush and
Stain the strangers with sinister hue
Of the shadow.

Trace onto the face of the enemy the greed,
Hatred, carelessness you dare not claim as
Your own.

Obscure the sweet individuality of each face.

Erase all hints of the myriad loves, hopes,
Fears that play through the kaleidoscope of
Every finite heart.

Twist the smile until it forms the downward
Arc of cruelty.

Strip flesh from bone until only the
Abstract skeleton of death remains.

Exaggerate each feature until man is
Metamorphosed into beast, vermin, insect.

Fill in the background with malignant
Figures from ancient nightmares – devils,
Demons, myrmidons of evil.

When your icon of the enemy is complete
You will be able to kill without guilt,
Slaughter without shame.

The thing you destroy will have become
Merely an enemy of God, an impediment
To the sacred dialectic of history.

— BY SAM KEEN

To conclude this section on Avoiding Violence, ask the group to brainstorm what might be some of the problems with this response. Share the following in your own words if the group hasn't brought out any of these points:

Sometimes we have no real choice but to avoid violence. But when we use the strategy of avoidance we do not deal with the root causes of the conflict. Nor do we deal with the consequences, including the consequences that others face.

II. Accommodating Violence (living with violence)

When we use the strategy or script of accommodation, we:
- Get used to violence. We conclude, "That's just the way it is. Just accept it." Or think, "I can't change the system. There is nothing I can do."
- Adapt to the violence — Think, "If I do anything it will just get worse. Just keep quiet and maybe it will go away."
- Think, "It's not so bad."

This approach assumes that nothing can be done about the violence — it is the way things always have been and the way things always will be — and the best option is "Don't rock the boat."

Ask the group:

Can you think of a time when you have responded to violence (done to you, to another, or to the planet) by accommodating? If so, please write a word or two or draw a picture that describes the incident on one of the cards I handed out.

To conclude this section on Accommodating Violence, ask the group to brainstorm what might be some of the problems with this response. Share the following in your own words if the group hasn't brought out any of these points:

One of the problems with using this strategy is that we become accustomed to the violence to the point where we no longer notice the violence or see a problem with it.

III. Counter-Violence: Responding to Violence with Violence

When we use violence to deal with violence, we:
- Take the offensive by initiating attempts at achieving power and control over the other in order to stop the violence. These can be through violent words or deeds, and can also include the wielding of political or financial power and control. This can be true even in the smallest of political systems, like the family.
- Think: "An eye for an eye."
- Think: "The end justifies the means."
- Think justice can prevail through violence.

This strategy is often based on the assumption that the only way violence will end is if a "better force" (usually ourselves) uses more violence to overpower the other and end it.

Ask the group:

> Can you think of a time when you have responded to violence (done to you, to another, or to the planet) by using violence yourself? If so, please write a word or two or draw a picture that describes the incident on one of the cards I handed out.

To conclude this section on Counter-Violence, ask the group to brainstorm what might be some of the problems with this response. Share the following in your own words if the group hasn't brought out any of these points:

> Some of the problems with this method are that it reinforces what becomes a cycle of violence ("you did this to me, so I have to do that to you," which prompts the other person, group, or country to say the same). In addition, it does not address the roots of the conflict, nor does it create a solution that meets the needs of the parties involved.

SMALL GROUP SHARING — 15 MIN.

Share in your own words:

> Reflect on the three scripts or ways of responding and notice if you tend to respond in one of the ways more than the others. When we often respond in the same way it can be called a script, meaning that it is like the script of a play or movie, where we repeat lines or behaviors that we have learned.

Invite the participants to form small groups of three and say the following in your own words:

> Share with your small group, at whatever level you feel comfortable, the example of when you have responded to violence in one, or more, of the 3 ways listed above. Brainstorm with your partners a more nonviolent way you could have responded in at least one of the situations you shared, i.e., a response that would have met the needs of both yourself and the other person, a "win-win" solution.

Call the group back and ask for one or two volunteers to share any insights that they might have had during their small group discussion. Thank the participants for their willingness to look at their own lives and to share difficult situations with their fellow participants.

THE TWO HANDS OF NONVIOLENCE — 20 MIN.

Share the following in your own words.

> To conclude our investigation of violence, we'll explore what each of these responses might feel like in our bodies with an exercise called, "The Two Hands of Nonviolence." I'll demonstrate first the three typical approaches to violence.
> First, there's *avoiding violence.* This can be depicted by bending over at the waist, covering your ears with your hands, and closing your eyes. It's a sense of retreating from the situation and of not being involved. One could also just turn around.

Demonstrate each of these postures while describing it.

Next, there's *accommodating violence*. This can be depicted by extending your arms in front of you at about a 45-degree angle (halfway between pointing down or parallel to the ground) with your palms facing up. It's that experience of simply passively accepting whatever is happening.

Next, there's *counter-violence*, meeting violence with violence. This can be depicted by extending your arms straight out in front of you, parallel to the ground, palms facing out away from you, pushing outward.

Finally, there's *active nonviolence*. This can be depicted by combining two of the aforementioned poses: one arm is outstretched at a 45-degree angle with the palm facing up and the other arm is straight out in front, parallel to the ground. Finally, pulling these two hands (keeping them in their same mode) closer to the body — in a relaxed but steady way.

Active nonviolence is a process that holds these two realities in tension and is like saying to a person:

On the one hand (symbolized by the hand that is out in front of me), I will not cooperate with your violence or injustice; I will resist it with every fiber of my being.

On the other hand (symbolized by the hand that is open), I am open to you as a human being.

Perform each of these slowly. Invite people to hold each pose for 15 to 30 seconds. Ask people to notice any feelings or sensations that they experience as they hold the poses and imagine in front of them someone with whom they are in conflict. After going through the entire set, ask people to return to the approach they think they use most in responding to conflict or violence. Then ask them to return to the approach they think they use the least.

Debrief in Pairs

Invite the participants to pair up and share with their partner on the following:

- What did you notice in doing the postures?
- What did you feel in your body?
- Did you notice any difference between the first three responses and the fourth (Two Hands) response?

Bring the group back together and conclude the exercise with two or three sharings from the participants. Convey the following in your own words if it has not been raised:

RICE BAGS DEFEAT NUCLEAR WEAPONS

In the 1950s, the interfaith peace organization Fellowship of Reconciliation launched an ambitious campaign to challenge the American people and government to look beyond politics and to feed the hungry. They organized a "Feed Thine Enemy" program, in which tiny bags of rice were sent to President Dwight Eisenhower at the White House with a message concerning famine in Communist China: "If thine enemy hunger, feed him."

It flopped. No one in the White House acknowledged the existence of the campaign, and it didn't change the public silence on Chinese suffering. Hostility grew between the nations, and there was no alteration of any policy toward China. Except one.

A crisis arose over the possession of the islands of Quemoy and Matsu, islands disputed by China and its U.S.-backed Taiwanese enemies. Twice the generals advising Eisenhower recommended preemptive nuclear strikes against China, and each time Eisenhower turned to his aides and asked how many little bags of rice had come in. Thousands, he was told.

In deference to the opinion of so many Americans, Eisenhower cited the little bags of rice as the reason he ruled out nuclear weapons in this case.

Thinking in terms of "scripts," and trying to experience what they might feel like bodily can be helpful in our recognizing what we are doing, and how we can possibly unlearn these scripts and write new ones.

THE TWO HANDS OF NONVIOLENCE

The Two Hands of Nonviolence Exercise was inspired by the writing of the late Barbara Deming, a feminist writer and activist. In her book Revolution and Equilibrium, *Deming's metaphor of the two hands underscores the creative tension that fuels both interpersonal transformation and social change:*

With one hand we say to one who is angry, or to an oppressor, or to an unjust system, "Stop what you are doing. I refuse to honor the role you are choosing to play. I refuse to obey you. I refuse to cooperate with your demands. I refuse to build the walls and the bombs. I refuse to pay for the guns. With this hand I will even interfere with the wrong you are doing. I want to disrupt the easy pattern of your life."

But then the advocate of nonviolence raises the other hand. It is raised out-stretched — maybe with love and sympathy, maybe not — but always outstretched… With this hand we say, "I won't let go of you or cast you out of the human race. I have faith that you can make a better choice than you are making now, and I'll be here when you are ready. Like it or not, we are part of one another."

CONCLUSION — 15 MIN.

⊙ Nonviolence Journal

Suggestion:

1) The last sentence of Johan Galtung's description of Cultural Violence reads: "It is also a way a community or individuals view themselves in relation to themselves, to 'others' and to the world. It often supports a sense of superiority over, and dehumanization of, other cultures." What might be some concrete examples in your own culture of a self-image that supports a sense of superiority? Is this violence for you? Why or why not?

or

2) Re-read the Prevalent Cultural Attitudes and Beliefs about Violence and respond to the following questions:
   - What does it mean to "believe in" or have "faith" in violence?
   - Are there any attitudes or beliefs that you feel particularly strongly about? Why?

⊙ Nonviolent Action

Suggestion:

Examine any conflict you are currently involved in. Reflect on how you are responding in that conflict. If you are using any of the 3 responses in this chapter, see if you might discover a response using the Two Hands of Nonviolence. If possible, engage the person you are in conflict with using the Two Hands approach you envisioned.

⊙ **Next Session's Reading**

Please read the readings located at the end of this session.

⊙ **Adding to the Wall of Learning and Growing**

Please add your insights, learnings, or questions to the "Wall" at this time.

⊙ **Closing**

Invite the participants to gather their 3x5 cards that they have written their scripts on. Place a large bowl in the middle of the circle. Share the following in your own words:

I invite those who would like, or those who are ready to, give up a certain way of responding, to tear up one or all of your cards and place them in the bowl, one at a time.

I invite you to think about what it might mean to change these patterns or scripts.

When all who are interested in doing this have finished, invite all to stand in a circle and to experiment with embodying the gesture for the Two Hands of Nonviolence while looking at each other around the circle. After a minute, conclude by saying "Pace e Bene (pronounced pah chay bay nay)!" or some other greeting.

KEY ORGANIZATIONS: TRAINING TO TRANSFORM VIOLENCE

University of Rhode Island Nonviolence Institute, Center for Nonviolence and Peace Studies, Multicultural Center, University of Rhode Island, 74 Lower College Road, Kingston, RI 02881, 401-874-2875, *www.uri.edu/nonviolence.* The program helps build a world of mutual understanding among people, in which nonviolent processes are used to reconcile conflicts and build community. We seek to study and apply approaches which will foster more harmonious relationships at every level. The Center will accomplish this mission by providing educational and research opportunities and leadership development at the University of Rhode Island, and help facilitate such programs throughout the state.

Capacitar International, Inc. 23 East Beach Street, Suite 206, Watsonville, CA 95076, 831-722-7590, *www.capacitar.org.* Capacitar — meaning, in Spanish, to empower, to encourage, to bring each other to life — is an international network of empowerment and solidarity connecting people from grassroots groups. Capacitar uses simple practices of healing, team-building, and self-development to awaken people to their own source of strength and wisdom so they can reach out to heal injustice and create a more peaceful world.

HOMEWORK

NONVIOLENCE JOURNAL

Suggested Topics:

1) The last sentence of Johan Galtung's description of Cultural Violence reads: "It is also a way a community or individuals view themselves in relation to themselves, to 'others' and to the world. It often supports a sense of superiority over, and dehumanization of, other cultures." What might be some concrete examples in your own culture of a self-image that supports a sense of superiority? Is this violence for you? Why or why not?

or

2) Re-read the Prevalent Cultural Attitudes and Beliefs about Violence and respond to the following questions:
   a. What does it mean to "believe in" or have "faith" in violence?
   b. Are there any attitudes or beliefs that you feel particularly strongly about? Why?

HOMEWORK

NONVIOLENT ACTION

Suggestion:

Drawing on your journal writing, identify a group that works to challenge the structural violence of domination and institutionalized separation. Get some information about them and make a plan to talk with them and attend a meeting. Consider participating in a public activity, forum, or rally supporting human rights.

My Faith in Nonviolence

by Mohandas Gandhi

I have found that life persists in the midst of destruction and, therefore, there must be a higher law than that of destruction. Only under that law would a well-ordered society be intelligible and life worth living. And if that is the law of life, we have to work it out in daily life. Wherever there are jars, wherever you are confronted with an opponent, conquer him [or her] with love. In a crude manner I have worked it out in my life. That does not mean that all my difficulties are solved. I have found, however, that this law of love has answered as the law of destruction has never done. In India we have had an ocular demonstration of the operation of this law on the widest scale possible. I do not claim, therefore, that nonviolence has necessarily penetrated the 300 million, but I do claim that it has penetrated deeper than any other message, and in an incredibly short time. We have not been all uniformly nonviolent; and with the vast majority, nonviolence has [only] been a matter of policy. Even so, I want you to find out if the country has not made phenomenal progress under the protecting power of nonviolence.

It takes a fairly strenuous course of training to attain to a mental state of nonviolence. In daily life it has to be a course of discipline though one may not like it, like, for instance, the life of a soldier. But I agree that, unless there is a hearty cooperation of the mind, the mere outward observance will be simply a mask, harmful both to the person

and to others. The perfect state is reached only when mind and body and speech are in proper coordination. But it is always a case of intense mental struggle. It is not that I am incapable of anger, for instance, but I succeed on almost all occasions to keep my feelings under control. Whatever may be the result, there is always in me a conscious struggle for following the law of nonviolence deliberately and ceaselessly. Such a struggle leaves one stronger for it. Nonviolence is a weapon of the strong. With the weak it might easily be hypocrisy. Fear and love are contradictory terms. Love is reckless in giving away, oblivious as to what it gets in return. Love wrestles with the world as with the self and ultimately gains mastery over all other feelings. My daily experience, as of those who are working with me, is that every problem lends itself to solution if we are determined to make the law of truth and nonviolence the law of life. For truth and nonviolence are, to me: faces of the same coin.

The law of love will work, just as the law of gravitation will work, whether we accept it or not. Just as a scientist will work wonders out of various applications of the law of nature, even so a person who applies the law of love with scientific precision can work greater wonders. For the force of nonviolence is infinitely more wonderful and subtle than the material forces of nature, like, for instance, electricity. The people who

> *The law of love will work, just as the law of gravitation will work, whether we accept it or not. Just as a scientist will work wonders out of various applications of the law of nature, even so a person who applies the law of love with scientific precision can work greater wonders. For the force of nonviolence is infinitely more wonderful and subtle than the material forces of nature, like, for instance, electricity.*

discovered for us the law of love were greater scientists than any of our modem scientists. Only our explorations have not gone far enough and so it is not possible for everyone to see all its workings. Such, at any rate, is the hallucination, if it is one, under which I am laboring. The more I work at this law the more I feel the delight in life, the delight in the scheme of this universe. It gives me a peace and a meaning of the mysteries of nature that I have no power to describe.

Practically speaking, there will be probably no greater loss in humanity [using nonviolence in a struggle] than if forcible resistance was offered, [and] there will be no expenditure in armaments and fortifications. The nonviolent training received by the people will add inconceivably to their moral height. Such men and women will have shown personal bravery of a type far superior to that shown in armed warfare. In each case the bravery consists in dying, not in killing. Lastly, there is no such thing as defeat in nonviolent resistance. That such a thing has not happened before is no answer to my speculation. I have drawn no impossible picture. History is replete with instances of individual nonviolence of the type I have mentioned. There is no warrant for saying or thinking that a group of men and women cannot by sufficient training act nonviolently as a group or nation. Indeed the sum total of the experience of humankind is that humans somehow or other live on. From which fact I infer that it is the law of love that rules humankind. Had violence, i.e., hate, ruled us, we should have become extinct long ago. And yet the tragedy of it is that the so-called civilized persons and nations conduct themselves as if the basis of society was violence. It gives me ineffable joy to make experiments proving that love is the supreme and only law of life. Much evidence to the contrary cannot shake my faith. Even the mixed nonviolence of India has supported it. But if it is not enough to convince an unbeliever, it is enough to incline a friendly critic to view it with favor.

SESSION 4: READING 2

The Power of Noncooperation
by Shelley Douglass

Noncooperation with evil is as much a duty as cooperation with good.
— M. K. GANDHI TO THE PEOPLE OF INDIA, 1921

Gandhi used to tell his followers that *swaraj*, home-rule for India, would come only when every Indian exercised swaraj, self-rule, in his or her own life. The dependence of India upon the British, he said, was the sum of the dependence of each Indian upon British cloth, British thought, British custom, British government. British rule continued because Indians felt powerless to remove it, and because by their actions they in fact rendered themselves powerless. Gandhi was able to bring about a nonviolent freedom struggle insofar as people were able to see the truth in this insight of his: The imposition of British rule was made possible by Indian cooperation, and could be ended by noncooperation. Indians had to learn to respect themselves, to throw off the limitations of untouchability and of their own reverse racism; Indians had to learn to govern their own desires for wealth and property; Indians had to refuse to surrender to their centuries of conditioning to caste divisions so that they could work together for freedom.

For the Gandhian movement protest was not enough. One could not stand by shouting objections as a major miscarriage of justice occurred. . . . Violence did not recognize the responsibility of Indians for their own problems, and so would not change anything at the deepest level. What Gandhi called for and sometimes achieved was a struggle within each person's soul to take responsibility for the evil in which she or he was complicit, and having taken responsibility, to exercise self-control and begin to change. The Salt March to the sea and the magnificent control exhibited by demonstrating Indians grew slowly from humble roots: the scrubbing of latrines in the face of social taboo, the sharing of gold jewelry by the wealthy, living and eating together in defiance of caste regulations, wearing Indian khadi (homespun) to withdraw support from the British economic empire. These actions and many others were symbolic of the deep change brought about by the Gandhian movement, a change in which people acknowledged their own responsibility for the wrong they sought to change, and thus in changing themselves were able to change their situation.

When violence broke out during the freedom struggle and later during partition, it happened because that vital insight was lost for a time. People again located the source of evil outside of themselves and tried to eliminate it with force. Gandhi's fasts and teachings were then concentrated on taking responsibility for the violence he might have caused, and calling people to take steps to stop their own violence. He understood that in giving up our own responsibility for evil we also give up the possibility of changing it. Gandhi's refusal to see the British as solely responsible for the situation of India was the key to Indian independence.

I believe that Gandhi's insistence upon recognizing our cooperation with evil and withdrawing it is essential to the struggle for social change . . . in which we are engaged today. So often people feel powerless to create change - the leaders of political parties, the generals, the multinational executives, and such groups and persons are held responsible for our situation, and they do not listen to the voices of the poor and the disenchanted. . . . Governments and corporations exist to hold power or make a profit, and they rarely listen to polite words of protest. If our hope for change rests upon the reasonableness of any government or economic system, then our hope is slim indeed.

The underlying fact that we tend to overlook is that while systems do not listen to people very well, they are made up of the very people to whom they do not listen. The existence of a given system depends upon the cooperation of all those who do not benefit from it and all who are hurt by it, as well as upon the smaller number of people who gain status or wealth from it. If those of us who protest the injustice of our system were instead to withdraw our support from the system, then change would begin...

Noncooperation may include marches, vigils, and tax refusal, but it includes also an inner dimension: the refusal to allow our minds to be manipulated, our hearts to be controlled. Refusing to hate those who are identified as enemies is also noncooperation.

The discipline of nonviolence requires of us that we move into the various forms of noncooperation. We will probably move slowly, one step at a time. Each step will lead to another step; each step will be a withdrawal from support of what is wrong and at the same time a building of an alternative. Negativity is never enough. It is not enough to oppose the wrong without suggesting the right. . . . [R]eligious roots can help [many] here, with their insistence on confronting the

> *Noncooperation may include marches, vigils, and tax refusal, but it includes also an inner dimension: the refusal to allow our minds to be manipulated, our hearts to be controlled. Refusing to hate those who are identified as enemies is also noncooperation.*

evil within ourselves and on our unity with all peoples.

The difficult thing about nonviolence is that it is a new kind of power to us, a new way of thinking. Even as we resist the structures in our society that separate us from others, we incorporate those structures in our own minds. Nonviolence becomes not only a process of resisting our own unloving impulses. Jesus' injunction to remove the beam from our own eye before presuming to treat our sisters' and brothers' eyes, and his direction to overcome evil with good can point [the] way [for many]. It is true that we resist what we understand to be evil. The system does evil. But the individual people who make up the system are people like you and me: combinations of good and evil, of strength and weakness. To hate people is to incorporate part of the evil that we resist. We must learn instead to love the people while we confront the system with our lives.

At the base of love for those caught within an evil system is the understanding that we are they: that we too are caught in the same system. Just as people in the peace movement have important insights and criticisms for people in the military, military folk have critical insights to share with [people in the peace movement]. No one person owns the truth — each one has a piece of it, as Gandhi said, and if we can put all our pieces together we may find a bigger truth. Recognizing our own complicity in an evil system means that we can take responsibility for it through noncooperation. It also means that we can confront our own failures, forgive ourselves, and from that process learn compassion. We can be honest enough to admit our own imperfections and our lack of certainty, and accept the same in other people.

Just as we do not have to hate Russian people or Chinese people, we do not have to hate those who stand against our beliefs within our own country. We can be friends. We can work together in ways acceptable to all of us: to feed the hungry, to help at a school, to plan a liturgy, to sponsor activities for our children, to encourage freedom and creativity. As we work together we can get to know each other, and when that happens we can begin to explore our feelings about [the issues at hand] with mutual acceptance. Even when we feel that the people who range themselves against us have become close-minded or unreasonable, we do not have to retaliate in kind. We can find the places in ourselves where we are close-minded and unreasonable, and understand the fear behind such feelings. We can forgive and refuse to be drawn into a cycle of hate and fear. It is possible to hold out the hope of community to all people, and to work at conflicts within our communities and neighborhoods in the same spirit that we would like to bring to international conflict.

The new power of nonviolence comes from taking responsibility: personal responsibility for our own lives, and our share of responsibility for the country and the systems in which we live. The power of nonviolence lies in facing ourselves with love and compassion while honestly confronting our own evil, and then in facing the evil of our country honestly, while confronting it with love and compassion. Nonviolence is an invitation to nurture the good, to confront the evil, and in doing so to build a new community which will bear in it the best of the old.

Shelley Douglass is a longtime peace and justice activist. The preceding essay was written in 1983 when she was part of the Ground Zero Center for Nonviolent Action in Washington State, which conducted a Gandhian campaign focused on the Trident nuclear submarine fleet whose Pacific base was nearby.

HOMEWORK

REFLECTIONS ON THE READINGS

Session 4:
Another Way

SESSION 4: **Another Way**

OBJECTIVES
- To reflect on modern day examples of nonviolence
- To explore some of the principles that Mohandas Gandhi developed during his experiments with nonviolence
- To share an experience of nonviolence in light of these principles

AGENDA
- Welcome [1 min.]
- Opening [5 min.]
- Reflection on Homework [10 min.]
- Large Group Reflection on Homework [5 min.]
- Nonviolence in Action: The Story of Karen Ridd [20 min.]
- Pieces of the Truth [50 min.]
- Break [10 min.]
- Share an Experience of a Two-Hands Moment [30 min.]
- Conclusion [10 min.]
    Nonviolence Journal
    Nonviolent Action
    Next Session's Reading
    Adding to the Wall of Learning and Growing
    Closing
- Agenda Options and Adjustments: See pages _____.

READINGS
- Reading #1: Mohandas Gandhi, "My Faith in Nonviolence"
- Reading #2: Shelley Douglass, "The Power of Noncooperation"

NOTES FOR THE FACILITATOR

SESSION PREPARATION: BEFORE

- Review the entire session in depth. Role-play or practice setting up and facilitating exercises beforehand. Where possible, put material into your own words. Feel free to make notes for this purpose on 3x5 cards or in the book next to the instructions.
- For the Opening: Cut up 16 slips of paper. Write the first of Mohandas Gandhi's principles on two of the slips of paper, numbering them 1A and 1B. Write the second principle on the next two slips, numbering them 2A and 2B, and so on until each of the eight principles are on two numbered slips of paper.
- For the *Pieces of the Truth* exercise: Think of an issue (for example, homelessness, the death penalty, war, etc.) that may be of interest to your group. Develop a specific scenario with respect to the issue (i.e., there is a fictitious bill that will be voted on soon re: the issue; or, there is going to be a community meeting on the issue of homelessness in the local park). Choose 4, 5, or 6 possible roles (depending on the number of people in your group) that contain a variety and balance of perspectives (for example, if you chose the death penalty, possible roles could include: the person to be executed, the governor, the perpetrator's family, the victim's family, a death penalty opponent, a guard from the prison, the chaplain from the prison). You will want to ensure that you have the same number of people in each role-playing group. Using a marker, write these roles on 1/3 piece of 8 1/2 x 11 paper.

PREPARATION: ON THE DAY OF THE SESSION

- Write Mohandas Gandhi's eight principles of nonviolence from the opening exercise on easel paper.

SESSION 4: **Another Way**

WELCOME — 1 MIN.

Welcome back for our fourth session of the *Engage: Exploring Nonviolent Living* Study Program. In the last session, we explored three typical scripts of reacting to violence: avoiding it, accommodating it, or meeting it with counter-violence; and explored a different way of responding in which we stand up for ourselves or others, and at the same time remember that the one who is causing the violence is part of our community, too. In this session, we will begin to reflect more on that fourth way of responding, using principles developed by Mohandas Gandhi during his struggle with the British to gain Indian independence.

OPENING — 5 MIN.

Ask people to stand (as they are able) and to form a circle. Then share:

In our second Session we began to investigate possible nonviolent responses to situations when we looked at different scenarios. In the last two sessions we have begun to write our insights about nonviolence on our Wall of Learning and Growing. We will continue this exploration of the dimensions of nonviolence by opening with insights that Mohandas Gandhi came to after almost sixty years of experimenting with nonviolence, fighting against injustice, colonization, and everyday violence.

Hand out the slips of paper with the principles of Gandhi. If you have less than 16 people in the circle, have some take two different ones.

In a moment I will ask the person who has the slip of paper with 1A to read that principle out loud. This should be followed by a moment of silence, and then the person who has 1B should repeat the principle. After another pause, the person who has 2A should read that principle, followed by the person who has 2B. Continue this until all 8 principles have been read. Let's begin!

1. All life is one.

2. We each have a piece of the truth and the un-truth.

3. Human beings are more than the evil they sometimes commit.

4. The means must be consistent with the ends.

5. We are called to celebrate both our differences *and* our fundamental unity with others.

6. We reaffirm our unity with others when we transform "us" versus "them" thinking and doing.

7. Our oneness calls us to want, and to work for, the well-being of all.

8. The nonviolent journey is a process of becoming increasingly free from fear.

After the last principle has been read, ask the participants to share a word or phrase that has come up for them as they have listened to these principles.

REFLECTING ON HOMEWORK — 10 MIN.

But first, I again invite you to get together with your Nonviolence Partner to take a few minutes to reflect on your experiences or insights since the last session, as well as to reflect on the readings, journaling, or nonviolent action.

LARGE GROUP DEBRIEF ON HOMEWORK — 5 MIN.

Invite the pairs back to the large group and take about 3 or 4 responses.

I invite you to share in the large group any reflections or insights that you have shared with your Nonviolence Partner so that the whole group can benefit.

NONVIOLENCE IN ACTION: THE STORY OF KAREN RIDD — 20 MIN.

Read the following story aloud (or invite participants to share in reading it aloud):

In 1989 Karen Ridd and four other international volunteers were working with a group called Peace Brigades International (PBI) when they were suddenly arrested by the Salvadoran military. Three of the five were Spanish nationals, and they were promptly deported from El Salvador, leaving Karen, who was Canadian, and her friend Marcela Rodriguez, who was from Colombia, to face whatever was coming. Fortunately, Karen had had time to call the Canadian consul and alert another PBI volunteer who happened to call in at the right moment. This was some comfort, as was the civility — at first — of the soldiers. But no one from the team had had to face arrest before (to date, no international volunteer had been killed in Central America despite enormous violence all around them) and from another room Marcela heard the soldiers describing them as "terrorists from the Episcopal Church." Their spirits did not improve when the two women, along with other detainees, were loaded onto a truck, taken to an army barracks, blindfolded, and subjected to five hours' interrogation about their alleged connection with the guerrilla *Frente Farabundo Martí para la Liberación Nacional* (FMLN) while sounds of torture and the sobbing of victims came from nearby rooms. Karen knew that PBI would quickly alert their worldwide network about the arrests, but she also knew that time was short — there was no telling what would happen in that barracks if someone didn't get them out before nightfall.

PBI had in fact activated its worldwide network, and before long hundreds of people were sending faxes to the Canadian and Colombian embassies, calling and sending e-mail messages to their representatives to urge Karen and Marcela's immediate release. All this got no response at all from the Colombian embassy, but

Canada brought official pressure on the Salvadoran government, no doubt hinting that their extensive trade relations with El Salvador could be compromised if Karen were not released immediately. Whatever it was that got through to whomever was in charge, Karen found herself walking across the barracks grounds toward a waiting embassy official a few hours later, a free woman. But when the soldiers removed her blindfold inside the barracks, she had caught a glimpse of Marcela, face to the wall, "a perfect image of dehumanization." Glad as Karen was to be alive, something tugged at her. Feeling terrible, she made some excuses to the exasperated Canadian Embassy official who had come all the way from San Salvador to get her, turned and walked back into the barracks, not knowing what would happen to her in there, but knowing it could not be worse than walking out on a friend.

The soldiers were startled, and almost as exasperated. They handcuffed her again. In the next room a soldier banged Marcela's head into the wall and said that some "white bitch" was stupid enough to walk back in there, and "Now you're going to see the treatment a terrorist deserves!" No more mister nice guy. But Karen's gesture was having a strange effect on the men. They talked to Karen despite themselves, and she tried to explain why she had returned. "You know what it's like to be separated from a *compañero*." That got to them. They released Karen and Marcela and the two women walked out together under the stars, hand in hand.

MOHANDAS GANDHI: WE EACH HAVE A PIECE OF THE TRUTH

Mohandas Gandhi (1869-1948) helped India achieve its independence from the British empire by organizing a process that was an alternative to passivity ("there is nothing we can do"), reformism ("we will vote the British out through parliamentary procedures," the original strategy of the Indian National Congress), or counter-violence (the strategy of terrorism or guerrilla war as a response to the structural violence of imperialism, an approach long advocated and put into practice by some groups).

Gandhi's approach hinged on a deep and thorough spiritual transformation of self and society. It meant breaking the internal chains (fear, hatred, and accommodation) that had kept people from withdrawing their consent. And it involved experimenting with, tapping into, and being rooted in the revolutionary power of nonviolent transformation he named *Soul-Force*.

"Soul-Force" is the English translation of *Satyagraha*, the word Gandhi used to describe the unitive power of love and truth that is at the root of all being and that can be unleashed to transform conflict and to create true peace, justice, and reconciliation. *Satyagraha* combines two Sanskrit words: "sat" (meaning "truth," "soul," or "that which is") and "agraha" (meaning "firm," "steadfast," "force," "holding onto," or "gripping"). It can thus mean "soul-force" or "truth-force," but it can also mean "holding firmly to truth," "clinging to that which is," or "firmly holding onto reality." Satyagraha includes the process of waging a struggle for justice in which we seek not to exterminate or conquer the opponent but — through love in action — to achieve a just resolution.

Gandhi's nonviolence maintains that no one possesses the *entire* truth. Rather, each of us possesses a piece of the truth *and* the un-truth. In a conflict, nonviolent action seeks to reveal the pieces of the truth of both parties so that solutions can be constructed that incorporate them.

Debrief

Explore with the participants:
- What did you see happening in the story?
- What might each person in the story have said about her or his actions?
- Do you see any of the Gandhian principles that we used in our Opening acted out in the story?

PIECES OF THE TRUTH — 50 MIN.

Share the following with the group:

One of the key Gandhian insights was that no one possesses the entire truth. Instead, each person possesses a piece of the truth *and* the un-truth. The following exercise explores this central principle of active nonviolence.

We will be working on the issue of _____ *(explain issue as necessary until participants understand)*. In this issue, there are a number of varying roles representing different perspectives. I have chosen these roles: _____*(state roles)*.

Break into group(s) of 4-6 people, trying to ensure that all groups have the same number of people. If you have one group that is smaller than the others, only do as many rounds as the number in that group. Ask the members of each group to pull their chairs into a circle. Distribute papers with roles to each group. Say:

Take one piece of paper and place it on the floor in front of you facing out into the circle (so that the other members of the group can clearly see it). It does not matter which role you get because you will have the opportunity to play all the roles.

Each person, one at a time, will role-play the person identified on the piece of paper for 45 seconds. I invite you to really "get into the role" and to go beyond stereotypes you may have of this person. Try to really be that person, feel the feelings, intentions, motivations, and needs of that person. Get in touch with that person's heart.

> "The stick, the carrot, and the hug may all be necessary but the greatest of these is the hug."
> —KENNETH BOULDING

You will have 45 seconds to portray your role. I will sound a bell, signaling when one person should stop and the next person should begin. Go around the circle in a clockwise direction. When the other participants are speaking you should listen actively and not be thinking about what you will be saying next. Does anyone have any questions about the directions?

Respond to any questions. Then invite everyone to close their eyes and get into their first roles for 30 seconds. Identify which character you will begin the round with. Start each successive round with the same character. Ask the participants to open their eyes. Sound the bell and say, "Begin." After 45 seconds, sound the bell and say, "Next person." Repeat this until all have spoken.

When the first round is ended (that is, when everyone in each circle has done their role-play), ask everyone in each circle to move one seat to the right. Each person now has a new role. Take 30 seconds for people to let go of their old roles and think about their new roles. Then commence the second round, beginning with the same role that you began with the first round. Continue these rounds until everyone has had a chance to play all the roles.

After the second round is completed, stop for a moment and say:
- See if you can get even more deeply into playing your character. Discover the person's deepest truth and reality.
- Regard the person you are portraying in the same way you regard the dearest people in your life.

Continue as above until all participants have played all roles. If you need to save time on this exercise, consider creating smaller groups or choose not to have everyone play all the roles.

Debrief

When the exercise is finished, debrief this exercise by asking participants to respond to each of the following questions, one at a time. Spend 3-5 minutes on each question. We have found that it is usually necessary to describe "feelings" and "noticings" as we have done below. Write the responses down on three easel paper pads side by side:

- What are your feelings and noticings, i.e., observations without judgments?
  - Feelings are usually just one word. Some examples of feelings are: Happy, overwhelmed, relieved, anxious. When you put the word "like" or "that" after the phrase "I feel" as in "I feel that . . ." or "I feel like . . ." what usually follows is a thought or a judgment, not a feeling.
  - Noticings are anything that you observed. Some examples of noticings might be: I had difficulty playing a particular role; a particular role was always played in a particular way, though it could have been played a variety of ways.
- What are your insights? What did you learn? Did you notice any of the Gandhian principles at work in this exercise?
- How can you apply these learnings in your life and in the world?

To close the exercise, share the following ideas if they have not already been shared:

- This exercise can help us to see the possibility that everyone has a piece of the truth. It can help us put ourselves into another's shoes so that we can see and feel what their piece of the truth may be.
- When we can identify with another's views and feel them with compassion, we can start to overcome our "us vs. them" thinking and doing. This has applications for our personal lives and also for participating in social movements.

> *"We are constantly being astonished these days at the amazing discoveries in the field of violence. But I maintain that far more undreamt of and seemingly impossible discoveries will be made in the field of nonviolence."*
> — MOHANDAS GANDHI

BREAK — 10 MIN.

SHARE AN EXPERIENCE OF A TWO-HANDS MOMENT — 30 MIN.

Share in your own words:

Last session we looked at the metaphor of two hands as a way to describe how we could oppose injustice, and at the same time, keep our hearts open to the people involved in committing the injustice — at how we could stop those people from doing harm, and at the same time, remind ourselves that we are tied to them through our common humanity.

In a moment we will break into small groups, and I will invite you to reflect on and share, at whatever level you feel comfortable, a time in your own life when you might have had such an experience. It could have happened in your home with your partner or your children or parents; in your workplace with co-workers; at school; or maybe even while you were shopping in a store or participating in some political action.

Take a couple of minutes to either close your eyes or to journal, and reflect on a time when you stood your ground and yet were open to the other person.

Bring people's attention back to the whole group, and then divide them into small groups. Allow 15 minutes for small-group sharing.

Call everyone back to the large group and debrief, asking for insights, reflections, or parallels to the Gandhian principles.

CONCLUSION — 10 MIN.

⊙ Nonviolence Journal

Let the participants know that the Nonviolence Journal suggestion is only a suggestion, and that if they have topics related to nonviolence or the course that they would like to write about, they should feel free to do so.

Suggested Topic:
Explore further the example of a "two-hands experience" that you or another shared in the session.
and/or
Re-read the Karen Ridd story. What were some of the stereotypes and qualities of nonviolence that you came up with in Session One, and how might you apply those stereotypes to this story?

⊙ Nonviolent Action

Make a list of people you have had struggles with over the years. Imagine that you are in a "Pieces of the Truth" exercise with one of them. Imagine each of you looking into one another's eyes and sharing from your deepest truth about your conflict. Try to really imagine that person's piece of the truth. Write down your responses and the other's imagined responses. After finishing, you may consider choosing another person or persons on your list to do this with. If it is possible, consider contacting one of the people on your list and taking time together to share on the things that have been difficult between you. As an alternative, you could write a letter to that person (that you could decide, or not, to mail).

⊙ **Next Session's Reading**

For next time, please read the readings located at the end of this session. Also, please read the section entitled *CARA: A Four-Step Process for Nonviolent Engagement* found in Session Five.

⊙ **Adding to the Wall of Learning and Growing**

Please add your insights, learnings, or questions to the Wall.

⊙ **Closing**

Ask people to form a closing circle. Invite one participant to read the following quotation from Mohandas Gandhi:

"Nonviolence is not only a negative state of harmlessness, but it is a positive state of love, of doing good even to the evildoer. But it does not mean helping the evildoer to continue the wrong or tolerating it by passive acquiescence."

In light of Gandhi's words, share that we will close by doing the "Two Hands of Nonviolence Wave" using the four "hand poses" explored earlier in this study program.

The four gestures are:

- **One: Avoidance.** Hands over your ears, head bent down into lap, and eyes closed.
- **Two: Accommodation.** Extending our arms out from our bodies with our palms up.
- **Three: Counter-Violence.** Extending our arms out from our bodies with our palms pushing outward.
- **Four: Active Nonviolence.** Keeping our left arm stretched out with our palms pushing outward, but then simultaneously turning our right palms upward in an open, receiving way. Finally, pulling these two hands (keeping them in their same mode) closer to our bodies, in a relaxed but steady way.

After you model the first gesture, ask the person to your right to duplicate and hold the gesture you will offer. Then the next person to the right is asked to do the same, and so on around the circle.

When it is your turn again, offer the next gesture (which begins another round). And so on for the remaining two rounds.

Thank you, everyone, for coming and participating!

KEY ORGANIZATIONS: EXPLORING NONVIOLENCE

Institute for Peace and Justice (IPJ)/Families Against Violence Advocacy Network (FAVAN), 4144 Lindell Boulevard #408, St. Louis, MO 63108; 314-533-4445; *ppjn@aol.com; www.ipj-ppj.org,* IPJ is an independent, interfaith, not-for-profit organization that creates resources, provides learning experiences, and advocates publicly for alternatives to violence and injustice at the individual, family, community, institutional, and global levels.

Mahatma Gandhi Research and Media Service: *www.gandhiserve.org*

M. K. Gandhi Institute for Nonviolence, c/o Christian Brothers University, 650 East Parkway, South Memphis, TN 38104, 901-452-2824, *www.gandhiinstitute.org.* Led by Mahatma Gandhi's grandson, Arun Gandhi, the Institute promotes and applies the principles of nonviolence locally, nationally, and globally, to prevent violence and resolve personal and public conflicts through research, education, and programming.

METTA Center for Nonviolence, PO Box 183, Tomales, CA 94971. *www.mettacenter.org; codirectors@mettacenter.org.* The METTA Center works to inspire and support the study and practice of nonviolence. By providing resources and other educational activities, we empower ourselves and others to enliven the legacy of Mahatma Gandhi, Dr. Martin Luther King Jr., and all those who have blazed a trail to the "beloved community" and a nonviolent future for humanity.

Resources Advancing Initiatives for Nonviolence (RAIN) is a nonprofit organization dedicated to developing resources that explore the creativity and spirituality of active nonviolence to promote the well-being of all. These resources include media that tell the stories of active nonviolence through video, print, and web formats. Contact information: 1545 Farwell Ave., Chicago, IL 60626; 773-338-8445; *www.RainOnline.org.*

HOMEWORK

NONVIOLENCE JOURNAL

The Nonviolence Journal suggestion is only a suggestion. If you have other topics related to nonviolence or the course that you would like to write about, feel free to do so.

Suggestion:

Explore further the example of a "two-hands experience" that you or another shared in the session.

and/or

Re-read the Karen Ridd story. What were some of the stereotypes and qualities of nonviolence that you came up with in Session One, and how might you apply those stereotypes to this story?

HOMEWORK

NONVIOLENT ACTION

Suggestion:

Make a list of people you have had struggles with over the years. Imagine that you are in a "Pieces of the Truth" exercise with one of them. Imagine each of you looking in one another's eyes and sharing from your deepest truth about your conflict. Write down your responses and the other's imagined responses. After finishing, you may consider choosing another person or persons on your list to do this with. If it is possible, consider contacting one of the persons on the above list and taking time together to share on the things that have been difficult between you. As an alternative, you could write a letter to that person (that you could decide, or not, to mail).

The Love Walks
by Ken Butigan

In the early 1990s in East Los Angeles, a group of women who are members of Dolores Mission Catholic Church were searching for a solution to the heavy toll that gang violence was taking in their neighborhood. Thirteen gangs were active in the parish, and gang killings and injuries were an almost daily occurrence. During a particularly violent period, the women were gathered in their prayer group, praying for a solution to this carnage.

That day, electrified with a sudden sense of discovery and consternation at the parallels of the Scripture reading of that day to their own predicament, one of the women felt that they were being called to stop huddling afraid behind their locked doors and drawn windows, fearful of their sons and neighbors, and to walk together in the midst of the war zone of the gangs.

After a long discussion, that night seventy women (and a few men) began a *peregrinacion* — a pilgrimage or procession — from one gang turf to the next throughout the barrio. When they encountered startled gang-members who were preparing for battle, the mothers invited them to pray with them. They offered them chips, salsa, and soda. A guitar was produced — they were asked to join in singing the ancient songs that had come with them from Michoacan and Jalisco and Chiapas. Throughout the night, in thirteen war zones, the conflict was bafflingly, disorientingly interrupted. People were baffled; the gang members were disoriented.

Each night, the mothers walked and within a week there was a dramatic drop in gang-related violence. The members of the newly formed *Comite pro Paz en el Barrio* had responded to the emergency of the violence being waged in their locality by "breaking the rules of war." By nonviolently intervening and intruding, they had challenged the old script of escalating violence and retaliation and created, for a time, a new and more creative script. Theirs had been more than a physical journey through their neighborhood. Most significantly, it had been the fundamental spiritual journey from the *war zone* to the *house of love.*

By entering this zone of danger, they had created a momentary space for peace. In that space, all the parties were able to glimpse their humanness. The gang-members were able to see, many for the first time, other human beings caring about them. At the same time, the women were able to let go of their paralyzing fear and anger long enough to see the human face of members of the gangs. It is no accident that the women christened their night-time journeys "Love Walks."

But this project did more than briefly interrupt the escalating cycles of violence.

By provoking a confrontation with their humanness, they unleashed a process of communication and transformation. Their activity changed the gang-members and themselves. The women listened to the deep anguish of the gang-members about the lack of jobs and about police brutality. This led them, in turn, to develop a tortilla factory, bakery, and child-care center, creating some jobs and giving the gang-members an opportunity to acquire job skills. It was also a space where conflict resolution techniques were learned, because people from different gangs worked together in these projects. The women then opened a school. And they shifted from a "Neighborhood Watch" mode —

> *Each night, the mothers walked and within a week there was a dramatic drop in gang-related violence.*

where they were the eyes and ears of the police — to a group trained to monitor and report abusive police behavior, a development that has redefined the relationship between the Los Angeles Police Department and the *barrio*.

The people in this neighborhood are the first to say that they have not achieved a utopia. There is still poverty, racism, and violence. Nevertheless, they have taken an enormous step toward creating a much more human environment. They did this by risking being human together.

SESSION 5: READING 2

Communication: An Introduction to a Historical Model and to the New Powerful, Non-Defensive Communication Model
by Sharon Ellison

"For centuries, Aristotle's model for communication has been taught in Western culture as the art of winning arguments. Powerful Non-defensive Communication replaces this traditional model with one that gives each person the ability to communicate effectively without engaging in a power struggle."

DR. MARTIN JACOBI, CLEMSON UNIVERSITY

THE WAR MODEL

Defensive Self-Protection: The historical use of the *rules of war* as the basis for our verbal interactions currently affects our lives in all realms. Using the *war motto* "To be open is to be vulnerable, and to be vulnerable is to be weak," people automatically close down, become defensive, and react to others in an adversarial manner. Such defensiveness not only inhibits our ability to understand and learn, it literally creates and accelerates conflict. Rather than protecting us, defensiveness depletes our energy and prevents us from achieving our goals.

Types of Defensive Reactions: Our defensive strategies, often not conscious, typically fall into three basic categories: *surrender, withdrawal,* and *counterattack*. Each of these strategies includes one format designed primarily for protection and another

to also *retaliate* against others. While a person might use any or all of six defensive reactions, most people have a habitual one; thus a common personality type can be associated with each type of defensive reaction.

Communication Tools Misused: Our three basic forms of communication—*questions, statements, and predictions*—are all misused when we are defensive—so dramatically that we might as well be trying to build a house by pounding nails with a saw. For example, when we ask a question, we often, through our tone, body language, and wording, convey an attitude of interrogation. People are often quite unconscious of the degree to which they do this. When we make a statement, we may state opinion as fact or convince others to agree with us. Or we may use a prediction to coax, punish or falsely threaten others.

Power Struggles: These defensive ways

of speaking and reacting are manipulative—and cause others to resist what we say. Each person involved can feel like a victim, even while lashing out in verbal attack; this dynamic causes ongoing power struggles that become addictive. Because we have never changed the basic model for how we communicate, we consider such conflict to be *normal — just human nature.*

When we use the *rules of war* as the basis for human conversation, we often become manipulative and controlling even when we have others' best interests at heart. We decide whether to speak or not depending on our own, advance determination of whether we think the person will listen or not. We may continue to ask questions when someone seems upset but doesn't want to talk. We try to "convince" someone we love to behave or think the way we think would be best. Trying to take information a person doesn't want to give is like a theft. Trying to put our ideas into someone's head when the person doesn't want to listen is like a beating or force-feeding.

We fear that if we don't try to control others, we won't have any impact and we will watch others make mistakes or do hurtful things. I think this is a myth, because most people do not want to be controlled, so they resist it. Ironically, using a non-defensive approach, we will have far more influence. People can hear our ideas and/or feel our caring without needing to resist. We can also still set effective boundaries when we need to. Far from losing power, we gain it.

THE POWERFUL NON-DEFENSIVE COMMUNICATION MODEL

Non-Defensive Communication Tools: The character and function of *questions, statements,* and *predictions* are very different when we use them non-defensively. For example, rather than asking questions that convey our own opinion or lead others to answer in a prescribed way, we can ask questions that are genuinely *curious, open,*

innocent, neutral, and *inviting.*

Formats for Non-Defensive Communication: This part of the material covers specific formats for using each communication tool. We are using non-defensive communication when we 1) ask questions, 2) make statements, and 3) predict consequences in an open, sincere way without trying to control how other people respond. We can gather accurate information, speak with clarity, protect ourselves, and hold others more accountable. People are more likely to respect us and we can strengthen personal and professional relationships.

THE QUESTION
CURIOSITY DIDN'T KILL THE CAT — IT WON THE PEACE PRIZE

Since dictionary definitions mirror common usage of a word, the fact that the word "question" is almost entirely defined as interrogation, or, if inquisitive, is seen as prying, reflects a troubling common belief. Many people think those who ask questions based simply on curiosity are "sticking their nose where it doesn't belong" — an offensive, inappropriate, and possibly dangerous thing to do. The message is that only those who are authorized to interrogate have the right to ask questions. So it isn't hard to see why we often hesitate to ask questions for fear of being rude or invasive. And when we do ask questions, it is easy to slip into interrogation mode — frowning, looking intense, and sounding accusatory.

Sincere curiosity is often the missing piece in our questions. Many of us were even actively taught to fear it. Parents who wanted to teach their children not to ask inappropriate questions repeated the old adage, "Curiosity killed the cat." Curiosity is actually at the heart of any genuine question. I believe we would have a decidedly different and healthier world if the saying went, "Ask all the questions you can think of — curiosity wins the peace prize."

We can select from dozens of ways to use *questions* to gather accurate information quickly and to stimulate others to respond sincerely and honestly.

The Nature of the question is curious, open, innocent, neutral, inviting.

The Purpose is to gather thorough information to understand accurately what the person means, believes, or feels.

An Example: If someone acts upset, the first step is to simply ask the person directly about your own assumption so he can *confirm*, *deny*, or *qualify*; for example, "Are you irritated (frustrated, angry, upset) about something?"

Try to Avoid using a question to *express your own opinion* or *to entrap* others.

THE STATEMENT
VULNERABILITY AND POWER JOIN HANDS

When we make statements, that old war motto — "To be open is to be vulnerable, and to be vulnerable is to be weak" — comes into play with a vengeance. Just as curiosity is often missing in our questions, vulnerability is often absent from our statements. While we might make vulnerable statements to a partner during safe, intimate moments, most of us would rarely choose to expose all our thoughts and feelings during conflict. Complete openness would show that the "case" we are trying to prove is not as airtight as we would have the other person think; it would make us vulnerable to attack.

For the same reasons, we generally don't choose to make statements that expose our vulnerability in the boardroom, at an office staff meeting, or with a political opponent. If we want to appear powerful to others, we usually consider that showing doubt or concurring with a point made by an opponent is equivalent to planting a land mine in our own territory. It will blow up our agenda and goals.

In a wide range of personal and professional situations, I think the majority of us believe that such acknowledgment will weaken our position. One workshop participant commented that when we are open and vulnerable "we wind up as roadkill."

I believe this deeply ingrained habit of guarding against emotional vulnerability causes us far more problems than it solves. Regardless of the issue, when we hide information we lose, in bits and pieces, our honesty, our integrity, and our ability to work creatively with others to resolve problems.

An odd reversal happens when we put up a strong front and avoid saying anything that makes us vulnerable: we *compromise* what we say. We sift and sort to decide what is appropriate to help us achieve our goals at any moment, paralleling the classic story of the politician who begins his career inspired to do good, and winds up compromising his way into hell.

Statements provide others with thorough information about how we interpret what they are saying and our own reactions to it.

The Nature of the statement is open, direct, vulnerable, subjective, descriptive.

The Purpose of the first three steps is to state neutrally our subjective interpretation of:

1) what we hear the other person saying,

2) any contradictions we see (perceive) in the person's tone, body language, and words, and

3) our conclusions regarding the person's overt and covert messages.

The fourth step is not neutral and is to

4) fully express our own reactions, our feelings, beliefs, and reasoning.

An Example: If the person continues to act irritable and yet denies it when asked, saying harshly, "I'm *fine*!," we might respond with this four-part statement:

• **Hear:** "*When* I hear you saying that you are in a good mood

• **See:** *and* (at the same time) I see that you are rolling your eyes and shrugging

• **Conclude:** *then* I believe that something is wrong but you don't want to tell me

• **Reaction:** *and* so I feel frustrated and am not sure if I should ask you more questions or leave you alone."

Try to Avoid stating *opinion* as *fact* or trying to *convince* others to agree.

THE PREDICTION
A NEW PRESCRIPTION FOR SECURITY

Security is the missing element in our habitual way of making predictions, just as curiosity is absent from our questions and vulnerability is absent from our statements. Either by manipulation with a covert bribe or by coercing with an overt threat, we have conventionally used predictions to get others to comply with our will.

Parents have typically said to me, "I told Johnny he couldn't watch TV unless he got dressed, but it didn't work." When I ask what they mean by "it didn't work," the response is invariably, "Well, he didn't get dressed" — in other words, he didn't make the choice they wanted him to make.

We act in a similar fashion with other adults. [Here is an example.] Hans was upset that Franklin's laxness about time always made them late for important events. One night, Hans made the following prediction: "If you are not ready to leave for the theater promptly at seven, I will drive my own car." When Franklin remained true to form and was late, Hans drove to the theater by himself, frustrated that his prediction "didn't work." He had succeeded in carrying it through, but he believed he had failed because Franklin hadn't made the choice Hans preferred. Hans remained locked in the power struggle even though his prediction had fulfilled its purpose — he had made it to the theater on time.

Many of us think a prediction is not effective unless the other person does what we want. But when we try to control what choice another person makes, our prediction backfires. We usher in more resistance and power struggle, and we pay the price of eroded trust and diminished productivity.

The Nature of the prediction is protective, foretelling, neutral, definitive, firm.

The Purpose is to create boundaries and security by telling another person ahead of time how we will react if s/he does make a certain choice, and how we will react if s/he does not make that choice.

An Example: If the person still acts upset and continues to deny it, after hearing our statement, saying "I said I'm *fine,* there's no *problem*!", we can set a limit using an "If...... then" sentence: "If you would like to tell me what's going on, then I'd like to hear it." "If you don't want to tell me, then I don't want to try to make you."

Try to Avoid using a consequence prediction to *coax*, *punish*, or *falsely threaten others*.

Quantum Leaps: Each of us can protect ourselves without getting defensive and have greater influence without being manipulative or controlling. Using non-defensive communication, we can be honest and powerful while being compassionate and sincere.

> *Curiosity is actually at the heart of any genuine question. I believe we would have a decidedly different and healthier world if the saying went, "Ask all the questions you can think of — curiosity wins the peace prize."*

One aspect of the *power* of non-defensive communication is that the process allows us to communicate with great clarity and walk away with increased self-esteem, even if the other person chooses not to cooperate. Anyone who uses this process can make a quantum leap in personal and professional growth. By changing how we communicate as individuals, we can work effectively toward greater understanding among diverse groups, and ultimately toward a more peaceful world.

HOMEWORK

REFLECTIONS ON THE READINGS

Session 5:
Trying It Out

SESSION 5: **Trying It Out**

OBJECTIVES
- To explore definitions of nonviolence
- To identify some of the principles of nonviolent power
- To practice nonviolent power

AGENDA
- Welcome [1 min.]
- Opening [5 min.]
- Reflecting on Homework [10 min.]
- The Love Walks: Nonviolence in Action [25 min.]
- What is Nonviolence? [20 min.]
- Break [10 min.]
- CARA: A Four-Step Process for Nonviolent Engagement [20 min.]
- Nonviolent Engagement: Parallel Lines Real-Play [45 min.]
- Conclusion [15 min.]
    Nonviolence Journal
    Nonviolent Action
    Next Session's Reading
    Adding to the Wall of Learning and Growing
    Evaluation
    Closing

READINGS
- Reading #1: Ken Butigan, "The Love Walks"
- Reading #2: Sharon Ellison, "Powerful Non-Defensive Communication"

NOTES FOR THE FACILITATOR

SESSION PREPARATION: BEFORE
- Review the entire session in depth. Role-play or practice setting up and facilitating exercises beforehand. Where possible, put material into your own words.
- Materials needed: bell.
- Write up the questions under the Love Walks exercise on easel paper.

SESSION 5: **Trying It Out**

WELCOME — 1 MIN.

Share in your own words:

Welcome back for our fifth session of the *Engage: Exploring Nonviolent Living* Study Program. In this session, we will look more closely at the meaning and definition of active nonviolence. As part of this, we will identify some of the principles of nonviolent power, and try them out by experimenting with nonviolence.

OPENING — 5 MIN.

To begin, I invite you to stand in a circle facing each other. Put your arms straight up in the air, and bow down to each other by bending at the hips and swinging your arms out and down in front of you. *[Demonstrate].*
You are bowing to each other.
Now bend back up at the hips and swing your arms out and up in front of you.
Repeat this motion. I invite you to repeat the syllable "ha" over and over again.
Faster.
Faster.

Let this run for a few minutes. Allow spontaneous laughter to break out.

REFLECTING ON HOMEWORK — 10 MIN.

I again invite you to get together with your Nonviolence Partner to take a few minutes to reflect on your experiences or insights since the last session, as well as to reflect on the readings, journaling, or nonviolent action.

THE LOVE WALKS: NONVIOLENCE IN ACTION — 25 MIN.

"The Love Walks" is one of the readings for this session. Ask the participants to recount the steps of this story. If needed, the following summary is provided:

"The Love Walks" tells the story of a group of women of one of the neighborhoods of East Los Angeles who were moved to take nonviolent action to restore peace and create justice in addressing the challenges of gang conflict. After reading a Bible passage the women came to the conviction that they were being called to respond to the daily violence which was killing and injuring many young people and was creating an atmosphere of fear, anger, grief, and powerlessness.
Equipped only with food, musical instruments, and prayer books, seventy women and a few men walked through the streets of their neighborhood where two gangs were about to do battle. They invited the young people to pray, sing, and eat with them.

They talked and listened to the young people. This creative initiative sparked numerous conversations between the women and the young people, which led to growing understanding and the development of jobs and a transformed community. The walks continued for several years and the violence was dramatically reduced.

Have the participants break into small groups and ask:

The women in the story could have read the Scripture, recognized a challenge to make a change, and still have tried to give the problem to someone else.
- Why did they take action?
- What could it have been within each of them that caused them to overcome their fear and take action?
- What can they teach us that we might need to know?

Bring them back to the large group and ask:

- What are the examples of active and creative actions that the women took that honored both themselves and the gangs?
- Are there aspects or facets of what might be called nonviolent power present in this story? If so, what are they?

WHAT IS NONVIOLENCE? — 20 MIN.

Read to yourselves the statements on nonviolence in the nearby box. When you are done, pick out one that particularly resonates with you and create something that reflects that. You can use the art supplies, your journal, or even your own body to image what an embodiment of the statement would look like.

Call the group back together and invite several people to share with the larger group what they created.

BREAK — 10 MIN.

CARA: A FOUR-STEP PROCESS FOR NONVIOLENT ENGAGEMENT — 15 MIN.

Part of our homework for this session included reading the CARA Four-Step Process presented below.

CARA — Center, Articulate, Receive, and Agree — is a four-step process for nonviolent engagement and transformation. CARA means "face" in Spanish. This process is a way to relate face-to-face with others in a nonviolent way, and is also a method for understanding how nonviolent action in social movements happens. It helps us to face people with whom we are in conflict in a way that does not avoid, accommodate, or use violence to meet violence. Some of the ways of conducting these four steps are drawn from other processes, including Powerful, Non-Defensive Communication and Nonviolent Communication (see contact info at end of session). Let us now go through this process step by step.

REFLECTIONS ON NONVIOLENCE

Engage: Nonviolence is active and creative power for justice and the well-being of all that employs neither passivity nor violence. Nonviolence is a process that seeks to break the cycle of escalating and retaliatory violence; to reach out to the opponent and to potential allies; to focus on the issue at hand; and to seek to reveal more clearly the truth and justice of the situation. Nonviolence is organized love.

Dictionary: The policy or practice of refraining from the use of violence, as in reaction to oppressive authority.

Mohandas Gandhi: Nonviolence is the greatest force at the disposal of [human]kind. It is mightier than the mightiest weapon of destruction devised by the ingenuity of humanity.

Barbara Deming: For Deming, nonviolence weaves confrontation and compassion together. She writes that we "can put *more* pressure on the antagonist for whom we show human concern. . . . We put upon [the opponent] two pressures — the pressure of our defiance of him [sic] and the pressure of our respect for his life — and it happens that in combination these two pressures are uniquely effective. . . . Because the human rights of the adversary are respected, though his actions, his official policies are not, the focus of attention becomes those actions, those policies, and their true nature. The issue cannot be avoided."

Dr. Martin Luther King, Jr.: The nonviolent approach does not immediately change the heart of the oppressor. It first does something to the hearts and souls of those committed to it. It gives them new respect; it calls up resources of strength and courage that they did not know they had. Finally it reaches the opponent and so stirs his [or her] conscience that reconciliation becomes a reality."

Michael Nagler: Nonviolence is the power released by an individual in a successful struggle with a potentially destructive negative drive AND its systematic release into the social field.

Angie O'Gorman: The call for human beings to "love your enemies" means "wanting wholeness and well-being and life for those who may be broken and sick and deadly. It was meant to be the cornerstone of an entirely new process of disarming evil; one which decreases evil instead of feeding it as violence does."

Thich Nhat Hanh: The essence of nonviolence is understanding and compassion, so when you cultivate understanding and compassion, you are practicing nonviolence. You cannot be absolutely nonviolent — but the more you can understand, the more you can be compassionate, the more you can be nonviolent. . . . Nonviolence is not a principle. It is a flower that blooms on the ground of understanding and love. Nonviolence is something to cultivate.

Ken Butigan: Nonviolence is the unfinished democratic revolution started 300 years ago. Democracy is the idea that we can decide the future of a culture by nonviolent means — by ballots instead of bullets.

To illustrate the following process, consider using the example of how the women in the "The Love Walks" story used one or all of these steps.

Step One: Center Ourselves

Centering is the process of making contact with what is really happening within us, our *truest selves* — that part of us where are heart, mind, and body are connected, and our heart is allowed to function unobstructed. By anchoring ourselves in our heart, we are prepared to respond, not simply to react, to the conflict we are facing. We may decide to protect ourselves. We may decide to engage. In either case, we can act from a place where we are most truly who we are, and not simply from a worn-out and potentially destructive script.

> *I had a student at the University of Maryland a while back who wrote a 13-word paper that for both brevity and breadth — the rarest of combinations — has stayed with me: "Question: Why are we violent but not illiterate? Answer: Because we are taught to read."*
>
> — COLMAN McCARTHY

Brainstorm with participants how they center and ground themselves. Some possible ways include (write these on easel paper after soliciting from group):
- Breathing — and focusing on one's breath
- Asking the other person to sit down
- Silently repeating a meaningful or sacred prayer, word, mantra, or name
- Recognizing and naming one's emotional state in that moment (fear, anger, sadness, happiness, and so forth).

Step Two: Articulate Our Truth

The goal of Step Two is to identify and share what is happening for us in the moment. This involves discovering what we are truly feeling and needing, and then sharing it with the other person. By being open, direct, vulnerable, and inviting, we are disarming ourselves so that the other person can feel less defensive. We have an attitude of interest and curiosity, trying to learn from the other. We believe in cooperation. We don't want to engage in a power struggle, but believe we can reach a win-win solution.

Brainstorm with participants how they can do this. Some examples include (write these on the easel paper):
- Relaxing body posture
- Speaking slowly and softly
- Using "I" statements such as:
    - I feel…
    - I believe…

Step Three: Receive the Truth of the Other Person

Step Three involves deep listening to the other person's truth: what their feelings are and what they need. It requires us to be truly curious and interested in the other, in their position and in them as human beings. We are limited beings with a finite understanding of and possession of the Truth. Our commitment should be to the Truth, more than our version of the truth. This insight — the fact that we only have a piece of the truth — opens us to the piece of the truth of the other person, including our opponent. Our opponent often has a piece of the truth that we are missing, that we will only get by being curious and listening with our hearts. There is a reason that they are holding a position different from the one you are; try to get to it.

Brainstorm some possible ways to do this step. Some examples include (write on easel paper):
- Listening actively
- Asking questions with curiosity
- Asking questions by lowering your voice at the end of the sentence
- What the person means by certain words, believes, or feels
- Checking out any of your own assumptions concerning the situation
- Explore any inconsistencies you may notice between the other person's words and their non-verbal communication (for example, when someone says in a loud, forced voice, "I am fine!" we see a contradiction)

If you need time to think through the other's sharing, ask to resume the conversation later.

Step Four: Agree, Don't Assume

Step Four is the process of revealing the truth and untruth of both parties, and finding ways to put the "two truths together" and discover the points of agreement where the needs of both parties are met.

Realizing that truth gets revealed over time, and that our learning and growing is a process, we remain constantly open to revising our understanding as we are transformed in the truth.

Brainstorm some possible ways to do this step. Some examples include (write on easel paper):
- Point out the elements you both agree on
- Ask the other person if each of you can consider the truth of the other and can agree on any of those additional pieces of the truth
- Agree to disagree on the elements that are clearly in opposition to each other

Ask if there are any questions.

NONVIOLENT ENGAGEMENT: PARALLEL LINES REAL-PLAY EXERCISE — 50 MIN.

Now we will work with the CARA process ourselves. Again, the CARA four steps are:
1) Center yourself
2) Articulate your truth
3) Receive the truth of the other person, and
4) Agree, don't assume.

We will now have an opportunity to practice the Four Steps by performing a "real-play" exercise. A "real-play" is a role-play exercise that practices nonviolent responses to a challenging, concrete, and real-life conflict or situation. (This process often has many benefits, including helping us get a feel for how our adversary may see our position.)

When you are ready to work with the large group, share:

We will practice the Four-Step process by having one person share a conflict they are dealing with. Some of you will volunteer to be the other people involved in this conflict scenario. The rest of you will be observers.

Who has a conflict they would like to work on? You will be the main actor.

Set up a chair for the participant who comes forward. Make sure that the main actor can see the four steps on the easel paper on the wall. Invite the person to share the scenario briefly with the rest of the group and to give enough information so that the other participants can play the other roles.

As the main actor shares the conflict situation, identify the other actor(s) involved in the situation. Set up chairs for each of those actors. Then ask:

Who would like to play one of the other roles?

Invite them up to take the other seats. Then say:

The main actor will play herself/himself and will try to use the four steps. The other actors have not heard of the four steps, so they will not use them. The role of the observers is to think of other ways to use the four steps. After we run through the conflict once and debrief, the observers will have the opportunity to tag in and play the roles up here. Now, everyone take a minute to get into your roles. Ready, begin!

> *"If you really want to cultivate nonviolence, you should take a pledge that, come what may, you will not give way to anger or order about members of your household or lord it over them. You can thus utilize trifling little occasions in everyday life to cultivate nonviolence in your own person and teach it to your children."*
> — MOHANDAS GANDHI

Let the real-play last for several minutes to give enough time for the main actor to practice the steps. Then sound the bell and ask the observers:

- Which steps did the main actor do well?
- Which steps could be improved?

For the second round, invite other people to play the different roles. Add the following instruction:

During the real-play, if anyone has a suggestion of how to play the main role, tag-in when you are moved to do so.

Then run the scenario again and debrief as above. When you are finished, invite the participants to return to their seats in the large group and debrief:

- What did you learn in this real-play?
- How can you apply what you learned to your life?

Write the responses on easel paper.

During the debrief it may be helpful to bring out some of the following points:

For longer, ongoing conflicts (for example, with those in our family), it is better not to dwell on past differences, but to build on the truths that we can bring together. Be future-oriented instead of past-oriented.

In some cases, the other person's truth or behavior may cross your boundaries. If the other is unwilling to change his or her words or behavior, you can take action to protect yourself (in the Two Hands model — the hand that conveys 'stop'), while at the same time being open to continuing dialogue and relationship (the outstretched hand in the Two Hands). You set both the negative and positive consequence of the other person's behavior at the same time. Setting limits takes the following format:

- If…, then…

For example, if someone keeps meeting you for dinner later than your agreed-to time, and the steps have not been effective in finding a resolution that leads to

COMPASSION

Love is a mind that brings peace, joy, and happiness to another person. Compassion is a mind that removes the suffering that is present in the other. We all have the seeds of love and compassion in our minds, and we can develop these fine and wonderful sources of energy. We can nurture the unconditional love that does not expect anything in return and therefore does not lead to anxiety and sorrow.

The essence of love and compassion is understanding, the ability to recognize the physical, material, and psychological suffering of others, to put ourselves "inside the skin" of the other. We "go inside" their body, feelings, and mental formations, and witness for ourselves their suffering. Shallow observation as an outsider is not enough to see their suffering. We must become one with the object of our observation. When we are in contact with another's suffering, a feeling of compassion is born in us. Compassion mean, literally, "to suffer with."

We begin by choosing as the object of our meditation someone who is undergoing physical or material suffering, someone who is weak and easily ill, poor or oppressed, or has no protection. This kind of suffering is easy for us to see. After that, we can practice being in contact with more subtle forms of suffering. Sometimes the other person does not seem to be suffering at all, but we may notice that he has sorrows that have left their marks in hidden ways. People with more than enough material comforts also suffer. We look deeply at the person who is the object of our meditation on compassion, both during sitting meditation and when we are actually in contact with him. We must allow enough time to be really in deep contact with him. We must allow enough time to be really in deep contact with his suffering. We continue to observe him until compassion arises and penetrates our being.

When we observe deeply in this way, the fruit of our meditation will naturally transform into some kind of action. We will not just say, "I love him very much," but instead, "I will do something so that he will suffer less." The mind of compassion is truly present when it is effective in removing another person's suffering. We have to find ways to nourish and express our compassion. When we come into contact with the other person, our thoughts and actions should express our mind of compassion, even if that person says and does things that are not easy to accept. We practice in this way until we see clearly that our love is not contingent upon the other person being lovable. Then we can know that our mind of compassion is firm and authentic. We ourselves will be more at ease, and the person who has been the object of our meditation will also benefit eventually. His suffering will slowly diminish, and his life will gradually be brighter and more joyful as a result of our compassion.

— *Thich Nhat Hanh*

agreement, you might say in a very neutral tone:

"If you do not arrive by 6 pm, then I will go to dinner by myself. If you arrive by 6 pm, then I will be happy to go to dinner with you."

This way, you are setting limits with the other and protecting yourself in the process. You are also offering the positive alternative. This statement is not done in a punitive way, but is put forward as a natural consequence. See Sharon Ellison's work for more detail about setting limits.

To close this exercise, share:

- Hopefully this exercise has given you the opportunity to apply what you have learned about communicating nonviolently by practicing it in real-life situations.
- For more resources for responding nonviolently to interpersonal conflict, please see the box at the end of the session.

CONCLUSION — 15 MIN.

⊙ Nonviolence Journal

Suggested Topic:
1) Re-read the statements about nonviolence. Share the art that you made with someone and journal on the interaction (how you felt, their response, etc.).
2) Reflect on the CARA process. Is there anyone else in your life with whom you would like to experiment with this process? If so, write your first and second step.

⊙ Nonviolent Action

1) If you feel ready, invite a person you are having a conflict with and engage in the four-step process with that person. You can prepare beforehand by practicing the real-play with a friend.
2) Before the next session, explore one or two organizations or projects in your community that are working for change using some of the nonviolent principles we have explored in the past two sessions. Check their website, give them a call, or set up an appointment to go to their office and chat. Find out the following:
   - What problem they are trying to address;
   - What strategy they are using to address the problem;
   - If they have a philosophy of nonviolence, and if so, what it is;
   - What motivates them to do the work?

⊙ Next Session's Reading

Please read the material located at the end of this session.

⊙ Adding to the Wall of Learning and Growing

Please add your insights, learnings, or questions to the Wall.

⊙ Evaluation

Let's take a few minutes to first identify the positives — the things that have been working thus far in this study program. *(Write these on easel paper.)* *Then, ask for participants to identify things that could be improved. (Write these on easel paper.)*

⊙ **Closing**

Ask the group to form a circle holding hands. Invite the participants to share a word that reflects what they are feeling, an insight they had during the session, or something they are taking with them.

KEY ORGANIZATIONS: COMMUNICATING NONVIOLENTLY

Center for Nonviolent Communication. 2428 Foothill Boulevard, Suite E, La Crescenta, CA 91214; 818-957-9393; *www.cnvc.org.* CNC is a global organization whose vision is a world where all people are getting their needs met and resolving their conflicts peacefully. In this vision, people are using Nonviolent Communication (NVC) to create and participate in networks of worldwide life-serving systems in economics, education, justice, healthcare, and peace-keeping.

Powerful Non-Defensive Communication. Ellison Communication Consultants, 4100-10 Redwood Road #316, Oakland, CA 94619; 510-655-8086; fax 510-655-8082;: *sharon@pndc.com; www.pndc.com.*

The Center for Attitudinal Healing. 33 Buchanan Drive, Sausalito, California 94965; 415-331-6161; fax 415-331-4545; *home123@aol.com; www.healingcenter.org.* Founded by Gerald Jampolsky, Attitudinal Healing is a non-dogmatic, practical spirituality. Its principles offer people ways to step through fear, conflict, or separation. It offers workshops and study programs.

HOMEWORK

NONVIOLENCE JOURNAL

Suggestion:

1) Re-read the statements about nonviolence. Share the art that you made with someone and journal on the interaction (how you felt, their response, etc.).

2) Reflect on the CARA process. Is there anyone else in your life with whom you would like to experiment with this process? If so, write your first and second step.

HOMEWORK

NONVIOLENT ACTION

1) If you feel ready, invite a person you are having a conflict with and engage in the four-step process with that person. You can prepare beforehand by practicing the real-play with a friend.

2) Before the next session, explore one or two organizations or projects in your community that are working for change using some of the nonviolent principles we have explored in the past two sessions. Check their website, give them a call, or set up an appointment to go to their office and chat. Find out the following:
   - What problem they are trying to address;
   - What strategy they are using to address the problem;
   - If they have a philosophy of nonviolence, and if so, what it is;
   - What motivates them to do the work?

Learning a New Dance — A Story from Venezuela

Told by Veronica Pelicaric and Leonor Andrade

Veronica: I had been invited to facilitate a three-day workshop on nonviolence in Caracas by a group of "anti-Chavistas," the nickname given to those who strongly oppose Hugo Chavez, the controversial Venezuelan president. When I arrived, I found that not only were 60 anti-Chavistas, mostly professionals and well-to-do citizens, participating, but that 15 staunch and active supporters of the president had also been invited. These were mostly young, intense, and poor people who were engaged in a struggle to be seen and heard after decades of indifference and serfdom. They brought with them many stories of injustices and rancor.

For the first day and a half, the workshop ran smoothly and without major clashes. Late on the second day, we moved to an expanded process of an exercise called "The Two Hands of Nonviolence." The expanded version of the exercise is worked in dyads, and I suggested that, when possible, people from opposing "factions" pair together. Leonor, a staunch anti-Chavista, sat in front of a Chavista woman. The exercise involves raising both hands straight out in front of our bodies to say, "Stop! I will not be part of your violence" to the aggressor, and then slowly lowering one hand in a gesture which says "I say stop! But I extend one hand to signify that I will not exclude you from my heart and I trust we will find a way of working out our differences." When it came to Leonor's turn to lower her hand, she just could not do it. She began to tremble, almost convulsively, and just could not bring herself to lower her hand to the Chavista. The whole room was seemingly mesmerized and glued to her execution of the exercise; a sense of

> *Suddenly, Leonor found in herself the strength to lower her hand, shakily and obviously with enormous effort of spirit.*

expectation mixed with allowing her the space she needed prevailed, adding to the intensity of the moment. Leonor's face was flush and her body contracted while the other woman just sat there and waited. Suddenly, Leonor found in herself the strength to lower her hand, shakily and obviously with enormous effort of spirit. She broke down and the room was filled with her sobbing. Many more people started crying too and most of us honored the moment by lowering our heads and going into our hearts to honor her struggle and to extend a moment of oneness.

Two weeks later ...

Leonor: I had gone to work that day like I did every day, but the morning dragged on with free-floating anxiety. Just before midday my co-worker reminded me it was almost twelve o'clock and time to get going. There was to be a huge demonstration that day. I grabbed my knapsack and walked toward the subway station wondering: "How will it go?"... "How will I react?"... "What will happen?"... "What will they do to us? ... "Will they hit us?" I was afraid. I met my companions and after agreeing on a strategy we walked towards the place where "they" were waiting. The banner under which I stood accused Chavez of being a dictator. I don't remember exactly what it said; I was trying to concentrate and stay focused.

And then I heard the other voice, obviously aimed at me: "You are full of hatred, I can tell by your eyes ... I am afraid of that look... the devil is in your gaze... witch, witch!" I just said nothing, stood frozen, and one thought bounced in my consciousness: "We are one, we are one."

I cannot say with precision what happened a few moments later. I only know that our eyes met and locked for what seemed like a very long time — both of us conscious of our strength, our loyalty to our mission, our position and rightness. Both she and I stood there in silence, without budging, rooted to the cement ground. Then, seemingly without a thought, my hand moved and to my astounded eyes went towards her hand. Electricity criss-crossed the air as both our eyes filled with tears while my chest and face flooded with a strange warmth. From behind me, our group started to sing the national anthem to the chorus of their whistles and horrible insults which I could not decipher. Something suddenly shifted, and one of those miracles of nonviolence occurred: as we winded down our singing, theirs began. We joined them and for a few, though intense, moments our voices rose as a single sound, honoring our motherland. I felt her fingers touch my hand and my eyes touched hers in recognition: we are one.

We turned and amidst a raging crowd and under police protection left the site.

Months have elapsed and I give thanks for having lived this possibility. John Dear, a nonviolence practitioner, says that the moment we define ourselves as "we" and "they," we have created the enemy. Now I know this to be true. That day, standing across from each other, we were divided, physically and spiritually, as enemies. What that woman saw in me were years of indolence, of indifference to a suffering which I did not care to investigate or imagine — years of passive violence which I nourished in my ignorance. I thank that woman for helping me become aware of an aspect of my violence and reinforcing my motivation to embrace the path of active nonviolence wholeheartedly.

SESSION 6: READING 2

Romaine Patterson's Angels' Wings

by Askari Mohammad for Time Classroom

Now a college student studying recording engineering at the Conservatory of Recording Arts and Sciences in Tempe, Arizona, Romaine Patterson was once a close friend of Matthew Shepard, a 21-year-old gay student whose lynched body was found hanging on a fence in Laramie, Wyoming, on October 12, 1998. When Shepard's killers were being tried, Patterson and others dressed like angels and surrounded anti-gay protestors to drown out their message.

Since Shepard's death, Patterson has spoken with others about hatred toward gays and lesbians, the changes people can make in their lives, and about the real Matthew Shepard. Whether at memorial services or in schools, Patterson ultimately hopes to get across a message of love.

TIME Classroom: How did you know Matthew Shepard?
Romaine Patterson: Matthew and I were introduced by a college instructor at Casper College in Casper, Wyoming. He was looking for college students his age. I just happened to know a lot of them. He called me and started hanging out with my group of friends. From that moment on he just became a very close friend.

TC: What are some of the things about him you feel were misrepresented or not covered by the media?
RP: There was a strong urge to make Matthew a martyr. A lot of people associated the tying to the fence with the crucifixion of Christ. Because of that, people were really

afraid to think of Matthew as a real person. People thought that Matthew was just this perfect young man, when in reality, he was a 22-year-old guy who was still trying to find out what he was going to do with his life.

TC: What was he like as a person?

RP: As a person he was pretty damn great. He was very nice, very open-hearted. He could talk to just about anybody and would talk to just about anybody. He just had a really smart head on his shoulders. At the same time, he struggled with a lot of issues. To be his friend was not an easy task because he was manic-depressive. He had some very big ups and some very big downs.

TC: What are the most important things people should know about Matthew Shepard, the person?

RP: I think people should know what I've learned from everything that has happened and one of the biggest lessons that he's taught me. In one of my last discussions with Matthew we talked about what he wanted to do with his life and what kind of roads he was going to be going down. He was very much convinced and he was trying very hard to convince me at the time that one person can really make a change in the world, as far as making it a better place and helping humanity. I didn't really understand what he meant until after everything had happened and I saw the change that Matthew had made on the world. I realized that he was right: one person really can make a difference. We all have a little role and the ability to make that difference. That was about the greatest lesson to be learned from Matthew.

TC: Was Matthew afraid his lifestyle would endanger him?

> *He was very much convinced and he was trying very hard to convince me at the time that one person can really make a change in the world, as far as making it a better place and helping humanity. I didn't really understand what he meant until after everything had happened and I saw the change that Matthew had made on the world. I realized that he was right: one person really can make a difference.*

RP: Matthew had been through many trials in his life, long before I even knew him. When he was overseas he had gone through some trials because of his size and his stature and the fact that he was gay. In the time that I knew Matthew he was so funny, he just was cocky almost. He just had this feeling that he'd been through the worst in life and nothing could be any worse than some of the challenges he had already overcome. Pretty regularly people harassed him. I remember one of his neighbors put the word "faggot" on his door in shaving cream. I don't think he ever assumed that it would get violent or that he could be hurt any more than he had been. Maybe he was a little naive that way, in thinking that he had been through the worst.

TC: Did and do you feel gays and lesbians who live in Laramie have reason to be afraid if they are open about their sexual orientation?

RP: I don't think it's just Laramie, I think it's a nationwide thing still. While gay and lesbian people are becoming much more visible in the country, I think that you will always find people out there looking for an excuse to be violent. I think that, in Laramie particularly, it is a challenge. Having grown up in Wyoming myself I could speak on just how challenging it is to come out into an environment where being gay or lesbian isn't something that's widely accepted or something that is widely seen. However I will say that Laramie, Wyoming, has drastically changed since Matthew and in a positive manner. When Matthew died, people couldn't understand it anymore than anyone else. To them it was just brutal and horrible and there was no excuse for it. Even the people that didn't necessarily agree with everything that was going on, I think they understood that no one deserves to be treated like that. I mean it comes down to human respect. I think that was an education for the country, not just Laramie, Wyoming.

TC: What can the nation and society learn from what happened in Laramie?
RP: I think there's a lot to be learned on so many levels. The first thing we need to learn is a little more human respect for another. I think some of the key lessons that I hope are learned are with parents and children. I think parents really need to sit down with their children and talk about the issue of hate. Hate unfortunately runs rampant through our world today. You see it everyday. I think it's really a discussion that needs to happen within the family.

This hatred is like a cancer and it spreads. But we have the ability to stop it with us. It's something that we all can do. I think Matthew Shepard was the first time people in this country ever talked about hate crimes. People were taking the time to really think about what it takes to have that kind of hatred to do these kinds of acts. I saw this transformation in people that was really incredible. I saw straight people talking about gay issues where they never would have talked about them before.

TC: Why did you feel it important to surround the anti-gay protesters dressed as angels?
RP: The group that we surrounded was a group from Topeka, Kansas [led by Rev. Fred Phelps of Westboro Baptist Church in Topeka, Kansas]. They have a website. It's *www.godhatesfags.com*. It's pretty disgusting. Essentially what they do is travel around the country protesting at a lot of the big gay events. At the memorial service they showed up and they were protesting and on a day which was already hard enough. I didn't know what I could do about it really. Fred Phelps had realized the huge media impact that Matthew's case was having and he's a big hound for the press. I was informed that he would be in Laramie, Wyoming, to protest outside the courthouse. So at this point in time, I was pretty good and angry. I was also mad that no one was doing anything about it.

I got on the phone with a really close friend of mine who lived in Laramie. In that conversation, the idea of the angels was born. The idea was, since there was going to be so much media there, what we wanted to do was use the media to our advantage. We decided we wanted a message of love, respect, and compassion to go out. That was the first point of why we did it. The other point was I personally couldn't stand the idea of Judy and Dennis Shepard going into the courthouse and having to walk by them one more time. It made my skin crawl to think that. So the idea of the angels was that we'd make these big wings so that every time Fred and his group protested, we would surround the little fenced-in area that they were in and turn our backs to him and silently stand in protest, and just block him out, kind of trapping all that hatred behind our wings. It was the most peaceful, serene experience. He couldn't say anything because he couldn't see anyone and no one could see him, and they were just stunned. In a weird way, we were using the imagery that he used to spread his hatred to show just the opposite. We're using it to show love. Ever since then, I've been helping other people do the same thing. It's a good, loving response to so much hatred.

TC: Are you still involved in the gay rights movement?
RP: I work with the Gay and Lesbian Alliance Against Defamation (GLAAD) and do a lot with them. I'm always doing work with the media. I just try to keep myself busy doing little things that continue that education. My favorite thing is to go to schools and talk to the kids. I start off with their own attitudes, like what are their attitudes about gay and lesbian people. A lot of young people don't realize the impact that their attitudes have on people. I tell them it starts with little things like words. Those words may be affecting someone right next to them and they don't even know it.

TC: How has knowing Matthew Shepard changed your life?

RP: It's changed just about everything about my life. I was pretty happy and content working at a coffee shop in Denver, Colorado, serving Matthew coffee. It taught me more about myself than I ever could have imagined. And more than anything, it taught me about people. My life has been touched by so many people since Matthew. And I'd like to think that I've touched a good number of lives myself. Nothing will ever be the same. I'll always be the friend of Matthew Shepard and for the rest of my life I'll be telling his story because he can't tell it himself. Before I was this young, naive person who thought I could go out and be openly gay and you wouldn't have to worry about it, but then I realized that that's not the reality of the world today. I realized I could make it a reality.

TC: If Matthew could know the chain of events and national media attention that occurred following his murder, what would he think of it?

RP: Well, first of all, he'd be like, 'Damn! They needed to show a better picture of me!' That would have been terrific. I think if Matthew could have had the foresight to see what was going to happen, if he would have known that the change he wanted to make in the world was going to happen the way it did, I think he would have changed nothing. I think Matthew has made more of an impact in his death then he ever could have in his life. I think he would be incredibly proud to know that his life helped so many and continues to help so many.

TC: Suppose you're speaking to a group of high school students right now. What message would you send to them?

RP: Take care of one another. Treat each other well. That's what this world is about; it's about learning to love each other. With so much hatred in the world, we need to learn to love again.

SESSION 6: READING 3

Anti-Oppression Glossary

- **Class:** Socially constructed category that links economics and social status.
- **Classism:** System of privilege based on social class in favor of middle and wealthier classes.
- **Disability:** Social construction of inability.
- **Discrimination:** The practice of excluding a group of people.
- **Dominant Culture:** Ideologies, social practices, and structures that affirm the central values, interests, and concerns of those who are in control of the material and symbolic wealth in society. The subordinate culture refers to groups who exist in social and material subordination to the dominant culture.
- **Gender:** The social construction of sex.
- **Gender identity:** One's gender regardless of biological sex.
- **Harassment:** Unwanted, unwelcome, unjustified bothering of another person.
- **Hegemony:** The dominance of one group over another not through force but rather through the institutions of society.
- **Heterosexism:** System of privileging male-female relations.
- **Homophobia:** Fear of same-sex relations and oppression of people practicing non-heterosexual relations.
- **Internalized Oppression:** When members of the oppressed groups come to believe in the attitudes of the oppressors such that the system of institutions of oppression remain intact and unchallenged by the oppressed. The oppressed group believes they are inferior to the oppressor and the oppressed believes in the values of the oppressor group.

- **Internalized Privilege:** When a member of a privileged social group absorbs the dominant cultural view of the group. This leads to a sense of special entitlement, that is, a feeling that being in the dominant group is the natural state of affairs because one is more capable. The more privilege one has, the more one views the world as devoid of social and historical context.

- **Oppression:** The systematic subjugation of a social group by another social group with access to power (for example, racism, sexism, heterosexism, classism, ableism, etc.).

- **Patriarchy:** System of oppression based on male domination.

- **People of Color:** A way that people rename themselves as opposed to "non-white" and socially constructed as a non-homogeneous group that has been brought together under their common experience of racism.

- **Privileges:** Advantages, rewards, and/or benefits given to those in the dominant group (for example, whites, males, Christians, heterosexuals, etc.) without their asking for them. Privileges are bestowed unintentionally, unconsciously, and automatically. Often these privileges are invisible to the receiver.

- **Race:** A socially constructed way of grouping people, which has more to do with their political and economic status, as contrasted with any common biological basis.

- **Racism:** A system of oppression based on "race."

- **Rank:** A conscious or unconscious social or personal ability or power arising from culture, community support, personal psychology, and/or spiritual power. Whether you earned or inherited your rank, it organizes much of your communication behavior. *Social* Rank is the power you have (or lack) because of your race, gender, age, economic standing, sexual orientation, nationality, religion, education, health, or language. Social rank may be global or may depend on context. *Structural* Rank is the power that belongs to your position in an established hierarchy. The corporation president outranks her secretary who outranks the cleaning staff.

- **Sex:** Biological category.

- **Sexism:** System of oppression based on sex and environment of gender roles.

- **Systematic racism:** The policies and practices of institutions and organizations which directly or indirectly operate to sustain the advantage of peoples of certain socially constructed "races" and the exclusion of other groups.

- **Tokenism:** When members of the oppressor group accept some members of the oppressed group into their group in order to justify the overall structure of oppressor and oppressed while still retaining the power and control.

HOMEWORK

REFLECTIONS ON THE READINGS

PART TWO:

Structural Violence
and
Nonviolent Power

Session 6:
Seeing What's Hidden

SESSION 6: **Seeing What's Hidden**

OBJECTIVES:
- To explore structural violence
- To reflect on many of the forms of structural violence and the impact that they have
- To analyze structural violence as "Prejudice + Power-over"

AGENDA:
- Welcome [1 min.]
- Opening [5 min.]
- Reflecting on Home Work [10 min.]
- What's in the Bag? [30 min.]
- Example: Working Women [15 min.]
- Break [10 min.]
- Structural Violence [35 min.]
- Today's Newspaper [25 min.]
- Conclusion [10 min.]
    Nonviolence Journal
    Nonviolent Action
    Next Session's Reading
    Adding to the Wall of Learning and Growing
    Evaluation
    Closing

READINGS
- Reading #1: Veronica Pelicaric and Leonor Andrade, "Learning a New Dance"
- Reading #2: Askari Mohammad, "Romaine Patterson's Angels' Wings"
- Reading #3: "Anti-Oppression Glossary"

NOTES FOR THE FACILITATOR

SESSION PREPARATION: BEFORE

- Review the entire session in depth. Role-play or practice setting up and facilitating exercises beforehand. Wherever possible, put material into your own words. Feel free to make notes for this purpose on 3x5 cards or in the book next to the written instructions.
- Play close attention to time in the session. You don't need to take all the hands when facilitating debriefs.
- Materials needed:
  - For the "What's in the Bag?" exercise you will need:
    - One brown lunch bag for each participant
    - Bags of multicolored candies (for example, M&Ms, Skittles, or Smarties)
    - Four chocolate bars
    - Variety of "prizes"—enough for about half of the group. Prizes should range in perceived value (some examples: large bar of chocolate; a box of macaroni and cheese; a mitten; or a can of dog food). So as not to spend much money, you could find things that you want to discard or look for food in your pantry.
    - Easel pad, pens
- Preparation for the "What's in the Bag?" exercise. Prepare the bags by putting candy in them. Make the distribution unequal, using the rough ratio of 5% "wealthy" bags, 10% "impoverished" bags and 85% "middle bags." In the wealthy bag, put the four chocolate bars; in the impoverished bags, put one M&M or nothing at all; in the middle bags, put 3 to 6 different colored pieces of candy. Mark the bags in a code that you understand so that you can ensure that anyone who is particularly marginal or vulnerable in any way in your group doesn't get an "impoverished" bag.
- Write out on easel paper:
  - Galtung's definition of structural violence that appears in the "Structural Violence" section.
  - Starhawk's definition of structural violence/oppression (that it equals prejudice + power-over).

PREPARATION: ON THE DAY OF THE SESSION

- Bring in copies of the day's newspaper. You should have half as many newspapers as expected participants for that day.

SESSION 6: **Seeing What's Hidden**

WELCOME — 1 MIN.

Say in your own words:

Welcome back for our sixth session of the *Engage: Exploring Nonviolent Living* Study Program. In this session, we will continue our exploration of the experience and dynamics of violence. We will explore structural violence; reflect on many of the forms of structural violence and the impact that they have; and analyze structural violence as "Prejudice + Power-over."

OPENING — 5 MIN.

Share the following in your own words:

I'd like to open this session with a 3-minute doodle.

Invite the participants to get one piece of paper and some writing or drawing implements. When everyone has the materials, invite them to draw, without thinking. Sound the bell after three minutes. At that time invite them to place their drawings, one at a time, in the center (on a small table; or hang them up on the wall) and to each say a word or two about their creation.

REFLECTING ON HOMEWORK — 10 MIN.

I again invite you to get together with your Nonviolence Partner to take a few minutes to reflect on your experiences or insights since the last session, as well as to reflect on the readings, journaling, or nonviolent action.

WHAT'S IN THE BAG? — 30 MIN.

Then convey the following in your own words:

> *"Be the change you want to see in the world."*
> — MOHANDAS GANDHI

We are going to open Session 6 with an exercise called "What's in the Bag?" The purpose of this exercise is to collect four candies of the same type and the same color. When you have collected the four candies of the same type and color, you can come to the front and choose a prize. Here are the prizes.

Tell the participants about the prizes. Take very few questions. Give each participant a bag. With the exception mentioned in the "Session Preparation," don't try to orchestrate who gets which bag. Tell participants not to look inside until everyone has one. When everyone has a bag, ask people to begin trading with one another in order to come up with four identical candies.

Ask participants to come forward to claim their prize when they have accumulated four identical candies.

Check to see if they have done so and then let them choose a prize. The game is over when all the prizes have been claimed.

Debrief

When the game is over and people have settled down, mention that this exercise was adapted by Karen Ridd (the Canadian activist whose story about being in prison in El Salvador we studied in Session 4) and then ask the following questions:

What feelings came up as you did this exercise?

Explore the feelings as they come up. For example: "You felt like giving up — what's that about?" Or: "Why did you feel angry?" Then ask:

What connections, if any, do you see to everyday life?

Sometimes the following ideas come up. People with wealthy bags can feel that they deserve them. Or they don't think much about others having less. Or they can feel confused or guilty. People with little or nothing often give up. People in the middle get busy trading, or trying to. More rarely, participants think about taking action to change the situation — for example, consider combining their candies to share a prize, or giving their winnings to someone else. Help people notice these perspectives as they come up. Then ask:

What factors enabled people to succeed in this game?

Write the responses on easel paper. Make generalizations as you write, e.g., when people say "knowing people in the room," you might write "networking." Once the list is complete, ask people to cluster the topics. Then ask:

What enables people to "succeed" in real life?
What role do different opportunities play in that "success"?
How do these differences relate, if they do, to violence?

Thank the participants for participating in the game and the discussion.

EXAMPLE: WORKING WOMEN — 15 MIN.

We will now explore one concrete example of difference in opportunities.

Ask participants to review briefly the "Working Women" sidebar on the following page. Ask them to break into groups of four and discuss the following question:

What does this example say about differences in opportunity? How does this relate to violence?

Bring the group back together and solicit several insights from the participants. Thank them and go to break.

WORKING WOMEN

Women generally earn less money than men for performing the same job duties. Contrary to popular myth, this is not because women get pregnant and have to leave the work force, or because women leave the work force to spend time at home with the kids, or because women work part-time and fewer hours than men. Women earn less than men in the same occupation with the same education and experiences, and the same amount of time put into their work.

In the past it was common to pay men more than women for the same work. That was a widely accepted practice "because men had families to support." Today such practices are illegal; however, men still earn more than women, even for the same job.

Facts about working women in the U.S.:
- Two-thirds of all mothers are now in the labor force.
- In 1996, African-American women earned only 63 cents and Hispanic women only 57 cents for each dollar earned by white men.
- Women and people of color, on average, earned less than white men with the same educational backgrounds; often, white men with less education earned the same as or more than educated women and people of color. For example, the average college-educated Hispanic woman earned only $21 per week more than white male high school graduates.
- Over a woman's lifetime, unequal pay hurts tremendously. It directly affects how much her pension and Social Security payments will be. For many women and people of color, growing older means growing poorer. Remember that, on the average, women live longer than men.
- Nearly 60% of full-time working American women who work year-round get paid less than $25,000 per year.
- In 1992 for those receiving hourly rates, women's median hourly earnings were 79.4 percent of men's; for full-time wage and salary workers, women's median weekly earnings were 75.4 percent of men's; and median annual earnings for women were 70.6 percent of men's annual earnings. (Bureau of Labor Statistics (BLS) and Bureau of the Census (BC).)

BREAK — 10 MIN.

STRUCTURAL VIOLENCE — 35 MIN.

Convey the following in your own words:

In Sessions 2 and 3 we explored what Johan Galtung, the peace researcher, called direct violence (physical acts) and cultural violence (societal attitudes and beliefs). In this session, we would like to look more deeply at the third kind of violence that Galtung writes about: structural violence.

Point to the easel where you have written an adaptation of Galtung's description of structural violence. Ask one of the participants to read aloud this description that you have written on easel paper and that is presented in a box below.

Lead a process where the group breaks this description into its components. Ask participants to reflect on what its different words and ideas mean, line by line. Ask them if they can think of examples.

> **Structural violence** *exists when some groups, classes, genders, nationalities, etc. are assumed to have, and in fact do have, more access to goods, resources, and opportunities than other groups, classes, genders, nationalities, etc., and this unequal advantage is built into the very social, political, and economic systems that govern societies, states, and the world.*
>
> — JOHAN GALTUNG

Then ask the group the following questions:

> From your point of view, is what Galtung is describing "violence"? If so, why? If not, why not?
>
> Is this "structural violence"? Why or why not? How does this relate to the "Working Women" discussion?

THREE FORMS OF POWER

In her book Truth or Dare, *the writer and social analyst Starhawk describes three forms of power: Power-over, Power-with, and Power-from-within:*

Power-over sees the world as an object, made up of many separate, isolated parts that have no intrinsic life, awareness, or value . . . . Human beings have no inherent worth; value must be earned or granted . . . . Power-over motivates through fear . . . .

Power-from-within . . . sees the world itself as a living being, made up of dynamic aspects . . . where there are no solid separations and no simple cause and effects. In such a world, all things have inherent value . . . .Its motivations are erotic in the broadest sense of the deep drives in us to experience and share pleasure, to connect, to create, to see our impact on others and on the world . . . .

Power-with . . .bridges the value systems of power-from-within and power-over. Power-with sees the world as a pattern of relationships, but its interest is in how that pattern can be shaped, molded, shifted. It values beings, forces, and people according to how they affect others and according to a history based on experience.

Then point to the easel where you have written the below quotation from Starhawk. Convey the following in your own words:

> Structural violence (which is also called oppression) fuses two things:
> Prejudice + Power-over.

Ask:

> What is "prejudice"? *(List the responses from the group.)*

Then ask (in your own words):

> And what is "Power-over"? Starhawk describes three forms of power: *Power-over, Power-with,* and *Power-from-within.* Here's her definition of Power-over:

> "Power-over sees the world as an object, made up of many separate, isolated parts that have no intrinsic life, awareness, or value . . . human beings have no inherent worth; value must be earned or granted . . . . Power-over motivates through fear . . ."

Finally, ask:

What are some examples of Prejudice + Power-over? *(Some examples include systems of economic inequality, racism, sexism, homophobia, ableism, etc.)*

What are some of the impacts of structural violence?

TODAY'S NEWSPAPER — 25 MIN.

Ask people to form pairs. Distribute a copy of the newspaper published that day to each pair. Ask each couple to scour the newspaper and find stories that indicate structural violence.

After several minutes, ask people to present their stories and why they seem to indicate structural violence.

After everyone has shared, ask people if they noticed or learned anything doing this exercise.

WHAT'S A DOLL TO YOU?

Excerpted from the book "Ideas for Action — Relevant Theory for Radical Change" by Cynthia Kaufman.

My friend's daughter had a doll that she loved to carry around. Morissa and her mom Marcy are white and the doll was black. Almost every time her parents took Morissa out in public with the doll, someone would comment on the racial situation. An African American man said: "I like the doll's complexion." An older white man was outraged and said, "How can you let her carry that doll?" Another older white man said tearfully, "I never thought before what it must have been like for Black kids to carry white dolls for all those years."

Why was the skin color of a doll such a big deal to everyone? When we stay within the confines of the racial expectations around us, we can be fooled into believing that race doesn't matter very much. This is especially true for those of us who are white. But when white people step outside of those expectations for having lovers or close friends who are of different races, when we bring those friends or lovers into family situations, when we socialize in the wrong places, or when we speak against the mistreatment of others, the walls of racism become very visible.

And for many people of color, those walls are ever present: in the lack of representation and misrepresentations of people from their own racial groups in the media every day; in the ways people are harassed by the police and treated in the judicial system; in the subtle but persistent ways that people of color are treated with suspicion in mostly white situations; and in the maddening fact that people of color can't know if they didn't get a job because they weren't the best applicant or because they weren't the right color...

Sometimes when people talk about racism, they talk as if it were just a matter of attitudes. It is common for people to see racism existing because some people believe that other people are inferior. While prejudiced attitudes do exist, and are an important part of the picture, the way that racial differences have become woven into the fabric of society is far more important...

Racism is anchored and reproduced in people's psyches, but it is also embedded in our social institutions.... [I]t is built into the legal, political, and economic structures of society.

CONCLUSION — 15 MIN.

⊙ **Nonviolence Journal**

Suggested Topic:
Reflect on the graphic on the Nonviolence Journal page depicting a "social ladder." Think about your own place on it. Write your name on the "rung" that you think you occupy. Then write the names of persons that you think might be above you and below you. Write responses to some or all of the following questions:

- Why do you see yourself at that location on the ladder?
- Why are some people above you and some below you?
- How did you get to that step on the ladder?
- What keeps you there?
- How do you feel about being located at that rung on the ladder?
- In maintaining yourself at this step in the ladder, what are the benefits and costs to yourself and others, if there are any?
- Would you like to step off the ladder? What would that be like? How would you do this?

⊙ **Nonviolent Action**

Watch a TV news program each day (or read a newspaper each day) with the lens of "structural violence." Ask: Who is excluded in the coverage? Who is included, and why? Apply other aspects from the discussion on structural violence (such as prejudice, power-over, the definition of structural violence) to these news presentations. Record your daily observations below.

⊙ **Next Session's Reading**

Please read the readings located at the end of this session, and review Sue Monk Kidd's "That's How I Like to See a Woman" at the end of session 1.

⊙ **Adding to the Wall of Learning and Growing**

Please add your insights, learnings, or questions to the Wall at this time.

⊙ **Closing** — 5 Min.

Put on an audiocassette or compact disk with instrumental music. In your own words, say:

Please stand and hold your arms out wide in front of you in a circle. Breathe in deeply and, while doing so, slowly draw your arms in so your own fingertips touch. Breathe out slowly, widening your arms back out. *Breathe in* the desire for the well-being of all and healing from exclusion; *breathe out* every obstacle to inclusion. Repeat this cycle four times.

KEY ORGANIZATIONS: ANTI-OPPRESSION TRAINING

The People's Institute for Survival and Beyond. *www.thepeoplesinstitute.org;* 7166 Crowder Blvd., Suite 100, New Orleans, LA 70127; (504) 241-7472; fax: (504) 241-7412; *contact@thepeoplesinstitute.org*. The People's Institute was founded in 1980 by long-time community organizers Ron Chisom of New Orleans and Jim Dunn of Yellow Springs, Ohio. It was created to develop more analytical, culturally-rooted, and effective community organizers. The People's Institute Undoing Racism™/ Community Organizing process has impacted the lives of nearly 100,000 people both nationally and internationally. Through this process, it has built a national collective of anti-racist, multicultural community organizers who do their work with an understanding of history, culture, and the impact of racism on communities. These anti-racist organizers build leadership in and account to the constituencies where they are organizing.

Crossroads Ministry. *www.crossroadsministry.org;* 425 South Central Park, Chicago, IL 60624; (773) 638-0166; fax: (773) 722-0445; *crossroadschicago@sbcglobal.net*. Crossroads Ministry leads anti-racism training and formation. Its mission is to dismantle systemic racism and build anti-racist multicultural diversity within institutions and communities. This mission is implemented primarily by training institutional transformation teams, and is guided by the following principles:
- The work of Crossroads is based upon a systemic analysis of racism and its individual, institutional, and cultural manifestations;
- The work of Crossroads is faith-based while at the same time non-sectarian, seeking to honor all expressions of spirituality that support and empower anti-racism;
- Crossroads seeks to be accountable in its work to those who share a common analysis of racism, and especially to communities of color;
- Crossroads understands its anti-racism work to be part of a national and global movement for racial justice and social equality; and
- Crossroads recognizes that resistance to racism also requires resistance to all other forms of social inequality and oppression.

The Center for Third World Organizing (CTWO, pronounced "C-2"). *www.cto.org;* 1218 E. 21st Street, Oakland, CA 94606; (510) 533-7583; fax: (510) 533-0923; *ctwo@ctwo.org*. CTWO is a racial justice organization dedicated to building a social justice movement led by people of color. CTWO is a training and resource center that promotes and sustains direct action organizing in communities of color in the United States. CTWO's programs include training of new and experienced organizers, including the well-known Movement Activist Apprenticeship Program (MAAP); establishing model multi-racial community organizations; and building an active network of organizations and activists of color to achieve racial justice in its fullest dimensions.

Soulforce. *www.soulforce.org;* PO Box 3195, Lynchburg, VA 24503-0195; (877) 705-6393 (toll free); fax: (434) 384-9333; *info@soulforce.org*. Soulforce is an interfaith movement committed to ending spiritual violence perpetuated by religious policies and teachings against gay, lesbian, bisexual, and transgender (GLBT) people. It teaches and employs the nonviolent principles of Mahatma Gandhi and Martin Luther King, Jr. for the liberation of sexual and gender minorities.

Tools For Change. *www.toolsforchange.org*; 349 Church Street, San Francisco, CA 94114; 415-861-6347; 800-99TOOLS; *info@toolsforchange.org*. Northwest Office: 2408 E. Valley, Seattle, WA 98112; (206) 329-2201. Tools for Change offers consulting, training, mediation and facilitation services nationwide. It has forged multi-cultural and multigenerational alliances in many different settings. Tools for Change offers workshops on alliance-building that embrace four assumptions:

- Everyone has a great deal of information and misinformation about people different from themselves. Mainstream culture precludes open discussion of this information.
- The creation of alliances that are both powerful and lasting requires changes in the perceptions and attitudes and behaviors of those with power and privilege as well as those who are oppressed.
- There are specific organizational and personal strategies that can qualitatively change the nature of our working together across differences.
- It is to every ones benefit to establish just relationships. Work needs to be proactive and vision based.

Tools for Change helps people explore their personal, social and organizational histories. It explores the different meanings of power: differential access to resources, power from within vs. power over) and the relationship between those with privilege and those without. It learns ways to deal with the common dynamics of guilt and blame and create ways to build relationships that are sustainable over the long term.

The Theater of the Oppressed Laboratory: Interactive Theater Workshops for Social Change. *www.toplab.org*. 122 West 27 Street 10th floor, New York, NY 10001; (212) 924-1858; fax (212) 674-6506. The Theater of the Oppressed Laboratory of New York is a group of individuals assembled without regard to race, gender, sexual orientation or physical limitation. It is a collective of educators, theater workers and artists who have extensively trained and collaborated with Augusto Boal, founder of the Theater of the Oppressed. Its purpose is to provide a forum for the practice, performance and dissemination of the techniques of the Theater of the Oppressed. The Laboratory works with educators, human service and health care workers, union organizers and community activists who are interested in using interactive theater as an organizing tool to analyze, and explore solutions to, problems that arise as a result of conditions brought on by discrimination and injustice in the workplace, school and community.

NONVIOLENCE JOURNAL

Suggestion:

Reflect on the nearby graphic depicting a "social ladder." Think about your own place on it. Write your name on the "step" that you think you occupy. Then write the names of persons that you think might be above you and below you. Write responses to some or all of the following questions:

- Why do you see yourself at that location on the ladder?
- Why are some people above you and some below you?
- How did you get to that step on the ladder?
- What keeps you there?
- How do you feel about being located at that rung on the ladder?
- In maintaining yourself at this step in the ladder, what are the benefits and costs to yourself and others, if there are any?
- Would you like to step off the ladder? What would that be like? How would you do this?

HOMEWORK

NONVIOLENT ACTION

Watch a TV news program each day (or read a newspaper each day) with the lens of "structural violence." Ask: Who is excluded in the coverage? Who is included, and why? Apply other aspects from the discussion on structural violence (such as prejudice, power-over, the definition of structural violence) to these news presentations. Record your daily observations below.

The Journey from Indifference to Heart-Unity in the Struggle Against Structural Violence

by Ken Butigan

Power is the capacity to bring about change. Economist and peace researcher Kenneth Boulding writes that there are three kinds of power: *coercive power, exchange power,* and *integrative* or *collaborative power.* Nonviolence scholar Michael Nagler has summarized the consequences of these three forms of power in terms of the impact that they have on the quality of the relationships of those involved.

Coercive power, which operates by threat, leaves those involved more separated and estranged. Exchange power, where one item is traded for another item of equal value, has a neutral impact — it leaves the qualitative relationship between the buyer and the seller unchanged. Integrative or collaborative power, on the other hand, draws the parties closer.

Nonviolence is *integrative power* seeking to achieve what Gandhi called "heart unity."

Violence distances us; nonviolence brings us closer together. The monumental goal of nonviolence is "optimal relatedness" or, simply put, heart-unity. This does not mean suppressing our differences. Part of the power of nonviolence lies, in fact, in celebrating our differences. But it also upholds our deep connection. One of the goals of nonviolence, Gandhi maintained, is *difference without division.* Or perhaps another way of saying it is, *unity in diversity.*

Saying this is easy. Achieving it is not. Dismantling structural violence requires the journey from "threat power" to "heart-unity."

This is not a simple matter of saying, "Why can't we all get along?" It is a step-by-step process of transforming our attitudes, of grasping the complexity of structural violence, and avoiding the pitfalls of moving too fast or too slow.

It is a journey beyond our personal interests. It is a journey of solidarity and connection with those under attack. It is a journey of discovering what within my own soul holds me back from taking a stand. It is a journey of powerful and courageous engagement with those who wield coercive power. And it is a journey to seeing the humanity of both the violated and the violator, without condoning the violator's actions.

> *This is not a simple matter of saying, "Why can't we all get along?" It is a step-by-step process of transforming our attitudes.*

This is a process of slowly awakening to suffering, transforming our separation from those who suffer, taking steps to relieve suffering, and then moving beyond help to "being with," "walking side-by-side," and "being one with."

This is an external journey: changing systems that keep us apart or that enforce injustice. But this external journey is ultimately rooted in a spiritual journey in which we as individuals and whole peoples break the chains within that keep the systems of injustice in place.

In this journey we often can pass through a number of stages toward authentic (not superficial) connection and relationship. As part of her anti-oppression work, Dr. Leticia Nieto has identified five stages of this journey: *Indifference, Distance, Inclusion, Awareness,* and *Becoming an Ally.* Dr. Nieto's framework identifies the steps by which one becomes an ally in the struggle for justice. With Dr.

Nieto's permission, I have added another step to this model: Gandhi's notion of heart-unity.

Here are the six phases of this journey of transformation:

1. Indifference

Indifference to structural violence is often rooted in unfamiliarity, isolation, or intentional separation from those who are systematically violated. Often a specific social or personal "script' in which we attribute some deficiency in intelligence, morality, or personality to the oppressed reinforces this. There is a tendency to dehumanize them and a conscious or unconscious attitude of superiority and supremacy.

2. Distance

As awareness of injustice grows, there is basic recognition of difference, but coupled with a negative evaluation of the oppressed. There is a tendency toward supremacy. There is a tendency to proselytize them. Overt appreciation for the oppressed is expressed while at the same time mainstream supremacy is communicated through covert attitudes/gestures/thinking patterns.

3. Inclusion

Here there is recognition and acceptance of superficial differences and experiences of oppression while holding that all human beings are essentially the same (from the mainstream point of view) and that all human beings suffer equally, whether they are oppressors or oppressed. This is a way of negating the reality of oppression. This often includes an attitude of universalism ("we are all sisters and brothers") without recognizing the specific structural arrangement by which oppression benefits the mainstream while oppressing those at the margins.

4. Awareness

As Nieto writes, "At this step one recognizes and appreciates differences and accepts that oppression operates in systematic, pervasive, restricting, hierarchical, complex, and internalized ways. One works from a place of curiosity and inquiry with a willingness to believe the oppressed as experts on their own oppression, and understands that the most anti-oppressive action they can take is to maintain awareness of oppression. One tends to ask oppressed: 'what is it like for you?' There is a tendency towards a relative and open stance regarding values and behavioral differences and a person can begin to acknowledge the implications of privilege and benefit."

5. Allyship

Here, one develops communication and ally skills with the goal of social change. She or he makes effective use of empathy to understand, and be understood, across differences. "One maintains sensitivity for experiences of the oppressed, acknowledges internalized dominance and mainstream supremacy, acknowledges privilege and entitlement, and uses them for social change," Nieto writes. "She or he challenges oppressors, oppressive institutions, and norms, and consistently speaks to the underlying, inherent inequity of the oppressor/oppressed system. There is a tendency towards allyship, advocacy, and action."

6. Heart-Unity

All life is one. Yet this oneness is dramatically distorted by systems of structural violence based on physical, political, economic, cultural, and psychological threat, fear, and separation. Heart-unity is a process that 1) affirms the radical interconnectedness of all life and 2) embodies this by relentlessly challenging, resisting and dismantling any form of structural violence and oppression that distorts or undermines this oneness.

Heart-unity goes beyond being an ally, which often can be reduced to a form of "helping" and privilege. It is a profound awareness of *difference* (it does not pretend to suffer or experience in the same way that the violated suffers or experiences) but also *difference without division* (being conscious of the profound connection and solidarity that binds us together) that can transform one's own self-understanding, assumptions, and choices. Heart-unity is a fundamental orientation that can alter one's relationship to both oppressors and the oppressed: opening us to the humanity of all while *sharpening* (not diminishing) our will to take steps to challenge and transform structural violence that distorts and destroys the humanness of both oppressor and oppressed.

Why I Quit the Klan:
An Interview with C. P. Ellis

by Studs Terkel

C. P. Ellis lives in Durham, North Carolina, and is a former leader of the Ku Klux Klan.

All my life, I had work, never a day without work, worked all the overtime I could get and still could not survive financially. I began to see there's something wrong with this country. I worked my butt off and just never seemed to break even. I had some real great ideas about this nation. They say to abide by the law, go to church, do right and live for the Lord, and everything'll work out. But it didn't work out. It just kept getting worse and worse...

Tryin' to come out of that hole, I just couldn't do it. I really began to get bitter. I didn't know who to blame. I tried to find somebody. Hatin' America is hard to do because you can't see it to hate it. You gotta have somethin' to look at to hate. The natural person for me to hate would be Black people, because my father before me was a member of the Klan...

So I began to admire the Klan... To be part of somethin'. ... The first night I went with the fellas . . . I was led into a large meeting room, and this was the time of my life!

It was thrilling. Here's a guy who's worked all his life and struggled all his life to be something, and here's the moment to be something. I will never forget it. Four robed Klansmen led me into the hall. The lights were dim and the only thing you could see was an illuminated cross... After I had taken my oath, there was loud applause goin' through-out the buildin', musta been at least 400 people. For this one little ol' person. It was a thrilling moment for C. P. Ellis...

The majority of [the Klansmen] are low-income Whites, people who really don't have a part in something. They have been shut out as well as Blacks. Some are not very well educated either. Just like myself. We had a lot of support from doctors and lawyers and police officers.

Maybe they've had bitter experiences in this life and they had to hate somebody. So the natural person to hate would be the Black person. He's beginnin' to come up, he's beginnin' to . . . start votin' and run for political office. Here are White people who are supposed to be superior to them, and we're shut out... Shut out. Deep down inside, we want to be part of this great society. Nobody listens, so we join these groups...

We would go to the city council meetings and the Blacks would be there and we'd be there. It was a confrontation every time... We began to make some inroads with the city councilmen and county commissioners. They began to call us friend. Call us at night on the telephone: "C. P., glad you came to that meeting last night." They didn't want integration either, but they did it secretively, in order to get elected. They couldn't stand up openly and say it, but they were glad somebody was sayin' it. We visited some of the city leaders in their homes and talked to 'em privately. It wasn't long before councilmen would call me up: "The Blacks are comin' up tonight and makin' outrageous demands. How about some of you people showin' up and have a little balance?"

We'd load up our cars and we'd fill up half the council chambers, and the Blacks the other half. During these times, I carried weapons to the meetings, outside my belt. We'd go there armed. We would wind up just hollerin' and fussin' at each other. What happened? As a result of our fightin' one another, the city council still had their way. They didn't want to give up control to the Blacks nor the Klan. They were usin' us.

> *A Klansman and a militant Black woman, co-chairmen of the school committee. It was impossible. How could I work with her?*

I began to realize this later down the road. One day I was walkin' downtown and a certain city council member saw me comin'. I expected him to shake my hand because he was talkin' to me at night on the telephone. I had been in his home and visited with him. He crossed the street [to avoid me]... I began to think, somethin's wrong here. Most of 'em are merchants or maybe an attorney, an insurance agent, people like that. As long as they kept low-income Whites and low-income Blacks fightin', they're gonna maintain control. I began to get that feelin' after I was ignored in public. I thought: . . . you're not gonna use me any more. That's when I began to do some real serious thinkin'.

The same thing is happening in this country today. People are being used by those in control, those who have all the wealth. I'm not espousing communism. We got the greatest system of government in the world. But those who have it simply don't want those who don't have it to have any part of it. Black

and White. When it comes to money, the green, the other colors make no difference.

I spent a lot of sleepless nights. I still didn't like Blacks. I didn't want to associate with them. Blacks, Jews, or Catholics. My father said: "Don't have anything to do with 'em." I didn't until I met a Black person and talked with him, eyeball to eyeball, and met a Jewish person and talked to him, eyeball to eyeball. I found they're people just like me. They cried, they cussed, they prayed, they had desires. Just like myself. Thank God, I got to the point where I can look past labels. But at that time, my mind was closed.

I remember one Monday night Klan meeting. I said something was wrong. Our city fathers were using us. And I didn't like to be used. The reactions of the others was not too pleasant: "Let's just keep fightin' them niggers." I'd go home at night and I'd have to wrestle with myself. I'd look at a Black person walkin' down the street, and the guy'd have ragged shoes or his clothes would be worn.

That began to do something to me inside. I went through this for about six months. I felt I just had to get out of the Klan. But I wouldn't get out...

[Ellis was invited, as a Klansman, to join a committee of people from all walks of life to make recommendations on how to solve racial problems in the school system. He very reluctantly accepted. After a few stormy meetings, he was elected co-chair of the committee, along with Ann Atwater, a Black woman who for years had been leading local efforts for civil rights.]

A Klansman and a militant Black woman, co-chairmen of the school committee. It was impossible. How could I work with her? But it was in our hands. We had to make it a success. This gave me another sense of belongin', a sense of pride. This helped the inferiority feeling I had. A man who has stood up publicly and said he despised Black people, all of a sudden he was willin' to work with 'em. Here's a chance for a low-income White man to be somethin'. In spite of all my hatred for Blacks and Jews and liberals, I accepted the job. Her and I began to reluctantly work together. She had as many problems workin' with me as I had workin' with her.

One night, I called her: "Ann, you and I should have a lot of differences and we got em now. But there's somethin' laid out here before us, and if it's gonna be a success, you and I are gonna have to make it one. Can we lay aside some of these feelins?" She said: "I'm willing if you are." I said: "Let's do it."

My old friends would call me at night: "C. P., what the hell is wrong with you? You're sellin' out the White race." This began to make me have guilt feelings. Am I doin' right? Am I doin' wrong? Here I am all of a sudden makin' an about-face and tryin' to deal with my feelins, my heart. My mind was beginnin' to open up. I was beginnin' to see what was right and what was wrong. I don't want the kids to fight forever...

One day, Ann and I went back to the school and we sat down. We began to talk and just reflect... I begin to see, here we are, two people from the far ends of the fence, havin' identical problems, except hers bein' Black and me bein' White... The amazing thing about it, her and I, up to that point, had cussed each other, bawled each other, we hated each other. Up to that point, we didn't know each other. We didn't know we had things in common...

The whole world was openin' up, and I was learning new truths that I had never learned before. I was beginning to look at a Black person, shake hands with him, and see him as a human bein'. I hadn't got rid of all this stuff. I've still got a little bit of it. But somethin' was happenin' to me...

I come to work one morning and some guys says: "We need a union." At this time I wasn't pro-union. My daddy was antilabor too. We're not gettin' paid much, we're havin' to work seven days in a row. We're all starvin' to death... I didn't know nothin' about organizin' unions, but I knew how to organize people, stir people up. That's how I got to be business agent for the union. ...

It makes you feel good to go into a plant and ... see Black people and White people join hands and defeat the racist issues [union-busters] use against people... I tell people there's a tremendous possibility in this country to stop wars, the battles, the struggles, the fights between people. People say: "That's an impossible dream. You sound like Martin Luther King." An ex-Klansman who sounds like Martin Luther King. I don't think it's an impossible dream. It's happened in my life. It's happened in other people's lives in America...

When the news came over the radio that Martin Luther King was assassinated, I got on the telephone and begin to call other Klansmen... We just had a real party... Really rejoicin' cause the son of a bitch was dead. 'Our troubles are over with.' They say the older you get, the harder it is for you to change. That's not necessarily true. Since I changed, I've set down and listened to tapes of Martin Luther King. I listen to it and tears come to my eyes cause I know what he's sayin' now. I know what's happenin'.

SESSION 7: READING 3

Letter from Delano
by Cesar Chavez

Good Friday 1969
E.L. Barr, Jr., President
California Grape and Tree Fruit League
717 Market St., San Francisco, California

Dear Mr. Barr:

I am sad to hear about your accusations in the press that our union movement and table grape boycott have been successful because we have used violence and terror tactics. If what you say is true, I have been a failure and should withdraw from the struggle; but you are left with the awesome moral responsibility, before God and Man, to come forward with whatever information you have so that corrective action can begin at once. If for any reason you fail to come forth to substantiate your charges, then you must be held responsible for committing violence against us, albeit of the tongue. I am convinced that you as a human being did not mean what you said but rather acted hastily under pressure from the public relations firm that has been hired to try to counteract the tremendous moral force of our movement. How many times we ourselves have felt the need to lash out in anger and bitterness.

Today on Good Friday, 1969, we remember the life and the sacrifice of Martin Luther King, Jr., who gave himself totally to the nonviolent struggle for peace and justice. In his *Letter From a Birmingham Jail* Dr. King describes better than I could our hopes for the strike and boycott: "Injustice must be exposed, with all the tensions its exposure creates, to the light of human conscience and the air of national opinion before it can be cured." For our part I admit that we have seized upon every tactic and strategy consistent with the morality of our cause to expose that injustice and thus to heighten the sensitivity of the American conscience so that farm workers will have, without bloodshed, their own union and the dignity of bargaining with their agribusiness employers. By lying about the nature of our movement, Mr. Barr, you are working against nonviolent social change. Unwittingly perhaps, you may unleash that other force which our union by discipline and deed, censure and education has sought to avoid, that panacean shortcut, that senseless violence which honors no color, class, or neighborhood.

You must understand—I must make you understand—that our membership and the hopes and aspirations of the hundreds of thousands of the poor and dispossessed that have been raised on our account are, above all, human beings, no better and no worse than any other cross-section of human society; we are not saints because we are poor, but by the same measure neither are we immoral. We are men and women who have suffered and endured much, and not only because of our abject poverty but because we have been kept poor. The colors of our skins, the languages of our cultural and native origins, the lack of formal education, the exclusion from the democratic process, the numbers of our men slain in recent wars—all these burdens generation after generation have sought to demoralize us, to break our human spirit. But God knows that we are not beasts of burden, agricultural implements, or rented slaves; we are men. And mark this well, Mr. Barr, we are men locked in a death struggle against man's inhumanity to man in the industry that you represent. And this struggle itself gives meaning to our life and ennobles our dying.

As your industry has experienced, our strikers here in Delano and those who represent us throughout the world are well trained for this struggle. They have been under the gun, they have been kicked and beaten and herded by dogs, they have been cursed and ridiculed, they have been stripped and chained and jailed, they have been sprayed with the poisons used in the vineyards; but they have been taught not to lie down and die nor to flee in shame, but to resist with every ounce of human endurance and spirit. To resist not with retaliation in kind but to overcome with love and compassion, with ingenuity and creativity, with hard work and longer hours, with stamina and patient tenacity, with truth and public appeal, with friends and allies, with nobility and discipline, with politics and law, and with prayer and fasting. They were not trained in a month or even a year; after all, this new harvest season will mark our fourth full year of strike and even now we continue to plan and prepare for the years to come. Time accomplishes for the poor what money does for the rich.

This is not to pretend that we have everywhere been successful enough or that we have not made mistakes. And while we do not belittle or underestimate our adversaries—for they are the rich and the powerful and they possess the land—we are not afraid nor do we cringe from the confrontation. We welcome it! We have planned for it! We know that our cause is just, that history is a story of social revolution, and that the poor shall inherit the land.

Once again, I appeal to you as the representative of your industry and as a man. I ask you to recognize and bargain with our union before the economic pressure of the boycott and strike takes an irrevocable toll; but if not I ask you to at least sit down with us to discuss the safeguards necessary to keep our historical struggle free of violence. I make this appeal because as one of the leaders of our nonviolent movement, I know and accept my responsibility for preventing, if possible, the destruction of human life and property. For these reasons, and knowing of Gandhi's admonition that fasting is the last resort in place of the sword, during a most critical time in our movement last February 1968 I undertook a 25-day fast. I repeat to you the principle enunciated to the membership at the start of the fast: if to build our union required the deliberate taking of life, either the life of a grower or his child, or the life of a farm worker or his child, then I choose not to see the union built.

Mr. Barr, let me be painfully honest with you. You must understand these things. We advocate militant nonviolence as our means for social revolution and to achieve justice for our people, but we are not blind or deaf to the desperate and moody winds of human frustration, impatience, and rage that blow among us. Gandhi himself admitted that if his only choice were cowardice or violence, he would choose violence. Men are not angels, and time and tide wait for no man. Precisely because of these powerful human emotions, we have tried to involve masses of people in their own struggle. Participation and self-determination remain the best experience of freedom, and free men instinctively prefer democratic change and even protect the rights guaranteed to seek it. Only the enslaved in despair have need of violent overthrow.

This letter does not express all that is in my heart, Mr. Barr. But if it says nothing else, it says that we do not hate you or rejoice to see your industry destroyed; we hate the

> *And mark this well, Mr. Barr, we are men locked in a death struggle against man's inhumanity to man in the industry that you represent. And this struggle itself gives meaning to our life and ennobles our dying.*

agribusiness system that seeks to keep us enslaved and we shall overcome and change it not by retaliation or bloodshed but by a determined nonviolent struggle carried on by those masses of farm workers who intend to be free and human.

Sincerely yours,

Cesar E. Chavez
United Farm Workers Organizing
Committee, A.F.L.-C.I.O.
Delano, California

HOMEWORK

REFLECTIONS ON THE READINGS

Session 7:
Responding to Structural Violence

SESSION 7: **Responding to Structural Violence**

OBJECTIVES
- To explore how structural violence is maintained through the combination of internalized attitudes and social conditions
- To investigate we can challenge structural violence
- To reflect on the personal and social steps involved in the struggle to confront and dismantle structural violence

AGENDA
- Opening [10 min.]
- Welcome [1 min.]
- Reflecting on Homework [10 min.]
- Revisiting Sue Monk Kidd's Story [45 min.]
- Break [10 min.]
- From Indifference to Heart-Unity Exercise [60 min.]
- Conclusion [10 min.]
    Nonviolence Journal
    Nonviolent Action
    Next Session's Reading
    Adding to the Wall of Learning and Growing
    Evaluation
    Closing

READINGS
- Reading #1: "The Journey from Indifference to Heart-Unity in the Struggle Against Structural Violence"
- Reading #2: Studs Terkel, "Why I Quit the Klan: An Interview with C. P. Ellis"
- Reading #3: Cesar Chavez, "Letter from Delano"
- Also: Review Sue Monk Kidd, "That's How I Like to See a Woman" (At the end of Session 1).

NOTES FOR THE FACILITATOR

SESSION PREPARATION: BEFORE

- Review the entire session in-depth. Role-play or practice setting up and facilitating exercises beforehand. Wherever possible, put material into your own words. Feel free to make notes for this purpose on 3x5 cards or in the book next to the written instructions.
- Play close attention to time in the session. You don't need to take all the hands when facilitating de-briefs.
- Materials needed:
    - Masking tape
- Write out on easel paper:
    - The opening
    - For Sue Monk Kidd Story: the 3 different forms of power described by Starhawk in Session 6.
    - The Six Phases with their brief descriptions in the "From Indifference to Heart-Unity" exercise.
    - The questions for the small group sharing.

PREPARATION: ON THE DAY OF THE SESSION

- For the From Indifference to Heart-Unity exercise: Tape 12 pieces of easel paper together into a large rectangle. Draw six concentric circles and name them using the following (with 6 being the outermost circle, then 5, etc.):
    - 1 – Heart Unity
    - 2 – Being an Ally
    - 3 – Awareness
    - 4 – Inclusion
    - 5 – Distance
    - 6 – Indifference

SESSION 7: **Responding to Structural Violence**

WELCOME — 1 MIN.

Share in your own words:

> Welcome back for our seventh session of the *Engage: Exploring Nonviolent Living* Study Program. Last session we looked at what Structural Violence is and how it manifests itself. Today we will explore how structural violence is maintained through the combination of internalized attitudes and social conditions; investigate how we can challenge structural violence; and reflect on how we can be allies in the struggle to confront and dismantle structural violence.

OPENING — 5 MIN.

> To open this session we are going to do a "call and response" based on a poem from the Australian Aboriginal educator, Lilla Watson.

Divide the participants into two groups of equal numbers. Name the groups "A" and "B." Invite Groups A and B to gather, look at the lines for their group that you've written on the easel pad, and take a few minutes thinking what might be appropriate arm (or body) movements and facial expressions for each of their respective lines.

When the group is ready, have each group stand in a line facing the other group. Take turns saying the following lines together. Invite each group to say their lines slowly and to pause between groups.

> Group A: If you have come here to help me,
> Group B: You are wasting your time.....
> Group A: But if you have come because
> your liberation is bound up with mine,
> Group B: Then let us work together.

Have the groups switch sides and do it again.

> *"Not everything that is faced can be changed, but nothing can be changed until it is faced."*
> —JAMES BALDWIN

REFLECTING ON HOMEWORK — 10 MIN.

> I again invite you to get together with your Nonviolence Partner to take a few minutes to reflect on your experiences or insights since the last session, as well as to reflect on the readings, journaling, or nonviolent action.

REVISITING SUE MONK KIDD'S STORY — 45 MIN.

Convey the following in your own words:

As we begin our session, let's revisit the story from Sue Monk Kidd entitled, "That's How I Like to See a Woman," that we read in Session 2. Let's listen to the following paragraph taken from the end of that story:

"Throughout my awakening, I'd grown increasingly aware of certain attitudes that existed in our culture, a culture long dominated by men. The men in the drugstore had mirrored one attitude in particular, that of seeking power over another, of staying up by keeping others down. Sitting in my car replaying my statement back to those men that women did not belong on their knees—I knew I had uttered my declaration of intent."

Individual reflection [15 Min.]

Ask the participants to write or use creative materials to reflect on the following two questions:

- Have you ever seen someone in your life (or in the world) take an action similar to the one Sue Monk Kidd did?
- Can you think of a situation where you would like to respond in a similar way? What would you imagine doing or saying?

Small Group Sharing [15 Min.]

Ask participants to form small groups of three to share their reflections together on the two questions above. Ask them to reflect also on the following question:

Thinking back on Starhawk's "Three Forms of Power" from Session 6, which of the three kinds of power described there did Sue Monk Kidd use?

Large Group Sharing [15 Min.]

Convey the following in your own words:

Two aspects of structural violence are *internalized attitudes* and *social conditions*. They often combine to either cause violence or keep people from resisting violence.

Then ask:

- What is an "internalized attitude"?
- What were the internalized attitudes of the men in the Sue Monk Kidd story?
- What do you imagine were the internalized attitudes of Sue Monk Kidd that she had to confront and transform?

- What is a "social condition"?
- What social conditions were present in this story?
- Finally, how were "internalized attitudes" and "social conditions" combined in this story?

Thank the group and go to break.

BREAK — 10 MIN.

FROM INDIFFERENCE TO HEART-UNITY — 55 MIN.

Overview and Stories [15 min.]

Review with the participants the main points, one at a time, of Reading #1: "The Journey from Indifference to Heart-Unity in the Struggle Against Structural Violence" (found at the end of the previous chapter).

1. *Indifference* to difference and oppression

2. *Distance* from difference and the awareness of oppression

3. *Inclusion* of difference without recognition of oppression

4. *Awareness* of difference and of the reality of oppression

5. *Being an Ally* to difference and taking anti-oppressive actions

6. *Heart-Unity* through difference-without-division

Convey the following in your own words:

As you can see, we have a representation of six concentric circles here in the center of the room. Each concentric circle corresponds to the six steps. In a moment I'm going to ask you to represent one of the characters from one of the stories we have studied for this session and position yourself on one of these circles: whether this person is indifferent, or inclusive, or exhibiting heart unity, and so forth.

The stories include:

- Sue Monk Kidd's intervention against sexism;

TOWNIES VS. OUTSIDERS

In the late 1990s, Pace e Bene trainer Cynthia Stateman facilitated a *From Violence to Wholeness* Study Program in a church in a small town in southwest Colorado. One of the participants was the town's mayor.

At one point during the ten-week study program, the following incident took place in the downtown area. A fight had broken out between a young man who had lived his whole life in the town and "an outsider" who had been brought in by a mining company to work in one of the nearby mines. The fight escalated, with several young people from both sides joining in. Someone suddenly pulled a knife out and one young man was badly wounded. The police and medical personnel finally arrived on the scene and the bloody fight ended.

Normally, this would have been the end of the matter. The police and the courts would do their job, and that would be it. But the mayor began thinking that something more had to be done. The *From Violence to Wholeness* Study Program had gotten her thinking that there were deeper truths to be uncovered and a more satisfying — more whole — resolution than time in jail for those involved in the altercation.

The mayor decided to call a town meeting to air the frictions between "outsiders" and "townies." Just as Gandhi would have done, she set in motion a process where 70 people (out of a population of 700) gathered to share their pieces of the truth and their feelings: the resentment town people felt at being passed over for jobs in the mine; the fear and anxiety the outsiders felt when visiting town. After much discussion, the manager of the local mining operation, who was also in attendance, said that he had not been aware of this tension and immediately guaranteed a number of jobs to local town residents.

Inspired by her reflections on the possibilities of nonviolence, the mayor had created the space for sharing of "truths" and creating an agreement that began the process of meeting the needs of both sides. Martin Luther King, Jr. would have called this a step toward the "Beloved Community." At Pace e Bene, we call this the first stage of the journey "from violence to wholeness."

- "Townies vs. Outsiders";
- The United Farm Workers ("Letter from Delano"); and
- C. P. Ellis's account of his repudiation of his role as a Ku Klux Klan leader.

Take a moment to read the "Townies vs. Outsiders" short story found on the opposite page.

Find one character from any of these stories that you would like to represent in this exercise.

Exercise [20 min.]

After participants have chosen a character, ask them to go "position" where that character's actions were within the six circles. Then ask people one at a time why they are standing where they are.

Ask them to play other people from the same story. Call on them one at a time to reflect on this.

Large Group Debrief [15 min.]

Then reassemble in the large group. Debrief the exercise with the following question:

- Thinking about these stories, how does each one reflect the struggle against structural violence?

Conclude the exercise by summarizing the key points brought out in the large group debrief.

CONCLUSION — 15 MIN.

⊙ Nonviolence Journal

Suggested Topic:
Review the six steps described in "From Indifference to Heart-Unity." Write about situations where you have experienced one or more of these phases. What might be a step or two that you could take that would move you to the next phase?

⊙ Nonviolent Action

If given the opportunity, take one action moving more in the direction of heart-unity.

⊙ Next Session's Reading

Please be sure to read the readings located at the end of this session.

⊙ Adding to the Wall of Learning and Growing

Please add your insights, learnings, or questions to the Wall at this time.

⊙ Closing [5 Min.]

Ask a participant to slowly read the following passage by Pam McAllister. Afterward, ask people to offer one word about the complexity of nonviolence.

What has drawn me most strongly to nonviolence
Is its capacity for encompassing a complexity
Necessarily denied by violent strategies.
By complexity I mean the sort faced by feminists
Who rage against the system of male supremacy but,
At the same time, love their fathers, sons, husbands,
Brothers, and male friends.
I mean the complexity which requires us
To name an underpaid working man who beats his wife
Both as someone who is oppressed and is an oppressor.
Violent tactics and strategies
rely on polarization and dualistic thinking and
require us to divide ourselves into the good and the bad,
assume neat, rigid little categories
easily answered from the barrel of a gun.
Nonviolence allows
for the complexity inherent in our struggles
and requires a reasonable acceptance of diversity
and an appreciation for our common ground.
— *Pam McAllister*

KEY ORGANIZATIONS: HUMAN RIGHTS

The Human Rights Campaign. *www.hrc.org;* 1640 Rhode Island Ave., N.W., Washington, D.C. 20036-3278; 202-628-4160; fax: 202-347-5323. As America's largest gay and lesbian organization, the Human Rights Campaign is a bipartisan organization that works to advance equality based on sexual orientation and gender expression and identity, to ensure that gay, lesbian, bisexual, and transgender Americans can be open, honest, and safe at home, at work, and in the community.

Global Exchange. *www.globalexchange.org;* 2017 Mission Street, #303 San Francisco, CA, 94110; 415-255-7296. Global Exchange is an international human rights organization dedicated to promoting political, social, and environmental justice globally. Since its founding in 1988 it has been working to increase global awareness among the U.S public while building partnerships around the world.

The Human Rights Action Center. *www.dyr.org/index.html.* Email: *hrac@juno.com.* 451 First Street, S.E., Washington, D.C., 20003; (202) 547-2582; fax: (202) 547-7254. Founded by Jack Healey, former director of Amnesty International USA, HRAC's mission is: to campaign to include the Universal Declaration of Human Rights in citizen's passports; to support growing human rights groups all over the world; to create innovative, forceful, effective solutions to assist victims in protecting themselves; to rightfully restore Aung San Suu Kyi to power in Burma; and to create a fund to get people out of harm's way in exceptional human rights abuse cases.

Amnesty International USA. *www.amnestyusa.org.* 5 Penn Plaza New York, NY 10001. (212) 807-8400; fax: (212) 627-1451. AI's vision is of a world in which every person enjoys all of the human rights enshrined in the Universal Declaration of Human Rights and other international human rights standards. In pursuit of this vision, AI's mission is to undertake research and action focused on preventing and ending grave abuses of the rights to physical and mental integrity, freedom of conscience and expression, and freedom from discrimination, within the context of its work to promote all human rights.

Human Rights Watch. *www. hrw.org.* 350 Fifth Avenue, 34th floor. New York, NY 10118-3299 USA. (212) 290-4700; fax: (212) 736-1300. HRW is dedicated to protecting the human rights of people around the world. It stands with victims and activists to prevent discrimination, to uphold political freedom, to protect people from inhumane conduct in wartime, and to bring offenders to justice. It investigates and exposes human rights violations and hold abusers accountable. And it challenges governments and those who hold power to end abusive practices and respect international human rights law.

NONVIOLENCE JOURNAL

Suggestion:

Review the six steps described in "From Indifference to Heart-Unity." Write about situations where you have experienced one or more of these phases. What might be a step or two that you could take that would move you to the next phase?

HOMEWORK

NONVIOLENT ACTION

If given the opportunity, take one action moving in the direction of heart unity.

The Milgram Experiment
Wikipedia (online encyclopedia)

The Milgram experiment was a famous scientific experiment of social psychology. The experiment was first described by Stanley Milgram, a psychologist at Yale University in an article titled "Behavioral Study of Obedience" published in the *Journal of Abnormal and Social Psychology* in 1963, and later summarized in his 1974 book *Obedience to Authority: An Experimental View*. It was intended to measure the willingness of a participant to obey an authority who instructs the participant to do something that may conflict with the participant's personal conscience.

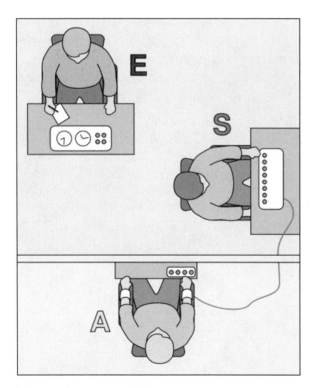

The experimenter (E) convinces the participant (S) to give what the participant believes are painful electric shocks to another participant (A), who is actually an actor. Many participants continued to give shocks despite pleas for mercy from the actor.

Method of the experiment

Details on the exact procedure tend to vary greatly, perhaps because of the prolificity of the test, perhaps because of its status as a near-urban-legend. The following account should be considered dramatized, not necessarily factually accurate.

Recruitment

Participants were recruited using various phony experiments; for instance, one study at Yale used a "study for memory" as its excuse. It is common in psychological experiments to mislead the participant as to the nature of the experiment, because when participants figure out what the experiment is testing for, they will sometimes provide that outcome of their own free will—for which they deserve a pat on the back, but which can skew the experiment's results. Consequently, the experiment is described as studying a very different thing than it actually is. The Yale experiment was advertised as taking one hour, for which those responding would be paid $4.50. Participants were men between the ages of 20 and 50, excluding college and high school students; later recreations of the experiment tested demographics of all ages, races, occupations, and genders.

Setup

In the waiting room, the participant meets the experimenter (decked out with clipboard and white lab coat) and someone who *claims* to be a fellow participant but is actually another experimenter. In psychological parlance, this person is called a "confederate." The experimenter explains to participant and confederate that the experiment will test the effectiveness of punishment on learning behavior. The participant will be the "teacher": he will pose various questions to the confederate (hereby called the "learner"). This testing will be facilitated by a communications device, which the Teacher and Learner are then shown.

The device, on the Teacher's side, consists of a large computerized control panel. It has a row of buttons, most with a numerical value associated with them. However, near the end of the row is a button labeled, "Do not go beyond this point" — though the presence of further buttons suggests that one *can* go beyond this point. The control panel also has a microphone and a speaker. The Learner's apparatus, on the other side of a wall from the Teacher's side, consists solely of a speaker, a microphone, and a chair... A chair which can and will deliver an electric shock, in voltage equal to the numbers on the Teacher's control panel. This shocking ability is sometimes demonstrated to both Teacher and Learner.

> Stark authority was pitted against the subjects' [participants'] strongest moral imperatives against hurting others, and, with the subjects' [participants'] ears ringing with the screams of the victims, authority won more often than not.

Rules

The experimenter straps the Learner into the chair and then takes the Teacher to the control panel. If the Learner answers a question incorrectly, he will receive an electric shock as punishment, with each incorrect answer resulting in a shock of increased magnitude: hence the row of buttons with its ever-growing voltage labels. Also, the experimenter tells the Teacher, the experiment must not be disrupted. No matter what happens, the Teacher and Learner must continue. The experimenter will stay in the room with the Teacher to help facilitate this. The Teacher turns on his microphone, and the questions and answers begin.

Events as seen by the participant

The Learner gets questions wrong, and the Teacher delivers the appropriate shocks. As the voltage builds up, however, the

Learner begins to protest. He yells out in pain every time the shocks are delivered. Between questions, he complains vociferously: the shocks are painful; he's starting to be hysterical; he wants the experiment to end right now. Even worse, he has a heart condition: too much voltage might kill him.

Explanation

In reality, there are no shocks being given to the confederate; he is merely acting. He might have been replaced by the control panel itself, if technology allowed it: each button would trigger an appropriate sound bite. Milgram did not need an injured confederate, only the illusion of it. The experiment up until now seems simple: if the Learner is begging to be released, why not release him? The answer lies with the experimenter in the white lab coat, a symbol of faceless scientific authority; the experimenter, present in the room with the Teacher, would refuse to let the Teacher (the participant) end the experiment prematurely. The test Milgram was running was not a "test for memory"; instead, he was attempting to answer a question: "How many people will continue up to and past the button that says *Do not go beyond this point*... if that guy in the white lab coat is constantly hovering over his shoulder, urging him to go on, refusing to let him stop?"

The end

At "Do Not Go Beyond This Point" (generally taking the place of the 300-volt button), the Learner gave a horrible scream; thereafter he would not answer any questions (which the experimenter would insist on interpreting as incorrect answers, necessitating the delivery of further shocks). His silence, combined with the knowledge of his heart condition and the blatant "Do Not Go Beyond This Point" label, led to an obvious conclusion. Once the participant had run out of buttons, the experiment ended.

Results

Before the experiment was conducted Milgram polled fellow psychologists as to what the results would be. They unanimously believed that only a few sadists would be prepared to give the maximum voltage.

In Milgram's first set of experiments, 65 percent of experimental participants administered the experiment's final 450-volt shock, though many were quite uncomfortable in doing so. No participant stopped before the 300-volt level. The experiment has been repeated by other psychologists around the world and with different participant demographics, but always with similar results. Variations have been performed to test for variables in the experimental setup. For example, participants are much more likely to be obedient when the experimenter is physically present, as opposed to when the instructions are given over a telephone.

Thomas Blass of the University of Maryland writes in *Psychology Today* (March/April 2002) that he has collected results from repeats of the experiment done at various times since, in the U.S. and elsewhere, and found that the percentage of participants who are prepared to inflict fatal voltages remains remarkably constant, between 61% and 66%, regardless of time or location (Blass, 2002). The full results were published in the *Journal of Applied Social Psychology* (Blass, 1999).

Reactions

The experiment raised questions about the ethics of scientific experimentation itself because of the extreme emotional stress suffered by the participants (even though it could be said that this stress was brought on by their own free actions). Most modern scientists would consider the experiment unethical today, though it resulted in valuable insights into human psychology.

In Milgram's defense, given the choice between "positive," "neutral," and "negative,"

84 percent of former participants contacted later rated their role in the experiments as a positive experience and 15 percent chose neutral. Many later wrote expressing thanks. Milgram repeatedly received offers of assistance and requests to join his staff from former participants.

Why so many former participants reported they were "glad" to have been involved despite the apparent levels of stress, one participant explained to Milgram in correspondence six years after he participated in the experiment, during the height of the Vietnam War:

> While I was a subject [participant] in 1964, though I believed that I was hurting someone, I was totally unaware of why I was doing so. Few people ever realize when they are acting according to their own beliefs and when they are meekly submitting to authority. ... To permit myself to be drafted with the understanding that I am submitting to authority's demand to do something very wrong would make me frightened of myself. ... I am fully prepared to go to jail if I am not granted Conscientious Objector status. Indeed, it is the only course I could take to be faithful to what I believe. My only hope is that members of my board act equally according to their conscience...

Milgram summed up in the article "The Perils of Obedience" (Milgram 1974), writing:

> The legal and philosophic aspects of obedience are of enormous import, but they say very little about how most people behave in concrete situations. I set up a simple experiment at Yale University to test how much pain an ordinary citizen would inflict on another person simply because he was ordered to by an experimental scientist. Stark authority was pitted against the

subjects' [participants'] strongest moral imperatives against hurting others, and, with the subjects' [participants'] ears ringing with the screams of the victims, authority won more often than not. The extreme willingness of adults to go to almost any lengths on the command of an authority constitutes the chief finding of the study and the fact most urgently demanding explanation.

The experiments began in July 1961, a year after the trial of Adolf Eichmann in Jerusalem. Milgram devised the experiment to answer the question "Could it be that Eichmann, and his million accomplices in the Holocaust were just following orders? Could we call them all accomplices?" (Milgram, 1974)

Milgram created a documentary film showing the experiment and its results, titled "Obedience."

Variations

Milgram describes 19 variations of the experiment that he conducted in *Obedience to Authority: An Experimental View*. In general, he found that when the immediacy of the victim was increased, compliance decreased, and when immediacy of the authority increased, compliance increased (Experiments 1-4). For instance, in one variation where participants received instructions from the experimenter only by telephone (Experiment 2), compliance greatly decreased; interestingly, a number of participants deceived the experimenter by *pretending* to continue the experiment. In the variation where immediacy of the "learner" was closest, participants had to physically hold the learner's arm onto a shock plate, which decreased compliance (Experiment 4). In this latter condition 30 percent still completed the experiment.

In Experiment 8, women were used as participants (all of Milgram's other experiments used only men). Obedience did not differ significantly, though they indicated experiencing higher levels of stress.

In one version (Experiment 10), Milgram rented a modest office in Bridgeport, Connecticut, purporting to be run by a commercial entity called "Research Associates of Bridgeport" with no apparent connection to Yale, in order to eliminate the prestige of the university as a possible factor influencing participants' behavior. The results of this experiment did not significantly differ from those conducted at the Yale campus.

Milgram also combined the power of authority with that of conformity. In these experiments, the participant was joined by confederates posing as additional "teachers." The behavior of the participants' apparent peers strongly affected results. When two additional teachers refused to comply (Experiment 17), only four participants of 40 continued the experiment. In another version, (Experiment 18) the participant performed a subsidiary task with another "teacher" who complied fully. In this variation only three of 40 defied the experimenter. This variation is the reference of singer Peter Gabriel's song, "Milgram's 37."

Spirit of the Redwoods:
An Interview with Julia Butterfly Hill
by Sara Marand

Julia "Butterfly" Hill occupied a redwood tree in Northern California for two years to prevent its being logged by the Pacific Lumber Company. She descended from the tree on Dec. 18, 1999, after the company agreed not to destroy the tree and the trees in the nearby area. The following article was written while Hill was still aloft. It begins with a quotation from Hill:

"For a year now, I have been living 180 feet up in this amazing ancient redwood tree, Luna. As I sit here looking out over the Eel River valley, at a view that I have watched change over the past year, I listen to a Columbia helicopter in the distance pull logs from once-forested slopes— slopes that Pacific Lumber has now turned into a legacy of clear-cuts, poisons, and mudslides. 1 have watched as the mudslides caused by Pacific Lumber and Maxxam's irresponsible logging continue to erode with the winter rains, sending more debris down the hill into the town of Stafford. 1 have watched as the creek beneath me, brown with silt, pours into the Eel River, and I know that clear-cuts line the creek for miles on the steep slopes above.

"I think about majestic trees hundreds or thousands of years old being cut down to become siding and decks. I think about the incredibly committed activists who have been tortured with pepper-spray by the police for merely sitting down in protest, and about David "Gypsy" Chain, who was killed by a tree purposely cut in his direction, while protesting an illegal timber harvest operation. I think about our government compromising away the health and quality of the environment and of our very lives in order to appease a criminal corporation. And I have to wonder why people still ask, "Why are you still up there?" Even now, some don't understand.

"Along with many others, I am committed to a world that lives with love and respect for all life, I am committed to a world where all old-growth forests are permanently protected, where trees on steep, unstable slopes are spared from the saw, where clear-cutting is replaced with true sustainable forestry, and where pesticide poisoning of the land, water, and people no longer exists.

"When I climbed Luna, I gave my word to her, the forests, and all people that I would not allow my feet to touch the ground until I felt I had done everything I possibly could to protect her and the forests. I still feel that there is more that I can accomplish from this perch. When my feet do eventually touch the ground again someday, this action for me will not end. The rest of my life is dedicated to living in service and love for all life."

On December 10, 1997, a twenty-four-year-old forest activist—Julia "Butterfly" Hill—scrambled up Luna, a thousand-year-old redwood tree located in the Headwaters Forest in northern California, and she has not yet come down. In the great American tradition of civil disobedience, Butterfly has been conducting a courageous vigil on behalf of Luna and the Headwaters Forest.

Located on California's north coast near the town of Eureka, the Headwaters Forest complex and surrounding lands contain the last remaining unprotected groves of ancient redwood trees on Earth. Under a controversial Habitat Conservation Plan, Charles Hurwitz's

Houston-based Maxxam Corporation, absentee owner of Pacific Lumber Company and of Headwaters, recently proposed to harvest almost half of its remaining ancient trees, while continuing to log on unstable slopes such as the one where Luna stands.

Luna was named by Earth First! activists who discovered the tree on a full moon night and who began the Luna tree-sit on October 5, 1997. Located near the clear-cut that caused a massive mudslide, destroying seven homes in the town of Stafford on New Year's Day, 1997, Luna has become a symbol of the struggle to save the Headwaters Forest from the greed of Maxxam Corporation.

For over fifteen months, Butterfly has lived in a tarped platform nestled in Luna's branches, one hundred and eighty feet above the forest floor. She has endured El Niño storms, helicopter harassment, a ten-day siege by company security men, and the sorrow brought about by witnessing the destruction of the forest. Yet she perseveres.

Although Butterfly is relatively new to the Headwaters Forest campaign, she has become one of America's most inspiring spokespersons for the protection of our forests and watersheds. Carrying on in the nonviolent tradition of Judi Bari and other Earth First! activists working to save northern California's redwood forests, Butterfly combines a strong understanding of the political aspects of the forest controversy with a deep spiritual connection to the forest and tree she calls home. Moreover, due to her record-shattering perseverance, Butterfly has been interviewed by reporters working for the *New York Times*, *ABC News*, *NBC News*, and the *London Times*.

The following interview with Butterfly was conducted by cellular telephone in early fall, 1998.

Sara Marand: *It's an honor to speak with you, Julia. To be doing this work, you must have a lot of inspiration. Can you share its source?*

Julia Butterfly: From where I sit, I can see

I have become one with nature in a way that I would never have thought imaginable….

everything that we are fighting for and everything that we are fighting against, in one view. That's extremely inspirational, because I see both sides. As you hike up the hill, you see the mudslides and the clear-cuts. Then, when you get to the top of the hill, you also see some forest lands that haven't been destroyed. You see the ocean off to one side. You see beautiful old trees, and baby trees trying to grow tall.

I've learned to just absorb all this into myself, instead of allowing it to absorb me. I've allowed it to fan the ember of commitment inside me into a flame. I don't give power to the negative, because I don't want that. I absorb that negative power into myself and channel it into something positive.

By not allowing my feet to touch the ground once during all this time, I've separated myself from the world down there. It has allowed me to tap, through the roots of this tree, into the heart of Mother Earth and to feel her pulsating power. I have become one with nature in a way that I would never have thought imaginable….

I feel that each of us is intricately enlaced with Mother Earth. We are all part of the body of life. Our human bodies, the planet, the trees, the plants, the animals—everything is part of this body of life, and all of it is part of the same spiritual power.

When we lose touch with that circle of power, we break the circle of magic and we break our ability to be part of that magic. When people numb themselves to the fact that we are a part of that body of life, that's when the destruction of our environment starts. Some people have set themselves higher than the Earth. They've set themselves higher than animals. They've set themselves higher than other people. In order to do that, they have to desensitize themselves to the purpose and the power of the circle that we are. That's what allows people to destroy.

I also feel that is why we have to focus on loving the Earth and each other—that's got to become our number one priority. We cannot destroy the Earth if we love her. We cannot destroy each other if we love each other. When we realize that we are all part of this body of life—and that we can't hurt that body in any way without hurting the whole, and we can't help it without helping the whole—that's when really magical things start to happen.

Marand: *What do you think Luna would like to say to the people who read this interview?*

Butterfly: "I love you." That's something that I have to share with all people—even with the loggers below. Some of the nearby communities have depended upon logging, and some people are angry about Earth First!ers. I want them to under-stand that I'm not trying to steal their legacy; I'm trying to save a legacy for their children, and I really do care about them.

Corporations prey upon the differences between environmentalist and logger to weaken us. They know that if they separate us, our power is diluted and they have ever better control.

I view the differences in our lives as diversity, and I recognize that our diversity is as important and incredibly beautiful as diversity in nature. I know we can use that diversity to combat all the different angles that these corporations and our government are using to destroy and manipulate us. I'm excited about bridging the gaps between us, because the way we are going to win is to get everyone, from all walks of life, to join together.

When I was placed under siege last year, dozens of security men were yelling horrible things at me. They were blowing air horns and bugles in the night to keep me awake. They were threatening that if I didn't come down right away, they were going to beat the living hell out of me when I did come down. They were saying all these crazy, mean, horrible things. I sang a song to them every time they got mean and horrible, and the song says:

Love in any language, straight from the heart, pull the thought together, never apart, and once we long to speak it, all the

world will hear that love in any language is fluently spoken here. Though the rhetoric of government may keep us worlds apart, there is no misinterpreting the language of the heart.

Marand: *You've watched some of the logging done around Luna. Can you tell us about it?*

Butterfly: It was really sad to see some of the biggest trees fall. I saw some truly incredible trees, both redwoods and Douglas firs, smashed into the ground. Under Maxxam's new rules, the loggers were under incredible pressure to triple the rate of cut, so they were cutting the biggest trees, which bring in the most money. They were also cutting in winds that were too extreme to be cutting in. One of the trees they felled actually hit Luna. At the time, I was out on a limb trying to videotape their cutting, and the impact almost knocked me out of the tree.

The wind was so high that they lost control of quite a few trees, and the trees shattered when they hit the ground. That was really difficult to watch, because when the trees shatter, they no longer have any value to the company. It was really sad seeing these ancient trees being cut for nothing.

Marand: *What's the most difficult thing for you to deal with living up there?*

Butterfly: Well, there's no doubt that the most difficult thing is watching the trees hit the ground and feeling absolutely powerless to stop it. That's really difficult. Nothing in my life has ever compared to that sadness; it's almost overwhelming.

At first, the cold, the lack of running water, and the physical inconveniences were difficult. Then, one night, when I thought I was going to die in the worst storm, Luna spoke to me.

Even though I'd said my goodbyes to my best friends, thrown out everything I owned, and given up the life I had been living, I hadn't given up life. I hadn't given up my being. I was still trying to hold on to those.

That night, I gave it all up. I talked to Luna, and I talked to the powers of the universe. I said, "Obviously, this is a test. This is testing how committed I am to what I believe in." I said, "Okay, I give myself completely; you can have all of me. I'm really just a part of the universe, anyway. If I die, all I'm doing is just giving myself to that from which I came." After that, my desire for things like running water just faded into the background. I don't think about those things anymore.

Marand: *What's an average day up there like?*

Butterfly: *(Laughs.)* Everyone asks that question. The truth is there isn't one. Every time I think I've been through it all or I've got it all figured out, something else comes my way to prove me totally wrong.

The two things I do every single day are to have tea and to pray. When I pray, I ask for four things—power, peace, truth, and love. I ask for the power of the universe to flow through me so that I can touch other people and empower them. I want to empower them in the light of truth, love, and peace, because that's where our healing is, that's where our hope is.

Marand: *Is there anything else you'd like to say, Julia?*

Butterfly: It's important that people understand that what's happening here with the Headwaters Forest is very critical. Less than three percent of our old-growth forest is left. People have to recognize that this is a life-or-death situation.

We can't expect people in other countries to defend the environment if we can't defend ours. When people stand up for the environment in third world countries, it becomes a life-or-death situation for them. They know that standing up for something means that they might get shot by their own government. Getting shot for protesting still isn't a common threat in this country. The biggest threat in our country is usually being jailed as a political prisoner. It's tragic when someone like Leonard Peltier is framed and held prisoner for decades, but it's unusual. Yet only a very small percentage of people in this country are willing to stand up for what they believe in.

Since being up here, I've realized that our actions are like ripples in the ocean. Every action, every word, every thought causes ripples. Those ripples join with the ripples of others and eventually create a tidal wave that changes things. We have to make sure that every ripple we create is a positive one, so that when our tidal wave finally happens, it will be a positive, powerful one. We must take care now if we want to change our Earth and our future in a positive and powerful way.

SESSION 8: READING 3

Stages of Community-Making
by Scott Peck

Communities, like individuals, are unique. Still, we all share the human condition. So it is that groups assembled deliberately to form themselves into community routinely go through certain stages in the process. These stages, in order, are:

- Pseudocommunity
- Chaos
- Emptiness
- Community

Not every group that becomes a community follows this paradigm exactly. Communities that temporarily form in response to crisis, for instance, may skip over one or more stages for the time being. I do not insist that community development occur by formula. But in the process of community-making by design, this is the natural, usual order of things.

Pseudocommunity

The first response of a group in seeking to form a community is most often to try to fake it. The members attempt to be an instant community by being extremely pleasant with one another and avoiding all disagreement. This attempt — this pretense of community — is what I term "pseudocommunity." It never works.

The essential dynamic of pseudocommunity is conflict avoidance. The absence of conflict in a group is not by itself diagnostic. Genuine communities may experience lovely and sometimes lengthy periods free from conflict. But that is because they have learned how to deal with conflict rather than avoid it. Pseudocommunity is conflict-avoiding; true community is conflict-resolving.

What is diagnostic of pseudocommunity is the minimization, the lack of acknowledgement, or the ignoring of individual differences. Another characteristic is that members will let one another get away with blanket statements, (they) will nod in agreement, as if the speaker has uttered some universal truth. Indeed, the pressure to skirt any kind of disagreement may be so great that even the very experienced communicators in the group — who know perfectly well that speaking in generalities is destructive to genuine communications — may be inhibited from challenging what they know is wrong.

Once individual differences are not only allowed but encouraged to surface in some way, the group almost immediately moves to the second stage of community development: chaos.

Chaos

The chaos always centers around well-intentioned but misguided attempts to heal and convert…. In the stage of chaos individual differences are, unlike those in pseudocommunity, right out in the open. Only now, instead of trying to hide or ignore them, the group is attempting to obliterate them. Underlying the attempt to heal and convert is not so much the motive of love as the motive to make everyone normal — the motive to win, as the members fight over whose norm might prevail.

The stage of chaos is a time of fighting and struggle. But that is not its essence. Frequently, fully developed communities will be required to fight and struggle. Only they have learned to do so effectively. The struggle during chaos … is uncreative, unconstructive, …boring. It has no grace or rhythm. The struggle is going nowhere, accomplishing nothing. It is no fun.

The proper resolution of chaos is not easy. Because it is both unproductive and unpleasant, it may seem that the group has degenerated from pseudocommunity into chaos. But chaos is not necessarily the worst place for a group to be. Fighting is far better than pretending you are not divided. It's painful, but it's a beginning. You are aware that you need to move beyond your warring factions, and that's infinitely more hopeful than if you felt you didn't need to move at all.

Emptiness

There are only two ways out of chaos….one is into organization — but organization is never community. The only other way is into and through emptiness.

The most common (and interrelated) barriers to communication that people need to empty themselves of before they can enter genuine community are:

Expectations and Preconceptions. Community-building is an adventure, a going into the unknown. People are routinely terrified of the emptiness of the unknown….Until such a time as we can empty ourselves of expectation and stop trying to fit others and our relationship with them into a preconceived mold we cannot really listen, hear, or experience.

Prejudices. More often unconscious than conscious, prejudice comes in two forms. One is judgments we make about people without any experience of them whatsoever. More common are the judgments we make about people on the basis of very brief, limited experience. One reason to distrust instant community is that community building requires time — the time to have sufficient experience to become conscious of our prejudices and then to empty ourselves of them.

Ideology, Theology, and Solutions. Obviously we cannot move very far toward community with our fellow human beings when we are thinking and feeling (in terms of) ideological and theological rigidities that …assume the status of "the one and only right way."

The Need to Heal, Convert, Fix, or Solve. Isn't it the loving thing to do to relieve your neighbor of her suffering or help him to see the light? Actually, however, almost all attempts to convert and heal are not only naive and ineffective but quite self-centered and self-serving. It hurts me when my friend is in pain. My most basic motive when I strive to heal is to feel good myself… there may be an opposite way: the appreciation and celebration of interpersonal differences.

The Need to Control. The need for control — to ensure the desired outcome — is at least partially rooted in the fear of failure. For me to empty myself of my over-controlling tendencies I must continually empty myself of this fear. I must be willing to fail.

The stage of emptiness in community development is a time of sacrifice. Such sacrifice hurts because it is a kind of death, the kind that is necessary for rebirth…This is an extraordinary testament to the human spirit. What it means is that, given the right circumstances and knowledge of the rules, on a certain but very real level we human beings are able to die for each other.

> *When I am with a group of human beings committed to hanging in there through both the agony and the joy of community, I have a dim sense that I am participating in a phenomenon for which there is only one word. I almost hesitate to use it. The word is "glory."*

Community

When its death has been completed, open and empty, the group enters community. In this final stage a soft quietness descends. It is a kind of peace. The room is bathed in peace. Then, quietly, a member begins to talk about herself. She is being vulnerable. She is speaking of the deepest part of herself. The group hangs on each word. No one realized she was capable of such eloquence.

When she is finished there is a hush. (Afterward:) Out of the silence another member begins to talk…deeply, very personally…

Then the next member speaks. And as it goes on, there will be a great deal of sadness and grief expressed; but there will also be much laughter and joy. And then something almost more singular happens. An extraordinary amount of healing and converting begins to occur — now that no one is trying to convert or heal. And community has been born.

It is like falling in love. When they enter community, people in a very real sense do fall in love with one another *en masse*.…

Because I have spoken so glowingly of its virtues, some might conclude that life in community is easier or more comfortable than ordinary existence. It is not. But it is certainly more lively, more intense. The agony is actually greater, but so is the joy.… life in community may touch upon something perhaps even deeper than joy.… When I am with a group of human beings committed to hanging in there through both the agony and the joy of community, I have a dim sense that I am participating in a phenomenon for which there is only one word. I almost hesitate to use it. The word is "glory."

HOMEWORK

REFLECTIONS ON THE READINGS

Session 8:
Facing the Possibilities and Consequences

SESSION 8: **Facing the Possibilities and Consequences**

OBJECTIVES
- To explore the consequences of nonviolent action that challenges "how things are"
- To reflect on the role of authority, conformity, and obedience in our lives and in society
- To experience the power of a community taking nonviolent action together

AGENDA
- Welcome [1 min.]
- Opening [5 min.]
- Reflecting on Homework [10 min.]
- Nonviolent Community Exercise [60 min.]
- Break [10 min.]
- Constructing Peace [25 min.]
- Facing the Consequences of Nonviolent Action [20 min.]
- Conclusion [10 min.]
    Journaling
    Nonviolent Action
    Next Session's Reading
    Adding to the Wall of Learning and Growing
    Identifying a Nonviolence Principle
    Closing

READINGS
- Reading #1: Wikipedia, "The Milgram Experiment"
- Reading #2: Sara Marand, "The Spirit of the Redwoods: An Interview with Julia Butterfly Hill"
- Reading #3: Scott Peck, "Stages of Community"

NOTES FOR THE FACILITATOR

SESSION PREPARATION: BEFORE

- Review the entire session in depth. Role-play or practice setting up and facilitating exercises beforehand. Wherever possible, put material into your own words. Feel free to make notes for this purpose on 3x5 cards or in the book next to the written instructions.
- Materials needed: masking tape; (optional) props for Nonviolent Community exercise.
- Preparation for the "Nonviolent Community" exercise: prepare for playing the role of a representative of a large institution that has decided to acquire and use for its own purposes the area where the Nonviolent Community is located. Do not use any names of actual companies. Bring a prop or two that will set you apart in that role from your facilitator role (a hat, or a jacket, a sign around your neck, etc.). Think out what your demands will be on the community and how they might be benefiting from your intrusion into their community. Be sure to make your demands significantly large so as to produce some sort of reaction in the group: for example, we will need 40% of the community to build the power plant on. One possible benefit is always jobs. Make sure to stress at the end or sometime during the exercise that not all institutions act in the way that you were role-playing.

PREPARATION: ON THE DAY OF THE SESSION

- Lay out a large area of paper or papers on the floor so that there are no gaps, but so that the border of the community is slightly irregular, as the plots of land in a community may be. (You can tape several pieces of easel paper together.)
- Play close attention to time in the session. You don't need to call on everyone with a hand raised when doing debriefs.

SESSION 8: **Facing the Possibilities and Consequences**

WELCOME — 1 MIN.

Convey in your own words:

Welcome back for our eighth session of the *Engage: Exploring Nonviolent Living* Study Program. In the last session we explored structural violence and how to work to overcome it. In this session, we will explore how nonviolent action for justice and the well-being of all can sometimes bring us into conflict with what we can call the set of "social arrangements," or "how things are." We will reflect on how nonviolence involves "facing the consequences" of activities carried out for justice. And we will practice how we can do this as part of a community, and not simply as an individual.

OPENING — 5 MIN.

Convey in your own words:

But first, I would like to open with a reflection on obedience. Obedience is typically understood as "following orders." Its original meaning, however, is "deep listening." Our exploration of active nonviolence can be deepened by reclaiming this original meaning of obedience, as the following quotation from Leonard Desroches stresses:

The present historical question regarding another potential Hitler and nonviolent resistance is not, "Could nonviolence overthrow another Nazi army or party?" The more valid question is, "Have we learned to live nonviolence to the extent that the uncontested growth of any such army and political party is now impossible?" Have we learned the crucial difference between obedience and following orders?

Obedience, the deepest possible listening to the human family's cries of anger and pain, is at the heart of our capacity to hear the clues of how to prevent great evil. In that sense, the quality of obedience lived in our families and intentional communities informs how we live on the more global level.

As we continue our exploration of active nonviolence, I invite all of us to listen deeply to the cries for justice and peace — and the exclamations of hope and joy — that are all around us.

REFLECTING ON HOMEWORK — 10 MIN.

I again invite you to get together with your Nonviolence Partner to take a few minutes to reflect on your experiences or insights since the last session, as well as to reflect on the readings, journaling, or nonviolent action.

CREATING NONVIOLENT COMMUNITY EXERCISE — 60 MIN.

Ask the following:

What would be needed to create an ideal, nonviolent town or community?

2000-YEAR-OLD EXAMPLE OF NONVIOLENT RESISTANCE
by Mulford Q. Sibley

Caligula ruled the Roman Empire from 37 to 41 C.E., a short but memorable reign of caprice and terror. At one point, he ordered a statue of himself built in the Temple of Jerusalem, knowing full well that the Jewish people would not allow any man's statue to be placed in the temple. Caligula appointed Petronius a governor of Syria and sent him to the eastern Mediterranean with explicit orders to erect the statue, even if it meant bloodshed.

On the way, Petronius was met by thousands of Jews who offered themselves as sacrifices rather than allow the idolatry proposed by Caligula. Petronius was prepared to do battle, but the Jews refused to fight, and lay down at Petronius's encampment, ready to die rather than see the statue built. For forty days Petronius was faced with this defiant but nonviolent mass, and finally he announced that he would petition Caligula on their behalf and offer his one life instead of thousands of their lives. Before Caligula received the petition, he decided to abandon the statue as a favor to his ally and friend Agrippa, King of Palestine.

In a story of coincidences, Caligula sent a letter to Petronius advising him to give up on the statue. Then, the petition from Petronius arrived. Angered that Petronius would not have carried out his order, Caligula ordered Petronius to go right ahead and kill himself. Luckily for Petronius, news of Caligula's assassination arrived before the death warrant, and the statue project was given up.

When people give examples, give them markers and encourage them to represent their ideas on the paper at their feet. Tell them:

The paper at your feet, for this exercise, is your community. I'd like to give you 10 minutes to draw and complete what your Nonviolent Community would look like. It is everyone's responsibility to help create it.

Give updates on the time. After 10 minutes say the following:

Now look around your community to make sure you have incorporated all the elements of a nonviolent community that you'd like to see. Take another minute to add something if you are missing anything.

While the participants are still drawing, transition into your role as a representative of a large institution that has decided to acquire and use for its own purposes the area where the Nonviolent Community is located. Assume an air of confidence and superiority, and don a prop or two to help distinguish your character from the facilitator you were just moments ago. Then say something like the following:

My name is …… and I represent ….. We are interested in entering into an agreement with the community. Our company wants …… and the benefits your community will see from this partnership are …… We will return in a week for further discussions (5 minutes of game time).

Leave the room for 5 minutes. Return and begin dialoguing with the community. Regardless of how the community responds, gradually increase your demands. Circle the drawn community as you walk pompously around the room until you finally step on a corner of the community that they've created. If this doesn't provoke a reaction, start drawing your company onto (and over) part of the community they've drawn.

Continue escalating your demands until the group has organized sufficiently against you so that they have had an experience of a nonviolent resistance action. It is ideal if the community mobilizes to protect itself, but if the group is unable to mobilize itself, end the game.

Debrief

Debrief this exercise with each of the following questions, spending approximately 3-4 minutes per question. Write the responses down on easel paper:

- What were your feelings and noticings (i.e., observations without judgments)?
- How did you work together as a community in the creating and protecting of the community?
- How could you have responded better as a community?
- What tools, skills, etc. do you need to transform your current community, and to respond more effectively when it is under attack?
- How can you apply what you learned to your life?

Close this exercise and transition to the break by putting the following point in your own words:

This exercise gives both an opportunity for participants to transform their current community into a more nonviolent village or town, and to resist violence perpetrated against it.

This exercise also stresses the importance of nonviolent community. In the *Engage Study Program*, we encourage you to explore being part of a nonviolence group, organization, or community. We especially encourage you to form or join a small support, reflection, and action group. Variously called small groups, affinity groups, or base communities, these Nonviolence Circles create an environment to support our work, to explore the depths of nonviolence, to take action, and to reflect on the meaning of the process of personal and social transformation.

BREAK — 10 MIN.

BUILDING THE NONVIOLENT COMMUNITY: CONSTRUCTIVE PROGRAM

For Gandhi, nonviolence is a coin with two sides: Constructive Program and Nonviolent Resistance. Sometimes people think of nonviolence only as a form of resistance: opposition to violence, injustice, and oppression. While it is true that resistance is vitally important, it is only part of the story. Constructive Program is equally, if not more, important.

Constructive Program is the process of envisioning and concretely building a society that reflects the values and principles of justice and the well-being of all.

Gandhi created 17 Constructive Programs during his decades-long struggle for Indian independence from British rule. His Constructive Program campaigns focused on education, gender, village self-sufficiency, Hindu/Muslim unity, the abolition of untouchability, and many other social challenges.

A prime example of Constructive Program was the spinning wheel. The British had established a monopoly on the production of clothing. Indians shipped raw material, cotton called *khadi*, to British textile mills that made finely tailored cloth and then shipped it back to India for sale at high prices. Gandhi orchestrated both a Resistance campaign, boycotting British clothing, and a Constructive campaign, building up the community by empowering the Indians to make their own clothing. Countless Indians heeded Gandhi's call to spin khadi at least 30 minutes a day. Some of the positive effects of the Constructive spinning program included:

- It stimulated a concrete and practical production of clothing
- It was an effective, long-term solution: one didn't need to buy British-made clothes
- It was creative; it increased self-esteem and self-reliance
- It was inclusive — everyone could do it regardless of class, caste, religion, gender, etc.
- It encouraged communal unity and solidarity between people, especially those doing it together in big spinning halls
- It was a spiritual practice. Repetitious spinning became for some a kind of "body prayer" that helped center and focus its "practitioners."

Near the end of his life, Gandhi argued that nonviolence work should be 90% Constructive Program and 10% Resistance.

CONSTRUCTING PEACE — 25 MIN.

Convey the following in your own words:

In the Nonviolent Community exercise, we explored some of the ways that we might transform the negative aspects of our community into positive ones. Please break into groups of two or three, read the nearby box entitled "Building the Nonviolent Community: Constructive Program," and discuss the following questions:

- What kinds of Constructive Programs are present in your communities?
- What are some of the positive effects of those programs?

Allow about 10 minutes for the small groups, then call them back to the large group and ask for learnings or insights.

FACING THE CONSEQUENCES OF NONVIOLENT DIRECT ACTION — 20 MIN.

Read aloud the following or convey it in your own words:

Often when one begins to work for the betterment of society, one is met with resistance, and sometimes suffering.

One of the worst evils on earth is involuntary suffering: suffering that is viciously imposed and forced on people. This involuntary suffering can be physical, psychological, or economic.

At the same time, one of the most powerful things on earth is a voluntary willingness to face suffering for justice and for the well-being of all.

It is often the deep opposition to involuntary suffering that leads one to voluntarily face the consequences of opposing unjust and imposed suffering.

Dr. King's fourth principle of nonviolence states: *Nonviolence holds that voluntary suffering can educate and transform.* Let's reflect on that using the following questions:

> *"Many people fear nothing more terribly than to take a position which stands out sharply and clearly from the prevailing opinion."*
> — REV. MARTIN LUTHER KING, JR.

- Why is there the possibility of suffering if one engages in nonviolent action? What can be the consequences of this sort of action, and why?
- In "The Milgram Experiment," one of this session's readings, what were the pressures or factors that hindered the participants from stopping the shocking of the "learners"?

DR. MARTIN LUTHER KING, JR.'S PRINCIPLES OF NONVIOLENCE

1) **Nonviolence is a way of life for courageous people.**
   - It is active nonviolent resistance to evil.
   - It is assertive spiritually, mentally, and emotionally.
   - It is always persuading the opponent of the justice of your cause.

2) **Nonviolence seeks to win friendship and understanding.**
   - The end result of nonviolence is redemption and reconciliation.
   - The purpose of nonviolence is the creation of the Beloved Community.

3) **Nonviolence seeks to defeat injustice, not people.**
   - Nonviolence holds that evildoers are also victims.

4) **Nonviolence holds that voluntary suffering can educate and transform.**
   - Nonviolence willingly accepts the consequences of its acts.
   - Nonviolence accepts suffering without retaliation.
   - Nonviolence accepts violence if necessary, but will never inflict it.
   - Unearned suffering is redemptive and has tremendous educational and transforming possibilities.
   - Suffering can have the power to convert the enemy when reason fails.

5) **Nonviolence chooses love instead of hate.**
   - Nonviolence resists violence of the spirit as well as of the body.
   - Nonviolent love gives willingly, knowing that the return might be hostility.
   - Nonviolent love is active, not passive.
   - Nonviolent love does not sink to the level of the hater.
   - Love for the enemy is how we demonstrate love for ourselves.
   - Love restores community and resists injustice.
   - Nonviolence recognizes the fact that all life is interrelated.

6) **Nonviolence believes that the universe is on the side of justice.**
   - The nonviolent resister has deep faith that justice will eventually win.

- What are some examples of people who have "faced the consequences," who were willing to sacrifice some of their freedom or even give their lives for justice and the well-being of all?

> *"There is no peace because the making of peace is at least as costly as the making of war—at least as exigent, at least as disruptive, at least as liable to bring disgrace and prison and death in its wake."*
> — DANIEL BERRIGAN

CONCLUSION — 10 MIN.

⊙ Nonviolence Journal

Suggested Topics or Questions:

1) After reading the box on King's Nonviolent Principles, reflect on the principles in light of the Nonviolent Community exercise and the stories we have presented thus far in the study program.

2) Are you involved in any activities that are helping to build up your community (any Constructive Program)? If not, reflect on a way you would like to be involved.

3) Consider one time in your life when you have let go of self-interest for the benefit of another.

> *"Non-cooperation with evil is as much a duty as cooperation with good."*
> —MOHANDAS GANDHI

⊙ Nonviolent Action

1) Investigate ways in which your community is coming under attack and who is working to resist this (or to construct an alternative to it).

2) Give up a little comfort (be it material, mental, or physical) and examine the ripples of that in your life.

⊙ Next Session's Reading

Please read the readings located at the end of this session.

⊙ Adding to the Wall of Learning and Growing

Please add your insights, learnings, or questions to the Wall.

⊙ Closing

Ask the group to form a circle holding hands. Invite the participants to share a word that reflects what they are feeling, an insight they had during the session, or something they are taking with them.

KEY ORGANIZATIONS

The Martin Luther King, Jr. Center, 449 Auburn Avenue, NE, Atlanta, GA 30312; (404) 526-8900; *information@thekingcenter.org; www.thekingcenter.org*. Established in 1968 by Mrs. Coretta Scott King, the King Center is the living memorial and institutional guardian of Dr. Martin Luther King, Jr.'s legacy. The King Center accomplishes this through programming, building a network of organizations, providing a clearinghouse for Dr. King's writings, and managing visitor services.

Michigan Peace Team (MPT), 1516 Jerome Street, Lansing, MI 48912; (517) 484-3178; *michpeaceteam@peacenet.org, www.michiganpeaceteam.org*. MPT empowers people to engage in active nonviolent peacemaking. It was started in 1993, in response to the growing need for civilian peacemakers both in the U.S. and abroad. MPT seeks a just world grounded in nonviolence and respect for the sacred interconnectedness of all life.

Nonviolence International (NI), 4545 42nd Street N.W., Washington, D.C.; (202) 393-3616, *nonviolence@igc.org, www.nonviolenceinternational.net*. NI assists individuals, organizations, and governments striving to utilize nonviolent methods to bring about changes reflecting the values of justice and human development on personal, social, economic, and political levels. NI is committed to educating the public about nonviolent action and to reducing the use of violence worldwide.

InterPlay. Body Wisdom, Inc. *www.interplay.org;* 2273 Telegraph Avenue, Oakland, CA 94612; 510-465-2797; *info@interplay.org*. InterPlay is easy, fun, and life-changing. It is based in a series of incremental "forms" that lead participants to movement and stories, silence and song, ease and amusement. In the process, we unlock the wisdom of our bodies and the wisdom in our communities. InterPlay offers seminars, keynote addresses, trainings, and consultations on many issues related to organizational life:

- Leadership development
- Tools for dealing quickly and easily with change
- Team building and collaboration
- Creativity and "thinking outside of the box"
- Flexible management
- Stress reduction
- A non-sectarian approach to spirit in the workplace

InterPlay has been applied around the world in corporations, non-profit organizations, healthcare settings, schools, colleges and universities, mental health organizations, and many other settings.

HOMEWORK

NONVIOLENCE JOURNAL

Suggested Topic:

1) After reading the box on King's Nonviolent Principles, reflect on the principles in light of the Nonviolent Community exercise and the stories we have presented thus far in the study program.
2) Are you involved in any activities that are helping to build up your community (any Constructive Program)? If not, reflect on a way you would like to be involved.
3) Consider one time in your life when you have let go of self-interest for the benefit of another.

HOMEWORK

NONVIOLENT ACTION

- Investigate ways in which your community is coming under attack and who is working to resist this (or to construct an alternative to it).
- Give up a little comfort (be it material, mental, or physical) and examine the ripples of this in your life.

The Birth of Sanctuary
by Christian Smith

Jim Corbett woke up on the morning of May 5, 1981, knowing that he had to do something about the arrested hitchhiker. He did not know, however, that what he was about to do would launch a social movement.

Corbett was a forty-six-year-old, semi-disabled Quaker who raised goats with his wife, Pat, on a ranch outside Tucson, Arizona. The night before, a fellow Quaker friend of Corbett's, Jim Dudley, had been stopped by the U.S. Border Patrol on his way back from a trip to Mexico, shortly after picking up a Salvadoran hitchhiker. Dudley was on his way to Corbett's house to return a van he had borrowed and to discuss the planned construction of a chapel in a Mexican village. The hitchhiker was arrested, Dudley was interrogated for half an hour and accused of smuggling an illegal alien before being released.

When Dudley finally arrived at Corbett's, he was visibly disturbed. The frightened hitchhiker, he told Jim and Pat, had begged Dudley the final moments before the abduction to lie about his Salvadoran identity. "Tell them I work for you and we are traveling together," he had pleaded. Dudley now wondered aloud whether he had made a mistake telling the truth. Couldn't he have tricked or eluded the Border Patrol somehow? Jim and Pat thought not. "Once you're stopped, there's not too much you can do."

But as they discussed the incident, their concern for the arrested hitchhiker grew. They remembered news stories reporting El Salvador's civil war and the assassination of El Salvador's Archbishop Oscar Romero and four North American churchwomen. They recalled that only ten months earlier twenty-seven middle-class Salvadorans had been discovered trying to cross the scorching desert seventy miles west of Tucson. The Salvadorans' paid smugglers—"coyotes"—had gotten lost and abandoned them, and they were forced to drink urine and cologne before the Border Patrol recovered them. Half of the twenty-seven had died of thirst and exposure. The remaining survivors were taken in by several Tucson churches. Frank Shutts, … also visiting Corbett that night, said that he had heard rumors of entire planeloads of deported Salvadorans being murdered at the San Salvador airport by death squads, as examples to others who might consider fleeing the country.

"There must be some way to intervene for these people," Corbett said. But none of them knew how. Helplessly, they shrugged their shoulders, noting that the night was getting late and Dudley had to catch a bus to Albuquerque. Frank Shutts drove him to the station. And the Corbetts went to bed. But Jim Corbett did not sleep well. He could not escape the thought of Dudley's arrested hitchhiker being sent home to a death-squad assassination.

In the morning Corbett resolved to follow up on the matter. He called the offices of the U.S. Immigration and Naturalization Service (INS) and the Border Patrol, who told him that they could not give out information on detainees. Corbett then remembered that his name was the same as that of a well-known former Tucson mayor. He called back the Border Patrol office and said in a commanding voice, "This is Jim Corbett here in Tucson, and I need the name of the Salvadoran you picked up late yesterday at the Peck Canyon roadblock. His name, and where he's being held." It worked. The officer looked up and gave him the information.

After a few more phone calls to a local immigration-rights organization, the Manzo Area Council, Corbett learned that the arrested hitchhiker could not be deported without a hearing if an INS G-28 form designating legal counsel was signed and filed. So, Corbett drove to the Santa Cruz jail, near Nogales, where Nelson, the hitchhiker, was being held. There Corbett met Nelson, who signed the G-28. Corbett also met two other arrested refugees who told him chilling personal stories of abduction and torture in El Salvador. He concluded that their lives would be in danger if they were deported, so he decided to file G-28s for them as well. The jailer said he had no more of the forms, so Corbett drove to the nearby Border Patrol office, where officers delayed him a half hour before giving him G-28s.

Back at the jail, Corbett was told he had to wait before he could see the two other prisoners again. Thirty minutes passed. Corbett grew impatient. He had to leave Nogales soon to get the G-28s filed at the Tucson INS office by five o'clock. He asked again to see the Salvadorans. "Who was it you were waiting for?" the jailer asked. "Oh, you wanted to see those guys? The Border Patrol took them twenty or thirty minutes ago. They're all gone. And there's no way to know where they went."

Corbett was stunned—he had been hoodwinked by agents of his own government. This was not a bureaucratic confusion, he fumed, but a deliberate effort to deprive refugees of their legal rights and deport them as swiftly as possible to what he considered a likely death. Jim Corbett, it turns out, was the wrong person for the Border Patrol to cross.…

The Corbetts borrowed $4,500 against the value of a trailer they owned and bailed four Salvadoran women and a baby out of jail. These refugees, who lived in a small apartment on the Corbetts' property, spent hours talking with Jim and Pat about the violence in El Salvador and the terrors of refugee life. Through them, the connection between "the refugee problem" and the U.S.-sponsored war in Central America became increasingly clear. Jim Corbett began to press the system harder to protect Salvadoran refugees from deportation. But the harder he pressed, the more disillusioned and frustrated he became with the INS and the Border Patrol.

On May 30, Corbett and a companion drove to Los Angeles to search in El Centro, a major INS detention center, for the refugees who twenty-five days earlier had been hastily transferred out of the Santa Cruz jail while he waited to see them. When a refugee-rights paralegal had recently traveled to El Centro to process G-28 forms, an INS official took the G-28s out of her hand, tore them up, and threw them in a trash can. Corbett was determined this time to find the refugees he was looking for, especially Nelson, Jim Dudley's arrested hitchhiker.

What he found instead—when a prisoner in the room who knew Nelson interrupted Corbett's conversation with the jail superintendent—was that Nelson had already been deported to El Salvador. Corbett couldn't believe his ears. Nelson's deportation was illegal, since Corbett had filed his G-28 on May 5! The superintendent, Mr. Aguirre, had told Corbett upon arrival that he had no record of Nelson. But when the outspoken prisoner insisted otherwise, Aguirre quickly ordered all the prisoners back to their cells and Corbett to leave immediately. Corbett, now angry, refused. Then Aguirre noticed that Corbett's companion had been recording the entire conversation with a tape recorder. Aguirre demanded he hand it over. Corbett replied the guards would have to take it by force, and that they wanted to leave now. Aguirre locked the room's doors and demanded the recorder. Corbett began to lecture Aguirre about refugees' rights. Aguirre stormed out of the room in a rage. After a few minutes, he

> The U.S. government, Corbett saw, was violating its own law and risking the lives of thousands of Central American refugees. It had to be fought.

returned and released them.

The experience was enraging. The U.S. government, Corbett saw, was violating its own law and risking the lives of thousands of Central American refugees. It had to be fought. Corbett began writing a series of "Dear Friend" letters to five hundred Quaker meetings and individual Quakers around the country explaining the plight of the refugees. In them, he criticized INS practices and solicited donations to help pay bond to free jailed Salvadoran refugees while their asylum applications were under review. This was the only legal recourse available for helping illegal aliens. In his first letter, however, Corbett alluded to the possibility of the need to violate immigration laws. "I can see," he wrote, "that if Central American refugees' rights to political asylum are decisively rejected by the U.S. government or if the U.S. legal system insists on ransom that exceeds our ability to pay, active resistance will be the only alternative to abandoning the refugees to their fate."

In the nineteenth century, Quakers had helped to organize an underground railroad to help slaves escape the antebellum South. Corbett was now beginning to envision a similar contemporary movement to assist Central American refugees. "The creation of a network of actively concerned, mutually supportive people in the U.S. and Mexico," he wrote, "may be the best preparation for an adequate response [to unjust INS policy]…"

By June, Corbett and the Manzo Area Council had raised $150,000 to bond refugees out of jail. The Corbetts had twenty Salvadorans living on their property and many refugees living with families from various Tucson churches. But the more money they raised, the more the INS increased the cost of bail for Central Americans—though not for Mexicans. Bail jumped from $250 to $1,000 to $3,000 per alien and more. It was a losing battle.

Another problem was that Central Americans applying for political asylum were being systematically discriminated against by the INS. Granting asylum implicitly acknowledged the existence of gross violations of human and political rights by regimes and forces supported by the U.S. Since this embarrassed the Reagan administration, political asylum for Central Americans was almost always denied. From 1983 to 1986, for example, only 2.6 percent of Salvadorans and 0.9 percent of Guatemalans requesting asylum were approved. This compared to 60.4 percent of Iranians, 51 percent of Romanians, and 37.7 percent of Afghans approved. Thus, bonding Central American refugees out of jail was really only postponing their deportation. Corbett began to despair of the bail-bond strategy. Rather than bonding refugees out of jail for exorbitant sums of money, he reasoned, why not help smuggle the refugees to safety, keeping them out of jail in the first place? Still, for the time, he continued to raise bond money.

June 26 was a turning point. On that day, Corbett took three Salvadorans, who had fled El Salvador under threat of death, to the Tucson INS office to apply for political asylum. He knew their applications would eventually be denied. But the INS had always allowed asylum applicants to go free, under custody of local ministers, while their applications were on appeal—long enough, Corbett still hoped, for the Salvadoran civil war to end. On this day, however, the Tucson INS director, William Johnson, ordered the three applicants arrested and placed bail at $3,000 each. Corbett desperately protested. This was his only means for working within the system, he argued. If the INS started arresting asylum applicants, Corbett insisted, the churches would have no choice—they would be forced to take their refugee operation underground. According to Corbett, Johnson replied that he was acting under orders from the State Department, that granting asylum to Salvadorans embarrassed the U.S. administration, and that hitherto all applicants would be arrested and sent to El Centro. Corbett and Johnson argued for an hour. At five o'clock Corbett was asked to leave. "We're not just going to abandon these people to their fate," Corbett warned.

Shortly thereafter, Corbett began putting

his intimate knowledge of the desert terrain to use guiding refugees across the border himself and escorting them around INS roadblocks to friends and relatives in Tucson. That such an act broke the law mattered little to Corbett by then. To him, protecting aliens whose lives were in danger was a moral imperative. The Nuremberg trials—which Corbett's lawyer father, Jim recalled, discussed at the family dinner table—had proven that. Corbett next organized a collection of sympathetic students, housewives, professionals, and retirees into a "Tucson refugee support group," which began coordinating a group smuggling operation. The number of refugees aided by their pro bono "evasion services" steadily increased. By mid-August, Corbett himself was making one to two trips a day transporting undocumented aliens to Tucson in his pickup truck.

Members of the Manzo Area Council and the newly formed Tucson Ecumenical Council Task Force on Central America (TEC), to which Corbett belonged, however, were more reluctant to break the law. They understood and supported Corbett's work, but chose themselves to continue working to bail Salvadorans out of El Centro. By mid-July they had raised another $175,000 in collateral and freed 115 refugees—every Salvadoran in the detention center.

By late summer, Corbett was beginning to run out of places to leave the refugees. His house was overflowing with Salvadorans, many of whom had serious emotional and drinking problems, and his wife, Pat, had come to the end of her rope. Corbett approached a number of area churches about housing illegal aliens, but each one declined his request. Then, in early autumn, after a TEC meeting, Corbett took aside John Fife, the forty-one-year-old pastor of Tucson's Southside Presbyterian Church, which hosted TEC's meetings. "John," he said, "we're running out of places to stash people. What about letting the refugees stay in your church?" Fife, it turns out, had already been weighing the possibility of sheltering illegals for weeks. He believed in principle that it was the right thing to do. But he hesitated, concerned for his family's welfare should he be

arrested. He told Corbett he would raise the idea at the church's next elders' meeting….

By Southside's next elders' meeting, however, Fife had made up his mind. His faith and ethics gave him no choice but to take in the refugees. To do otherwise, he judged, would be immoral. He explained this to the elders at the meeting, and, after five hours of discussion, they agreed. By a seven-to-zero vote, with two abstentions, the elders decided to shelter illegal aliens in their church building. The next Sunday, Fife announced the decision to the entire church. Within a few weeks, Fife and others from TEC were joining Corbett in transporting the undocumented refugees. Although members of Southside agreed to act as discreetly as possible, it only took a month for the Tucson INS to hear the rumors that city ministers were openly defying immigration laws. Shortly before Thanksgiving, an INS lawyer approached TEC activist Margo Cowan in the city courthouse and told her, "We're not sure what Fife and Corbett are up to. But tell them to quit or we're going to have your asses."

Cowan and Fife called an emergency TEC meeting in Fife's living room. "We can do two things," Fife surmised. "We can continue on and wait for them to indict us. Or we can quit." After a brief discussion, everyone agreed the legal route was grossly inadequate, that they couldn't quit. Fife then observed that there was an alternative to waiting passively for the inevitable arrests. They could go public. "Beat 'em to the punch," Fife said. That way, they could claim the high moral ground and openly explain themselves to the media and their denominations before the INS could brand them just another bunch of "coyotes" and lock them away….

The day of the public declaration was set for March 24—the second anniversary of Archbishop Romero's assassination. Tim Nonn, of TEC…. worked full-time for weeks before the big day, trying to generate media interest and church support.

On the morning of March 24, Fife and others set up a table on the church steps and hung two banners, which read in Spanish,

"This is a Sanctuary of God for the Oppressed of Central America" and "Immigration, Don't Profane the Sanctuary of God." By 10:00 A.M., forty news reporters and television crews, including several Europeans and one from Canadian broadcasting, had arrived to cover Southside's public declaration of the movement that was henceforth known as Sanctuary. A church openly breaking federal law was big news.

Corbett began the news conference by telling the reporters that he had been smuggling refugees across the border for months. Manzo Area Council lawyers then explained the injustice of immigration laws. Next, Fife read a letter he had sent the previous day to Attorney General William French Smith and other state and INS officials, which announced the church's violation of the law and declaration of sanctuary. "We believe the current policy and practice of the U.S. Government with regard to Central American refugees is illegal and immoral," it read. "We will not cease to extend the sanctuary of the church to undocumented people from Central America. Obedience to God requires this of us." Finally, a Salvadoran, Alfredo, masked to hide his identity, spoke of the violence in El Salvador which drove him to seek political asylum in the U.S....

The INS decided to treat Sanctuary publicly as a trivial novelty that would soon fade into insignificance. No arrests were made. In fact, however, it was later revealed that the INS was deeply worried about Sanctuary and initiated a covert investigation of the movement by paid infiltrators.

In its first year as a sanctuary, Southside Presbyterian harbored sixteen hundred Salvadorans on their way to more permanent homes around the country. And, with national and religious media giving front-page coverage on the movement, word about Sanctuary spread quickly. Steadily, churches scattered across the country began declaring public sanctuary.... By early 1983, more than

Fife had made up his mind. His faith and ethics gave him no choice but to take in the refugees.

forty-five churches and synagogues had declared public sanctuary and more than six hundred "secondary Sanctuary groups" had offered their endorsements and support. The movement was spreading, from New England to southern California....

In 1983, other churches and synagogues made public declarations of sanctuary. Religious groups were by then declaring sanctuary at a rate of more than two a week. In the first six months of 1984, the total number of sanctuaries had more than doubled to 150. And eighteen national religious denominations and commissions had publicly endorsed Sanctuary. Clearly, the Sanctuary movement was not fading into trivial insignificance, as the INS had hoped. Publicly downplaying Sanctuary's importance was not working. So the INS shifted to a more aggressive strategy. In February 1984, Texas Sanctuary workers Stacey Lynn Merkt and Sister Diane Muhlenkamp were arrested for transporting undocumented refugees.... [I]n January 1985, the Justice Department announced the indictment of sixteen Arizona Sanctuary workers, including Corbett and Fife, three nuns, two priests, a nurse, a housewife, and a graduate student. The long-awaited, direct confrontation with the government had arrived.

The arrests, however, only served to increase the movement's visibility and produce an outpouring of support from around the country.... In one week after the Arizona indictments, registration for a TEC-organized national symposium on Sanctuary jumped from three hundred to fifteen hundred participants. The city of Los Angeles and the state of New Mexico declared themselves Sanctuaries. By mid-1985, the number of declared Sanctuaries had climbed to 250. Two years later, the number had grown to four hundred. Despite opposition, the Sanctuary movement was continuing to attract an expanding number of people willing to break federal law to protect aliens and protest U.S. Central America policy.

The Political Objective and Strategic Goal of Nonviolent Actions
by Robert J. Burrowes

All nonviolent struggles are conducted simultaneously in the political and strategic spheres, and these spheres, which are distinct, interact throughout. I have discussed this at length elsewhere. Despite this, only rarely have nonviolent struggles been conducted with a conscious awareness of this vitally important relationship. Gandhi's campaigns were very effective partly because he understood the distinction and relationship between politics and strategy in nonviolent struggle. And the failure of many campaigns can be attributed, in part, to the fact that most nonviolence practitioners do not. To illustrate the distinction and the relationship between these two spheres, and to highlight their vital importance, this article discusses them within the simpler context of nonviolent actions.

Every nonviolent action has a political objective and a strategic goal. When planning an action, it is vitally important to distinguish between its objective and its goal. The political objective of the action is a statement of what the group wants to do: to demonstrate in the city square, to hang a peace sign on the nuclear warship, to picket a factory, to blockade the bulldozer, to occupy the embassy, to go on strike. But why does the group want to do this? Usually, it is to persuade one or more sections of the community to act differently in relation to the campaign issue. So the strategic goal identifies, first, whom the group wants to influence, and second, what they want them to do. For example, if the political objective is to demonstrate in the city square, one possible strategic goal might be to cause members of the public to speak out in support of the nonviolence practitioners' perspective. If the

political objective is to picket a factory, the strategic goal might be to cause workers (through persuasion) not to enter it. If the political objective is to blockade a bulldozer, the strategic goal might be to cause workers to stop logging, or, if the media is present, to cause television viewers to not buy old-growth timber from a particular company.

As can be seen from these simple examples, it makes more sense to decide the strategic goal first, and to then design an action to ensure that the goal is achieved. In other words, it is superior strategy to 1. Decide whom you want to influence AND what you want them to do (derived from the political and strategic assessment that guides your struggle), 2. Decide on a tactic that will do this, and 3. Design the action so that it will do this most effectively. Thus, a strategic goal should be stated using this form: to cause a specified group of people to act in a specified way. Further examples of strategic goals that conform to this formula include: to cause trade unionists to place work-bans on ships carrying uranium, to cause more men to speak out publicly against domestic violence, to cause builders to stop using old-growth timber.

Once the strategic goal has been carefully and specifically defined, equally careful thought should be put into working out what tactic (at this stage of the strategy) will most likely achieve this goal and how it should be designed (so that it will cause the specified audience to act in the specified way). Of course, good action design requires an awareness of what makes nonviolent action work in the first place.

Nonviolent action works because of its capacity to create a favorable political atmosphere (because of, for example, the way in which nonviolence practitioner honesty builds trust); its capacity to create a non-threatening physical environment (because of the nonviolent discipline of the nonviolence practitioners); and its capacity to alter the human psychological conditions (both innate and learned) that make people resist new ideas in the first place. This includes its capacity to reduce or eliminate fear and its capacity to "humanize" nonviolence practitioners in the eyes of more conservative sections of the community. In essence, nonviolent activists precipitate change because people are inspired by the honesty, discipline, integrity, courage, and determination of the nonviolence practitioners — despite arrests, beatings or imprisonment — and are thus inclined to identify with them. Moreover, as an extension of this, they are inclined to act in solidarity.

To summarize and illustrate the argument so far, consider a nonviolent struggle in which the nonviolence practitioners are working to end sexual violence in a local community. One strategic goal of the group might be: to cause the men in a specified group (perhaps those in a particular organization) to take specified action (sign a personal pledge to not use pornography? put a sign in their front window saying they abhor sexual violence? undertake to speak out publicly against all forms of sexual violence? join a group that organizes counseling for male perpetrators?) to help halt sexual violence in that community. The strategic goal will be achieved, at least in part, if some men respond by doing the specified act(s). So what should be the political objective of the action; that is, what nonviolent action will best cause the specified men to act in this way? To "out" known perpetrators by putting their photograph in public places? To conduct a street rally involving local women? To repaint a billboard that objectifies women? To picket the local hotel or brothel every Saturday night? To organize an exhibition of artwork by survivors

The strategic goal identifies, first, whom the group wants to influence, and second, what they want them to do.

of sexual violence? Or something else? For the action to be strategically effective, it must be planned to achieve the strategic goal.

And how might the action be designed to maximize its effectiveness? What qualities (truthfulness? dignity? respectfulness?) can the nonviolence practitioners demonstrate that will most influence these men? How can the action be carried out in a way that engages these men? For example, human needs theory suggests that if you want people to change their behavior, nonviolence practitioners must provide opportunities for involvement that allow people to enhance their self-esteem and/or security, at least.

If the strategic goal of a nonviolent action is achieved, then the action was strategically effective; this does not mean or require, however, that its political objective was achieved. In fact, it might not have been. This is because strategic effectiveness is unrelated to the achievement of the political objective. For example, the political objective of nonviolence practitioners might be to blockade a bulldozer. However, the (usually unspecified) strategic goal of the bulldozer blockade should be something like this: to cause consumers to stop buying (the specified) paper products that are made from woodchips taken from old-growth forest (by a specified company). In this case, as long as the action is well-designed, it does not matter if the nonviolence practitioners are arrested before the blockade takes place, because the message of their truthfulness, commitment, discipline, courage, and sacrifice, together with the solidarity action they are calling for (which will undermine the power of their opponent), will still go out to their audience. In short, the failure to physically stop the bulldozer is strategically irrelevant.

It is the failure to distinguish between the political objective and the strategic goal that often causes a great deal of confusion, particularly around such questions as the role of secrecy and sabotage, in planning nonviolent actions. Many groups attach great importance to the political objective of their action, and use secrecy to improve their prospects of being able to carry it out. But this is invariably counterproductive, in the strategic sense, and is based on a flawed understanding of how and why nonviolence works. This is because, as explained above, achievement of the political objective is not equivalent to achievement of the strategic goal.

And while many nonviolence practitioners achieve their (secret) political objective, they fail to achieve (what should be) their strategic goal (to cause specified people to act in the specified way) because the qualities (such as honesty and integrity) of nonviolence practitioners that inspire their audience are not allowed into play. (There are, of course, many other reasons why the use of secrecy is strategically counterproductive.)

For some types of action — such as a rally, a picket, or a strike — no one would even suggest using secrecy. But whatever the action, as explained above, strategic effectiveness is unrelated to whether the action is successfully carried out or not (provided it is strategically selected, well-designed, and sincerely attempted). This point was classically illustrated by the Indian satyagrahis who attempted to nonviolently invade the Dharasana Salt Works in 1930. Despite repeated attempts by many hundreds of nonviolence practitioners to walk into the salt works during a three-week period, not one nonviolence practitioner got a pinch of salt! But an account of the nonviolence practitioners' nonviolent discipline, commitment, and courage — under the baton blows of the police — was reported in 1,350 newspapers around the world. As a result, this action — which failed to achieve the political objective of seizing salt — functionally undermined support for British imperialism in India. If the nonviolence practitioners had resorted to the use of secrecy, there would have been no chance to demonstrate their honesty, integrity, and determination — and to thus inspire empathy for their cause — although they might have gotten some salt!

Whether or not nonviolence practitioners achieve their political objective is strategically irrelevant. This is because an effective nonviolent action is designed to achieve its strategic goal, irrespective of the response of opponents or the authorities to the political objective of the action. Whether or not nonviolence practitioners achieve their strategic goal, however, is always strategically determinative.

A Decalogue for a Spirituality of Nonviolence
by Rosemary Lynch and Alain Richard

Creative nonviolence calls us:

- To learn to recognize and respect the sacred in every person, including in ourselves, and in every part of creation. The acts of the nonviolent person help to free this sacredness in the opponent from obscurity or captivity.

- To accept oneself deeply, "who I am" with all my gifts and richness, with all my limitations, errors, failings and weaknesses. To live in the truth of ourselves, without excessive pride, with fewer delusions and false expectations.

- To recognize that what I resent, and perhaps even detest, in another, comes from my difficulty in admitting that this same reality lives also in me. To recognize and renounce my own violence, which becomes evident when I begin to monitor my words, gestures, reactions.

- To renounce dualism, the "we-they" mentality. This divides us into "good people/bad people" and allows us to demonize the adversary. It is the root of authoritarian and exclusivist behavior. It generates racism and makes possible conflicts and wars.

- To face our fear and to deal with it with love as well as courage.

- To understand and accept that the *New Creation*, the building up of the *Beloved Community* is always carried forward with others. It is never a "solo act." This requires patience and the ability to pardon.

- To see ourselves as a part of the whole creation to which we foster a relationship of love, not of mastery, remembering that the destruction of our planet is a profoundly spiritual problem, not simply a scientific or technological one. *We are one.*

- To be ready to suffer, perhaps even with joy, if we believe this will help liberate the best within the other. This includes the acceptance of our place and moment in history with its trauma, with its ambiguities.

- To be capable of celebration, of joy, when transformations occur, when one sees the connection she or he had not seen before.

- To slow down, to be patient, planting the seeds of love and forgiveness in our own hearts and in the hearts of those around us. Slowly we will grow in love, compassion and the capacity to forgive.

REFLECTIONS ON THE READINGS

PART THREE:

Putting Nonviolent Power Into Action

Session 9:
The Power of Action

SESSION 9: **The Power of Action**

OBJECTIVES

- To imagine what it is like to take nonviolent action
- To become familiar with the history and process of nonviolent social movements
- To begin to plan a group nonviolent action as a way of experimenting with nonviolent power

AGENDA

- Opening [5 min.]
- Welcome [1 min.]
- Reflection on Homework [10 min.]
- Imagining Ourselves Acting [20 min.]
- Nonviolent Social Movement Brainstorm [15 min.]
- The People Power Model vs. the Power Elite Model [15 min.]
- Break [10 min.]
- A Way to Make Decisions: Consensus Process [15 min.]
- Beginning to Plan a Group Nonviolent Action [40 min.]
- Conclusion [10 min.]
     Journaling
     Nonviolent Activity
     Next Session's Reading
     Adding to the Wall of Learning and Growing
     Identifying a Nonviolence Principle
     Evaluation
     Closing

READINGS

- Reading #1: Christian Smith, "The Beginning of Sanctuary"
- Reading #2: Robert J. Burrowes, "The Political Objective and Strategic Goal of Nonviolent Actions"
- Reading #3: Rosemary Lynch and Alain Richard, "The Decalogue for a Spirituality of Nonviolence"

NOTES FOR THE FACILITATOR

SESSION PREPARATION: BEFORE

- Review the entire session in depth. Role-play or practice setting up and facilitating exercises beforehand. Wherever possible, put material into your own words. Feel free to make notes for this purpose on 3x5 cards or in the book next to the written instructions.
- Materials needed: masking tape for timeline; pieces of paper (or half pieces of paper) for the Nonviolent Social Movement Brainstorm exercise.
- As with all the openings, use the one presented here or another that you find centering or grounding.
- Write out on easel paper:
  - Categories of Social Movements

PREPARATION: ON THE DAY OF THE SESSION

- The Nonviolent Social Movement Brainstorm exercise will require a timeline that people can write on. Use three or four pieces of easel paper taped together. Make the timeline from 1900 to the present, and then on into the next 50 years. Mark off every 20 years along a horizontal center line running the length of the timeline.
- Play close attention to time in the session. You don't need to call on everyone with a hand raised when facilitating debriefs.

SESSION 9: **The Power of Action**

WELCOME — 1 MIN.

Share in your own words:

Welcome back for our ninth session of the *Engage: Exploring Nonviolent Living* Study Program. In this session, we will try to imagine what nonviolent action feels like and involves. Then we will get a sense of the history of social movements, and begin to imagine what it is like to take nonviolent action, and where the power comes from. Finally, we will begin some preliminary planning of a nonviolent action of our own.

OPENING — WALKING EXERCISE: 5 MIN.

Put on a piece of quiet, meditative music and say the following:

For our opening I would like us to do a walking meditation. By slowing down our walking to a very slow pace we can become aware of things around us that we often take for granted.

Form a line behind me with at least two feet between each person. Stand as straight as you can and place your hands folded together across your stomach. Lower your eyes to about 45 degrees and keep a soft focus — not really focusing on anything in particular.

Be aware of each step you take and notice any feelings you have in your body. After we make one trip around the room, end back at your seat.

Lead them once around the room.

REFLECTING ON HOMEWORK — 10 MIN.

Now I invite you to get together with your Nonviolence Partner to take a few minutes to reflect on your experiences or insights since the last session, as well as on the readings, journaling, or nonviolent action.

IMAGINING ACTION — 20 MIN.

I invite you to recall "The Love Walks," the story of the women of East Los Angeles that we discussed in Session Five. Recall how they lived in fear, but then decided to step out of their locked houses into the streets to be with their sons, grandsons, brothers, and nephews so that they could change the way in which they and their families lived and died — so they could change their society. They left the safety of their homes to reach out and to listen. They walked, they sang, they organized, they secured jobs, they

> "Injustice anywhere is a threat to justice everywhere. We are caught in an inescapable network of mutuality, tied in a single garment of destiny. Whatever affects one directly, affects all indirectly."
>
> —MARTIN LUTHER KING, JR.

monitored police activity, they helped the young men open a bakery.

Please imagine this situation again. I invite you to close your eyes and put yourself in this story. Imagine you are one of these women. Imagine doing what they did.

After a minute:

Please open your eyes. How did you see yourself? What did you do?

Were you able to do it? If not, what would it take to put yourself in the shoes of one of these women?

Record the responses to both questions on easel paper or dry erase board.

WOMEN IN NIGERIA TAKE NONVIOLENT ACTION FOR CHANGE

Nigeria is the world's sixth-largest oil producer and the United States' fifth-largest supplier, yet most Nigerians do not share in this teeming wealth. Intent on changing this disparity, in the summer of 2002 hundreds of unarmed Nigerian women of the Ugborodo and Arutan communities dramatically occupied ChevronTexaco's key oil terminal in the country, bringing petroleum production to a sudden halt. The women said that if efforts were made to remove them, they would disrobe. This created a paralyzing dilemma for the male Nigerian employees (who would be asked to remove them) because it invoked a profound cultural taboo. After ten dramatic days, the women reached a landmark pact with the company to provide jobs, infrastructure, and economic empowerment in villages long mired in poverty.

As an editorial in the Minneapolis Star Tribune commented, "In the best traditions of Mohandas Gandhi and Martin Luther King, several hundred Nigerian women took a nonviolent stand for their country. Ranging in age from 25 to 90 — some with infants strapped to their backs — the women held a successful sit-in at ChevronTexaco's Escravos facility in Nigeria's oil-rich delta. Without firing a shot or injuring a soul, they shut down an operation that produces a half million barrels of oil a day. In the end, they accomplished what their men could not, and what their government should have done long ago." ("Nigerian women / Protest wins oil company attention," Minneapolis *Star Tribune*, July 20, 2002).

NONVIOLENT SOCIAL MOVEMENT BRAINSTORM — 15 MIN.

Display the timeline you have constructed. Present the following:

Social movements promote "a long-term process of social change in which the whole population is first alerted to and educated about a problem. A converted and growing majority of public opposition then creates the political and social conditions that force new public policies," according to social movement theorist and activist Bill Moyer.

I invite you to break into small groups of three or four. Please brainstorm a list of historical, contemporary, and possible future social movements and list them on separate pieces of paper. These movements can include Constructive Programs or use Nonviolent Direct Actions or a combination of both.

Here are some categories under which many movements around the world can be found. (*Put these categories up on easel paper.*)

- Peace movements
- Human rights movements
- Labor movements
- Nationalist self-determination movements
- Environmentalist movements
- Community improvement movements (for example, sustainable energy, organic food, alternative education, etc.)
- Anti-racism movements
- Anti-sexism movements
- Animal rights movements
- Health improvement movements (e.g., the anti-smoking movement or Mothers Against Drunk Driving)
- Others…

> "A single affinity group (a small group of individuals working together) can be more powerful than an entire social movement."
> — TERRY MESSMAN

After 5 minutes, reconvene the groups.

I now invite you to place on the timeline the social movements you've identified according to the approximate dates they were active.

When they are done:

I invite you to reflect on what social movements you would like to see now or in the future.

> "History is made by people. Not by mysterious collective forces or abstract social causes. Specific flesh-and-blood human beings, all of us, continually act — individually and collectively, intentionally and unintentionally — to construct and reconstruct our societies and cultures. In doing so, we become the creators of the social worlds we inhabit and co-authors of the social story we call history."
> — CHRISTIAN SMITH

Wrap up this exercise with the following observation:

All movements started from individuals and groups just like us — people concerned about an issue or just wanting to make a difference and leave the world a little better than they found it.

TWO APPROACHES TO SOCIAL AND POLITICAL POWER
THE PEOPLE POWER MODEL VS. THE POWER ELITE MODEL

1. The Power Elite Model

The Power Elite Model holds that society is organized in the form of a hierarchical pyramid, with powerful elites at the top and the relatively powerless mass populace at the bottom. The elites, through their dominant control of the state, institutions, laws, myths, traditions, and social norms, serve the interests of the elites, often to the disadvantage of the whole society.

In this model, power flows from the top to the bottom. Since people are powerless, social change can be achieved only by appealing to the elites at the top to change their policies through normal channels and institutions, such as the electoral process, lobbying Congress, and use of the courts.

The focus constituency, in this model, is the powerholders, and the method of change is persuasion, either convincing existing powerholders to change their view or electing new powerholders.

2. The People Power Model

The People Power Model holds that power ultimately resides in the hands of the populace. Even in societies with strong power elites, the powerholders' power is dependent on the cooperation, acquiescence, or support of the mass public.

This model is represented by an inverse triangle, with the people at the top and the power elite at the bottom. People power is the model used by social movements.

The movement's strategy is not only to use normal channels in an effort to persuade powerholders to change their minds, but also to alert, educate, and mobilize a discontented, impassioned, and determined grassroots population. This population creates change by "leading the leaders": withdrawing support for the status quo and creating the conditions for the powerholders to move off their position to one that reflects that of an increasingly vocal and active public.

Source: Bill Moyer

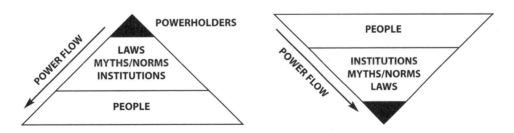

NONVIOLENT POWER: PEOPLE POWER VS. POWER ELITE — 15 MIN.

Convey the following in your own words:

To understand how individuals and groups can make a huge impact when they act for social change, it is helpful to understand how nonviolent social movements work and to understand what form of power they use.

Social change is rooted in the mobilization of power. But what kind of power? In exploring this, we will reflect on two models of power: The Power Elite Model and the People Power Model. Each of these models leads to opposite movement strategies.

Let's read and discuss the explanations of these two approaches to political and social change found on page 183.

After the group reads the material in this box, suggest:

Now, let's discuss the *people power model* in light of one of the movements that we brainstormed earlier, or in light of one of the stories we have studied in the *Engage* Study Program. Let's think about how one or more of these movements have exercised people power.

BREAK — 10 MIN.

NONVIOLENT ACTION HELPS GENERATE THE PEOPLE POWER OF SOCIAL MOVEMENTS

Active Nonviolence provides social movements with the optimum opportunity to win over and involve the general citizenry in people power because:

- Nonviolence is based on timeless national, cultural, human, and religious values and principles such as equality, security, preservation, justice, democracy, love, forgiveness, caring, compassion, and understanding.
- Nonviolence appeals to these values and principles held by people and nations.
- Nonviolence is less threatening than violence to ordinary citizens.
- Nonviolence (unlike militaristic or violent methods) allows everyone to participate: women, men, elderly, youth, and even children; people from all traditional levels of strength and weakness.
- In nonviolence, the means are consistent with the ends—they are the ends in the making.
- Nonviolence has the capacity to reduce the effectiveness of police and state violence— the powerholders' ultimate weapon — and to turn it to the movement's advantage.
- A clear policy of nonviolence makes it difficult for provocateurs to disrupt or discredit movements by promoting internal violence, hostility, dissension, dishonesty, and confusion.

Source: Bill Moyer. For a more comprehensive presentation of these assumptions, see Appendix.

A WAY TO MAKE DECISIONS: CONSENSUS PROCESS — 15 MIN.

Present the following in your own words:

Our goal in the next couple of sessions is to create a nonviolent activity together. To do so, we need a decision-making process. The consensus process is a method of group decision-making by which an entire group of people can come to an agreement. The steps of the consensus process are:

- Someone puts forward a proposal
- The facilitator asks if there are any clarifying questions; these are answered
- Then the facilitator asks if there are any reservations; these are discussed
- If there are reservations, the facilitator asks for any amendments
- After the proposal is amended, the facilitator restates the proposal (so everyone is clear on its content) and asks to see if there is consensus. If everyone agrees, then consensus has been reached.
- If someone has concerns or objections, discussion continues
- If someone objects, she or he can do one of several things:
  - Give qualified support ("I don't see the need for this, but I'll go along with it.")
  - Stand aside ("I think it's a mistake but I can live with it.")
  - Block ("I cannot support this personally AND I cannot allow the group to support it. It is immoral.") Blocking typically is a rare phenomenon. If someone blocks, she or he should present a new proposal

- If concerns or objections remain, the facilitator may ask if those people are willing to "stand aside" to permit the group to take action, or whether they feel unable to do so
- The group continues discussion until consensus is reached or the effort is suspended

Please move into your small groups to practice using consensus by deciding on what kind of pizza your group would like to order.

> *"Never doubt that a small group of thoughtful, committed people can change the world. Indeed, it is the only thing that ever has."*
> — MARGARET MEAD

BEGINNING TO PLAN A GROUP NONVIOLENT ACTION — 30 MIN.

Explain the following:

In the next two sessions (Ten and Eleven), we will plan and prepare our own nonviolent action for the purpose of experimenting with the principles of nonviolence applied to an issue or situation we consider important and in need of change.

In this session, we will begin this process by exploring what kind of nonviolent action we would like to create. This action should be neither too hard nor too easy, depending on the experience of the group.

> *Social movements have played a central role throughout history in achieving positive social change. Rooted in grassroots "people power," nonviolent social movements have been a powerful means for ordinary people to act on their deepest values and to successfully challenge immoral and unjust social conditions and policies, despite the determined resistance of entrenched powerholders.*
> — BILL MOYER

Finding Our Focus

Convey the following in your own words:

A group seeking to create a nonviolent activity often comes together with a specific focus: ending harassment of homeless people in their neighborhood, or challenging racist behavior in city government, or contributing to the process of creating a nuclear-free future, etc.

As participants in the *Engage* Study Program, we have a wide variety of interests. We therefore first need to brainstorm what issue, policy, or condition we would like to focus on. We need to find our strategic goal.

As a first step, I invite us to sit in a circle and relax. Let the room grow quiet. Please close your eyes. Allow your deepest self to speak.

> I would like to beg you to have patience with everything unresolved in your heart and try to love the questions themselves as if they were locked rooms or books written in a very foreign language. Don't search for the answers, which could not be given to you now, because you would not be able to live them. And the point is, to live everything. Live the questions now. Perhaps then, someday in the future, you will gradually, without even noticing it, live your way into the answer.
>
> — RAINER MARIA RILKE

Ask the group to listen silently to the following questions, allowing a couple of minutes between each question:

- What is it in the depth of your heart that you want to see addressed? It can be something close at hand or it can be international in scope.

- Who are the people you would like to affect on this issue or problem, and what would you like them to do?

Invite the participants to open their eyes. Debrief the session, writing the group's responses on easel paper. Look for commonalities. Identify two or three issues. Try to distill out for each of the issues what they want to accomplish and who they need to move to achieve this? Help the group see how its relatively small action may be part of a larger strategy for social change.

After some time, see if there are any proposals for a strategic goal for each of the issues (the specific person or persons they want to affect and what they want them to do)? Ask the group to use the consensus process in deciding which of the proposals the group will adopt.

Once the group has agreed to a strategic goal, you can move to the next step of deciding what action to do to help realize this goal.

Beginning to Design Our Action (Toward Our Political Objective)

State the following in your own words:

The action should be designed with our strategic goal in mind. Of course, typically we do not achieve our goal with just one action, but each action contributes to this eventual possibility.

Examples of actions that a small group can take include:

- To inform neighbors of an issue (a local issue that the community is struggling with; war; health care; human rights; etc.) and encourage them to get involved, an action could be setting up an information table on the issue in a setting where people have many different views on these issues. The action can include developing printed materials (information fliers, etc.), handing these out to passersby, and giving people of many different perspectives an opportunity to discuss these issues.

- If the issue is sexism and the strategic goal is to influence the owner of a billboard who has been resistant to dialogue to change a particular ad, a small group could picket the owners office, or hang a bedsheet with an alternative message on the billboard.

- If the issue is war, to influence local citizens to become more aware of the human costs of a current war and write letters or join the anti-war movement in some way, a small group could organize the reading of names of people killed on both sides of a war at an appropriate site.

- A small group could organize a public activity to support local social service organizations or agencies whose budgets are at risk of being cut (or have been cut).

- To amplify its message, a small group could join in with another group's nonviolent action.

Let's ask ourselves:

- Is anyone else working on this goal? Do we want to join them in an action that they are already doing, or initiate one ourselves?

If the participants are unsure about what other groups might be working on the issue, ask for volunteers to do research on the issue for the next session. (See the Nonviolent Action suggestion in the Conclusion section.)

If time permits, begin a brainstorm of possible actions that the group could take that would help to draw them closer to their goal. Ask people to reflect on how these possible activities can reflect the group's deepest values, principles, and beliefs. Also, if time permits, assign each person, or each group of two, a specific topic to research.

CONCLUSION — 10 MIN.

⊙ Nonviolence Journal

Suggested Topic:
Thinking back on "The Love Walks," reflect more on what role you assumed and what, if any, significance that might have for future roles you might play. If you were unable to place yourself in the story, reflect on what the obstacles were. If they were obstacles that would prevent you from action when action was needed, how might you overcome those obstacles?

⊙ Nonviolent Action

Please spend time before the next session researching the issue that the group is focusing on for the nonviolent action you are planning.

⊙ **Next Session's Reading**

For next time, please read the readings at the end of this session.

⊙ **Adding to the Wall of Learning and Growing**

Please add your insights, learnings or questions to the Wall.

⊙ **Closing**

Have an audiotape or compact disk of instrumental music prepared. With the music playing, say the following:

For our closing I'd like to read the following words from novelist and poet Alice Walker from her book *Anything We Love Can Be Saved: A Writer's Activism:*

There is always a moment in any kind of struggle when one feels in full bloom. VIVID. ALIVE. To be such a person or to witness anyone at this moment of transcendent presence is to know that what is human is linked, by a daring compassion, to what is divine. During my years of being close to people engaged in changing the world I have seen fear turn into courage. Sorrow into joy. Funerals into celebrations. Because whatever the consequences, people, standing side by side, have expressed WHO THEY REALLY ARE, and that ultimately they believe in the love of the world and each other enough TO BE THAT.

KEY ORGANIZATIONS

Nonviolence Peaceforce (NP). 425 Oak Grove Street, St. Paul, MN 55403; (612) 871-0005; fax: (612) 871-0006; *www.nonviolentpeaceforce.org.* NP is building a trained, international civilian peaceforce committed to third-party nonviolent intervention.

Nevada Desert Experience (NDE), PO Box 46645, Las Vegas, NV 89114-6645; (702) 646-4814: *nde@peacenet.org, www.nevadadesertexperience.org.* NDE works to stop nuclear weapons testing through a campaign of prayer, education, dialogue, and nonviolent direct action. NDE mobilizes people of faith to work toward nuclear abolition.

Peace Brigades International (PBI)/USA, 428 8th St. SE, 2nd fl., Washington, DC 20003; (202) 544-3765; *info@pbiusa.org; www.peacebrigades.org.* PBI provides nonviolent international peacekeeping in areas of violent conflict and repression, offering unarmed protective accompaniment to individuals, organizations, and communities threatened with political violence and human rights violations.

HOMEWORK

NONVIOLENCE JOURNAL

Suggested Question:

Thinking back on the exercise of placing yourself in the shoes of the women in "The Love Walks," reflect more on what role you assumed and what, if any, significance that might have for future roles you might play. If you were unable to place yourself in the story, reflect on what the obstacles were. If they were obstacles that would prevent you from action when action was needed, how might you overcome those obstacles?

NONVIOLENT ACTION

Suggestion:

Please spend time before the next session researching the issue that the group is focusing on for the nonviolent action you are planning.

The Story of Roberto Morales
by Jhon Evaristo Flores

Jhon Evaristo Flores Osorio is a conscientious objector and a social leader from Colombia, currently teaching in Belize. The name of his friend who was killed has been changed.

"Have you heard, Jhon?" my school friends asked me at lunch break. "They say Roberto Morales was shot and killed by the military this morning!"

The awful words echoed in my ears and crushed my heart. Roberto and I had grown up together in the same neighborhood in Ciudad Bolivar, the poorest and most crime-infested district of Bogotá, Colombia. We were friends and I knew his mother and brother. I knew nothing of his father. Because they were poor, Roberto quit school so that he could work and help out. I was poor too, but I was an excellent student and had received a scholarship for school. I had a dream of finishing school and living a life different from my mother's sad and angry life; even though I also had to work to help my mother, who was raising seven children alone. And so, I was in school the morning that 15-year-old Roberto was shot in the street.

"Who told you this?" I asked desperately. "How do you know this is true?" I prayed for some flaw in the story that would prove it was not true; but in my heart, I knew that yet another friend of mine was dead.

Young people were being killed all the time in the streets of Ciudad Bolivar. Our district was known as the most violent district in Bogotá and was called *"zona roja,"* the dangerous "red zone." It was a district infested with youth gangs and members of the Revolutionary Armed Forces of Colombia (FARC) guerrilla group. Because of the negative image of Ciudad Bolivar, most people in Bogotá thought that people from there were very dangerous criminals, especially youth. The government had a policy to eliminate "that problem." But eliminating "that problem" meant eliminating our youth!

"Grupos de Limpieza Social" (Groups to Clean Society) or "Escuadrones de la Muerte" (Squadrons of Death), as we called them, were formed. More than 500 youth were killed in Ciudad Bolivar by 1992 and no one came forward to claim responsibility. Even with all of this killing going on, it was uncommon for students to be killed. The perception was that if you went to school you were "good"; young people who didn't go to school were viewed as "bad" or in gangs. No one asked if you were out of school working to help your poor family; you were automatically "that problem."

Roberto had been playing ball in the street with a friend that morning. They didn't have a real ball. They were using a rock to play catch. One of the boys let go with a curve ball that was intercepted by a military bus just making the turn onto the street where the boys were playing. The rock went sailing through one of the open windows. The boys froze. The bus stopped immediately. A Captain got off the bus and before the boys could explain what had happened, he took aim and without a word, shot Roberto. He then got back on the bus, which lumbered on down the road, leaving Roberto dead on the street. His stunned friend ran to Roberto's home to tell his mother.

Grief-stricken, Maria Morales went to the authorities to demand answers for the killing of her son, but they ignored her pleadings. Searching for help, Roberto's mother remembered that I had joined the Conscientious Objection group that had been organizing Nonviolent Action activities. (In spite of all the violence in Ciudad Bolivar there were many organizations and people like me working and developing workshops, trainings, art, carnivals, public debates, sports, and other similar activities to create a better and safer place to grow and live.) She came to us for help.

Until the killing of Roberto, no one had done anything. The killing of Roberto mobilized us. We were sad and tired and couldn't bear the killings of our youth any more. We decided to protest to the authorities. We planned our demonstration very carefully. Our goal was to form a commission to negotiate with the government. We democratically elected representatives from our group for the commission, prior to the demonstration. I was one of the representatives elected. The day of the protest we would demand representatives from the government meet with us and organize the commission.

There were about 60 or 70 of us in the Nonviolent Action group. Most of us were youth between 13 and 17 years old; I was 14. There were some adults including Roberto's mother and some of her friends with their young children. They wanted to make people conscious of the social problems in Ciudad Bolívar. Even though we were all sad because of the death of Roberto, we were also full of hope that at last we were going to have answers from the government authorities.

The demonstration took place on a sunny morning only a few days after Roberto was killed. We all dressed in black and white, mostly jeans and T-shirts, to symbolize death and life. We carried placards that said, "Queremos Morirnos De Viejos" ("We Want To Die of Old Age") and "Para Que La Vida Siga Siendo Joven" ("Life Is For the Young"). We were met by 100 policemen carrying shields, batons, guns, and gas canisters. It was their practice to use their shields to enclose people and then beat them with their batons. We were very

frightened, but before they could hit us, we began the "Carnival of Life" we had planned. We started dancing and playing instruments and joining in games. The police didn't know what to make of us. They had never seen protestors all dressed alike and had certainly never seen them dance and sing! Bystanders joined the "Carnival." Even some of the police started dancing with us! Instead of beating us, they began talking to us and asking us why we were protesting. We realized that they didn't know why they were planning to hit us; they only obey orders.

The results of that "Carnival of Life" were felt almost immediately. Within two months, a public debate was organized by both representatives from our group and the government authorities in a public school in Ciudad Bolívar. Every social organization in the district, as well as all the teachers, students, and parents participated. More than 2000 people attended. The outcome was the government opening a Human Rights office for youth in Ciudad Bolívar and promising more investment in education, health, recreation and sports, culture and art, employment and social security, especially for youth. Other killings were investigated, and military/police promised better communication among themselves and the community.

After this public debate the situation in Ciudad Bolívar changed dramatically. For the first time, a high-ranking military officer was found guilty for the killing of a boy in Ciudad Bolívar. People were filled with confidence and continued to speak out to their government, which was now listening to them. The "Carnival of Life," which was created because of the killing of my friend, had returned hope and dreams to the mothers and children of Ciudad Bolívar.

> *We were very frightened, but before they could hit us, we began the "Carnival of Life" we had planned. We started dancing and playing instruments and joining in games. The police didn't know what to make of us. They had never seen protestors all dressed alike and had certainly never seen them dance and sing! Bystanders joined the "Carnival." Even some of the police started dancing with us! Instead of beating us, they began talking to us and asking us why we were protesting. We realized that they didn't know why they were planning to hit us; they only obey orders.*

The Eight Stages of Successful Social Movements
by Bill Moyer

Social movements are not spontaneous events. According to Bill Moyer, successful social movements follow eight stages. His schema helps us not only to plan social movements, it helps to overcome a sense of failure and powerlessness that we often feel — the sense that we are always losing.

We don't criticize a sophomore in college because she hasn't graduated from college; similarly, social movements are not unsuccessful just because they haven't met their objectives yet. Movements build toward their goals over time, building on a series of phases. Moyer's concept is important because it challenges one of the key weapons of the status quo, which seeks to continually make its opponents feel powerless. The Eight Stages of Successful Social Movements is a practical strategy and action planning model describing eight stages that successful movements progress through over many years. For each stage, it gives the roles of the movement, powerholders, and the public, and movement goals appropriate to that stage.

The following eight stages are grouped into five broad phases of hidden problem, increasing tensions, take-off, waging the movement, and success.

HIDDEN PROBLEM

Stage 1: Normal Times

- A critical social problem exists that violates widely held values.
- The general public is unaware of this problem.
- Only a few people are concerned.

   Movement uses official channels, demonstrations are small and rare.
   Powerholders: chief goal is to keep issue off social and political agenda.
   Public is unaware of the problem and supports powerholders. Only 10-15% of public support change.

Movement goals of Stage 1:
- Build organizations, vision, and strategy.
- Document problems and powerholders' roles. Become informed.

INCREASING TENSIONS

Stage 2: Efforts to Change the Problem Demonstrate the Failure of Official Remedies

- A variety of small and scattered opposition groups do research, educate others.
- New wave of grassroots opposition begins.
- Official mechanisms are used to address the problem: hearings, the courts, the legislature; if these work, the problem is resolved. But often, the official approaches don't work. This shows

how entrenched the problem is and demonstrates the failure of institutions to solve it.

> **Movement** uses official system to prove it violates widely held values.
> **Powerholders:** chief goal is to keep issue off social and political agenda and maintain routine bureaucratic functioning to stifle opposition.
> **Public** still unaware of issue and supports status quo. 15-20% of the public support change.

Movement goals of Stage 2:
- Prove and document the failure of official institutions and powerholders to uphold public trust and values.
- Begin legal cases to establish legal and moral basis for opposition.
- Build opposition organizations, leadership, expertise.

Stage 3: Ripening Conditions

- Recognition by the public of the problem and its victims slowly grows.
- Pre-existing institutions and networks (churches, peace and justice organizations) lend their support.
- Tensions build. Rising grassroots discontent with conditions, institutions, powerholders, and "professional opposition organizations" (e.g., large lobbying groups).
- Upsetting events occur, including ones which "personify" the problem.
- Perceived or real worsening conditions.

> **Movement:** grassroots groups grow in number and size. Small nonviolent actions begin. Parts of progressive community won over, pre-existing networks join new cause.
> **Powerholders** still favor existing policies and control official decision-making channels.
> **Public** still unaware of problems and supports powerholders. 20-30% oppose official policies.

Movement goals of Stage 3:
- Educate/win over progressive community.
- Prepare grassroots for new movement.
- More local nonviolent actions.

TAKE-OFF

Stage 4: Take-Off

- A catalytic ("trigger") event occurs that starkly and clearly conveys the problem to the public (e.g., the killing of Matthew Shepard in 2000; 1986 Chernobyl nuclear accident).
- Building on the groundwork of the first three stages, dramatic nonviolent actions and campaigns are launched.
- These activities show how this problem violates widely held values.
- The problem is finally put on "society's agenda."
- A new social movement rapidly takes off.

> **Movement** enacts or responds to trigger event, holds large rallies and demonstrations and many nonviolent actions. A new "movement organization" is created, characterized by informal organizational style, energy, and hope for fast change. "Professional opposition

organizations" sometimes oppose "rebel" activities.

Powerholders are shocked by new opposition and publicity, fail to keep issue off social agenda, reassert official line, and attempt to discredit opposition.

Public becomes highly aware of problem. 40-60% oppose official policies.

Movement goals of Stage 4:

- Put issue on social agenda. Create a new grassroots movement.
- Alert, educate and win public opinion.
- Legitimize movement by emphasizing and upholding widely held societal values.

WAGING THE MOVEMENT

Stage 5: Movement Identity Crisis — A Sense of Failure and Powerlessness

- Those who joined the movement when it was growing in Stage 4 expect rapid success. When this doesn't happen there is often hopelessness and burn-out.
- It seems that this is the end of the movement; in fact, it is now that the real work begins.

  Movement: numbers down at demonstrations, less media coverage, long-range goals not met. Unrealistic hopes of quick success are unmet. Many activists despair, burn out, and drop out. "Negative rebel" and "naive citizen" activities gain prominence in movement.

  Powerholders and media claim that movement has failed, discredit movement by highlighting and encouraging "negative rebel" activities, sometimes through agents provocateurs.

  Public alienated by negative rebels. Risk of movement becoming a subcultural sect that is isolated and ineffective.

Movement goals of Stage 5:

- Recognize movement progress and success. Counter "negative rebel" tendencies.
- Recognize that movement is nearing Stage Six and pursue goals appropriate to that stage.

Stage 6: Winning Majority Public Opinion

- The movement deepens and broadens.
- The movement finds ways to involve citizens and institutions from a broad perspective to address this problem.
- Growing public opposition puts the problem on the political agenda; the political price that some powerholders have to pay to maintain their policies grows to become an untenable liability.
- The consensus of the powerholders on this issue fractures, leading to proposals from the powerholders for change (often these proposals are for cosmetic change).
- The majority of the public is now more concerned about the problem and less concerned about the movement's proposed change.
- Often there is a new catalytic event (re-enacting Stage 4).

  Movement transforms from protest in crisis to long-term struggle with powerholders to win public majority to oppose official policies and consider positive alternatives. Movement broadens analysis, forms coalitions. Many new groups involved in large-scale education and involvement. Official channels used with some success. Nonviolent actions at key times and places. Many sub-goals and movements develop. Movement promotes alternatives, including paradigm shift.

Powerholders try to discredit and disrupt movement and create public fear of alternatives. Promote bogus reforms and create crises to scare public. Powerholders begin to split.

Public: 60-75% of the public oppose official policies, but many fear alternatives. However, support for alternatives is increasing. Backlash can occur and counter-movements may form.

Movement goals:
- Keep issue on social agenda.
- Win over and involve majority of the public.
- Activists become committed to the long haul.

SUCCESS

Stage 7: Success: Accomplishing Alternatives

- Majority now opposes current policies and no longer fears the alternative.
- Many powerholders split off and change positions.
- Powerholders try to make minimal reforms, while the movement demands real social change.
- The movement finally achieves one or more of its demands.
- The struggle shifts from opposing official policies to choosing alternatives.
- More costly for powerholders to continue old policies than to adopt new ones. More "re-trigger" events occur.

Movement counters powerholders' bogus alternatives. Broad-based opposition demands change. Nonviolent action, where appropriate.

Powerholders: Some powerholders change and central, inflexible powerholders become increasingly isolated. Central powerholders try last gambits, then have to change policies, have the policies defeated by vote, or lose office.

Public majority demands for change are bigger than its fears of the alternatives. Majority no longer believe powerholders' justifications of old policies and critiques of alternatives.

Movement goals:
- Recognize movement's success and celebrate, follow up on the demands won, raise larger issues, focus on other demands that are in various stages, and propose better alternatives and a true paradigm shift.
- Create ongoing empowered activists and organizations to achieve other goals.

Stage 8: Continuing the Struggle

- Our struggle to achieve a more humane and democratic society continues indefinitely. This means defending the gains won as well as pursuing new ones.
- Building on this success, we return to Stage 1 and struggle for the next change.
- Key: The long-term impact of the movement surpasses the achievement of its specific demands.

Movement takes on "reform" role to protect and extend successes. The movement attempts to minimize losses due to backlash, and circles back to the sub-goals and issues that emerged in earlier stages. The long-term focus is to achieve a paradigm shift.

Powerholders adapt to new policies and conditions, claim the movement's successes as their own, and try to roll back movement successes by not carrying out agreements or continuing old policies in secret.

Public adopts new consensus and status quo. New public beliefs and expectations are carried over to future situations.

Movement goals:
- Retain and extend successes.
- Continue the struggle by promoting other issues and a paradigm shift.
- Recognize and celebrate success. Build ongoing grassroots organizations and power bases.

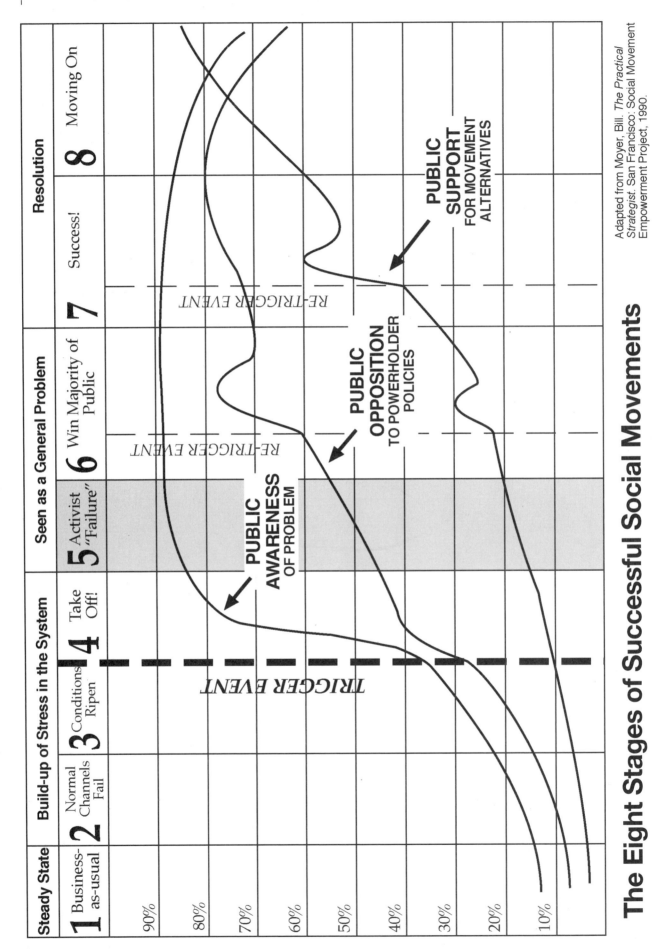

The Eight Stages of Successful Social Movements

Adapted from Moyer, Bill. *The Practical Strategist.* San Francisco: Social Movement Empowerment Project, 1990.

Eight Stages of Social Movement Success *Bill Moyer 1990*

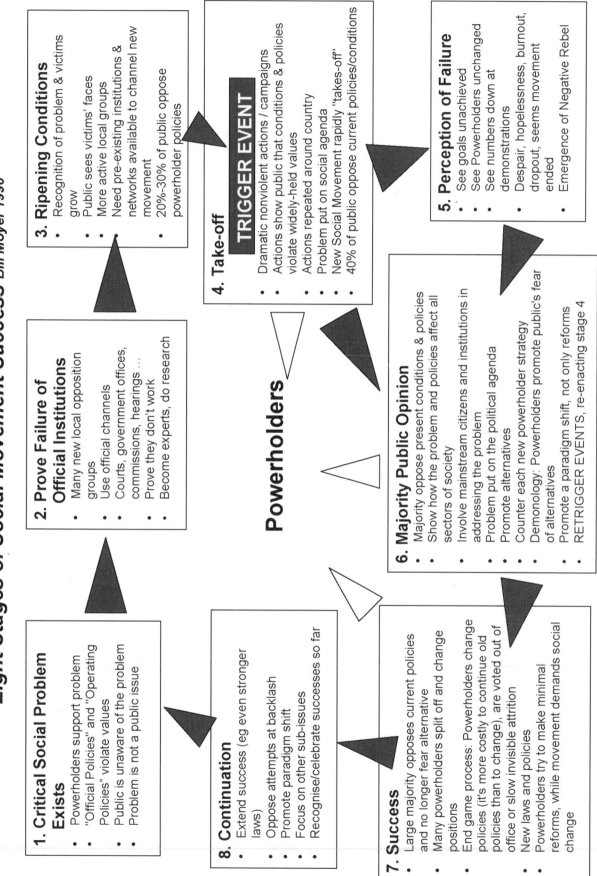

3. Ripening Conditions
- Recognition of problem & victims grow
- Public sees victims' faces
- More active local groups
- Need pre-existing institutions & networks available to channel new movement
- 20%-30% of public oppose powerholder policies

4. Take-off

TRIGGER EVENT
- Dramatic nonviolent actions / campaigns
- Actions show public that conditions & policies violate widely-held values
- Actions repeated around country
- Problem put on social agenda
- New Social Movement rapidly "takes-off"
- 40% of public oppose current policies/conditions

5. Perception of Failure
- See goals unachieved
- See Powerholders unchanged
- See numbers down at demonstrations
- Despair, hopelessness, burnout, dropout, seems movement ended
- Emergence of Negative Rebel

2. Prove Failure of Official Institutions
- Many new local opposition groups
- Use official channels
- Courts, government offices, commissions, hearings ....
- Prove they don't work
- Become experts, do research

Powerholders

6. Majority Public Opinion
- Majority oppose present conditions & policies
- Show how the problem and policies affect all sectors of society
- Involve mainstream citizens and institutions in addressing the problem
- Problem put on the political agenda
- Promote alternatives
- Counter each new powerholder strategy
- Demonology: Powerholders promote public's fear of alternatives
- Promote a paradigm shift, not only reforms
- RETRIGGER EVENTS, re-enacting stage 4

1. Critical Social Problem Exists
- Powerholders support problem
- "Official Policies" and "Operating Policies" violate values
- Public is unaware of the problem
- Problem is not a public issue

8. Continuation
- Extend success (eg even stronger laws)
- Oppose attempts at backlash
- Promote paradigm shift
- Focus on other sub-issues
- Recognise/celebrate successes so far

7. Success
- Large majority opposes current policies and no longer fear alternative
- Many powerholders split off and change positions
- End game process: Powerholders change policies (it's more costly to continue old policies than to change), are voted out of office or slow invisible attrition
- New laws and policies
- Powerholders try to make minimal reforms, while movement demands social change

HOMEWORK

REFLECTIONS ON THE READINGS

Session 10:
Getting Ready

SESSION 10: **Getting Ready**

OBJECTIVES

- To continue to plan a group nonviolent action by developing its key elements and sharing the tasks involved
- To create a role-play of the group's nonviolent activity that the group will enact in the next session

AGENDA

- Welcome [1 min.]
- Opening [5 min.]
- Reflecting on Homework [10 min.]
- Action Rooted in Nonviolent Principles [20 min.]
- The Eight Stages of Successful Social Movements [25 min.]
- Break [10 min.]
- Using The Nonviolent Action Checklist [50 min.]
- Preparing the Action Role-Play [15 min.]
- Conclusion [10 min.]
      Nonviolence Journal
      Nonviolent Action
      Next Session's Reading
      Adding to the Wall of Learning and Growing
      Identifying a Nonviolence Principle
      Closing

READINGS

- Reading #1: Jhon Evaristo Flores, "The Story of Roberto Morales"
- Reading #2: Bill Moyer, "The Eight Stages of Successful Social Movements"

NOTES FOR THE FACILITATOR

SESSION PREPARATION: BEFORE

- Review the entire session in depth. Role-play or practice setting up and facilitating exercises beforehand. Wherever possible, put material into your own words. Feel free to make notes for this purpose on 3x5 cards or in the book next to the written instructions.
- Materials needed: masking tape; (optional) table with candle, compact disk of appropriate music and CD player, extra copies of the NV checklist.

SESSION 10: **Getting Ready**

WELCOME — 1 MIN.

Present in your own words:

Welcome back for our tenth session of the *Engage: Exploring Nonviolent Living* Study Program. In this session, we will focus on creating our nonviolent action and prepare a role-play for this action. By doing this we will try to gain deeper familiarity with nonviolence by experimenting with it in a way that our group is capable of.

OPENING — 5 MIN.

With music playing, share the following:

I'd like to open our tenth session with a passage from Martin Luther King, Jr.

We are now faced with the fact that tomorrow is today.
We are confronted with the fierce urgency of now.
In this unfolding conundrum of life and history
there is such a thing as being too late.
Procrastination is still the thief of time...
We must move past indecision to action...Now let us begin.
Now let us rededicate ourselves to the long and bitter —
and beautiful — struggle for a new world.
This is the calling of the children of God,
and our brothers and sisters wait eagerly for our response.
Shall we say the odds are too great?
Shall we tell them the struggle is too hard?
...Or will there be another message,
of longing, of hope, of solidarity with their yearnings,
of commitment to the cause, whatever the cost?
The choice is ours, and though we might prefer it otherwise
we must choose in this crucial moment in human history.

REFLECTING ON HOMEWORK — 10 MIN.

I again invite you to get together with your Nonviolence Partner to take a few minutes to reflect on your experiences or insights since the last session, as well as to reflect on the readings, journaling, or nonviolent action.

ACTION ROOTED IN NONVIOLENT PRINCIPLES — 20 MIN.

Let's revisit the initial planning we did in Session 9 on the nonviolent action we would like to create.

What did we initially decide?

What ideas about this action have you had since the last session?

NONVIOLENT ACTIVITY GUIDELINES

When engaging in personal, interpersonal, or social-structural nonviolent action:
- Our attitude will be one of openness, friendliness, and respect towards all people we encounter;
- We will use no violence, verbal or physical, towards any person;
- We will protect opponents from insults or attack;
- We will not destroy property;
- We will not bring drugs or alcohol other than for medical purposes;
- We will not run — it creates panic;
- We will not carry weapons;
- We will behave in an exemplary manner; and
- We will not evade the consequences of our actions.

We will act in this spirit because we seek a win-win solution that contributes to a more just and peaceful situation and world. We commit to seek this solution guided by:
- The desire for the well-being of all;
- The awareness of the oneness and interdependence of all beings;
- The wisdom that this unity is strengthened and expressed through diversity and difference;
- The fact that everyone — including those with whom we struggle — has both a piece of the truth and a piece of the un-truth;
- The need to transform Us vs. Them thinking and doing; and
- The choice to transform fear, anger, and despair into empathy, compassion, and creative power.

We commit to take responsibility for our own actions guided by:
- The awareness of the sacredness and woundedness of ourselves and all others;
- Our longing for just and lasting peace;
- Our ability to actively challenge violence and injustice while acknowledging the humanity of those with whom we struggle;
- Our experiments in challenging the threat power or coercive power of violence through the unifying power or cooperative power of active nonviolence; and
- Our ability to transform fear and anger into compassion and empathy.

We pledge to ground our action in the power of nonviolence, including:
- The power to break the cycle of retaliatory violence through unilateral initiatives rooted in connectedness, cooperation, and compassion;
- The power to alert, educate, and mobilize a discontented and determined grassroots population that creates the conditions for change; and
- The power to resist violence and injustice and create a constructive alternative situation and world.

List these on easel paper. If the group did not reach consensus in the previous session on what action they would like to do, ask if anyone has a specific proposal. If there is more than one proposal, hold off on making a final decision until after this next part of this segment.

What nonviolent principles are we trying to employ in this action? To help us think about this question, let's brainstorm some of the nonviolent principles we have explored in this study program.

If necessary, ask participants to review the Nonviolence Guidelines (see sidebar opposite) and reflect on ways they can help shape their nonviolent action.

FREEDOM IN OUR LIFETIME: THE STRUGGLE AGAINST APARTHEID

In 1985, a wave of unrest against apartheid (the system of legalized segregation and racism in place in South Africa since 1948) begins to sweep across the black townships in South Africa. Security forces try to control the unrest via a provocative containment policy that incites dangerous confrontations. Impatient youths and others initiate sporadic violence. Black leaders are routinely harassed and imprisoned.

In the city of Port Elizabeth, Mkhuseli Jack, a charismatic 27-year-old youth leader, understands that violence is no match for the state's awesome arsenal. Jack stresses the primacy of cohesion and coordination, forming street committees and recruiting neighborhood leaders to represent their interests and settle disputes. Nationally, a fledgling umbrella party, the United Democratic Front (UDF), asserts itself through a series of low-key acts of defiance, such as rent boycotts, labor strikes, and school "stay-aways."

Advocating nonviolent action appeals to black parents who are tired of chaos in their neighborhoods. The blacks of Port Elizabeth agree to launch an economic boycott of the city's white-owned businesses. Extending the struggle to the white community is a calculated maneuver designed to sensitize white citizens to the blacks' suffering. Beneath their appeal to conscience, the blacks' underlying message is that businesses cannot operate against a backdrop of societal chaos and instability.

Confronted by this and other resistance in the country, the government declares a state of emergency, the intent of which is to splinter black leadership through arbitrary arrests and curfews. Jack and his compatriots, however, receive an entirely different message: the country is fast becoming ungovernable. Apartheid has been cracked.

Undaunted by government reprisals, the UDF continues to press its demands, particularly for the removal of security forces and the release of jailed African National Congress leader Nelson Mandela. White retailers, whose business districts have become moribund, demand an end to the stalemate. The movement also succeeds in turning world opinion against apartheid, and more sanctions are imposed on South Africa as foreign corporations begin to pull out many investments. In June 1986, the South African government declares a second state of emergency to repress the mass action that has paralyzed the regime.

By 1990, the stand-off between the black majority and the government impels the new prime minister, F. W. de Klerk, to lift the ban on illegal political organizations and free Mandela. In 1994, South Africa's first truly democratic national election elects Mandela to the nation's presidency.

Before moving on, ensure that the group is clear on what their goal is and what action they would like to take.

THE EIGHT STAGES OF SUCCESSFUL SOCIAL MOVEMENTS — 25 MIN.

The Eight Stages of Successful Social Movements are presented in the schematic on page 198 and in the session's readings. Divide the larger group into groups of 2 or 3 depending on how many participants are in the group. Invite each group to spend about 10 minutes discussing the model. Some questions for the participants to discuss in their smaller groups:

- Does the group's action fit into a larger social movement?
- If so, what stage might the movement be in, and how does the group's action contribute?
- If not, what might a movement around the issue they have look like?

Invite the participants back to the larger group and discuss further for about 10 minutes.

BREAK — 10 MIN.

USING THE NONVIOLENT ACTION CHECKLIST — 30 MIN.

Convey the following to the group:

> Now let's develop the different dimensions of our action guided by the checklist on the next page.

If necessary, review the consensus decision-making process. Then ask the group to answer the questions on the checklist found in the nearby sidebar.

Note: Action planning often takes longer than the time allotted here or in the next session. If necessary, encourage the group to stay an additional half-hour or hour at the next session, or plan for an additional

> *Cowardice asks the question, "Is it safe?"*
> *Expediency asks the question, "Is it politic?"*
> *And Vanity comes along and asks the question, "Is it popular?"*
> *But Conscience asks the question "Is it right?"*
>
> *And there comes a time when one must take a position that is neither safe, nor politic, nor popular, but he must do it because Conscience tells him it is right.*
>
> — MARTIN LUTHER KING, JR.

meeting to solidify its action plans. For each of the areas, especially outreach, logistics, and miscellaneous tasks, ask for volunteers (one person or a small committee) to take responsibility for the following task areas. Ask each person and committee to develop an "action plan" for meeting these tasks between the end of this session and the beginning of the next.

THE NONVIOLENT ACTION CHECKLIST

Framework

- What is the strategic goal (i.e., who are we trying to influence, and what do we want them to do)?

- What is the political objective (what is the action or event)?

- How does this event communicate its goals and nonviolent principles before, during, and after the event?

- What will the scenario be? (Including place and time)

- What person or small group will provide overall coordination of the event?

Outreach

- Will the group be trying to work with other groups or communities? If so, who will make the contacts?

- Will the group have a flyer, explaining to the public what it is doing? If so, who will prepare it?

- What publicity will you do? Will you try to reach other people to join you? If so, who will do it?

- What kind of media work will you do? Will you send out a press release ahead of time? Will there be spokespeople during the event, ready to talk to the press? Will they have a series of "talking points"? If so, consider appointing a Media Subcommittee.

- Do we need to contact authorities ahead of time? If so, who will do this?

Logistics and Miscellaneous Tasks

- Will the group need peacekeepers (a group of volunteers who will try to ensure that the event remains nonviolent)?

- Will the group need legal observers (people who will track and support anyone who might get arrested — purposely or by accident)? Who will organize these?

- Will the group need props and other materials? If so, who will make or get them?

- Does the group need to raise money? For what? How much? How will it do this?

- Will the group need a stage? A sound system? A truck to transport materials? If so, consider having a Logistics Subcommittee.

- What about transportation?

- Who will clean up after the event?

PREPARING THE ACTION ROLE-PLAY — 15 MIN.

Ask the group to create a role-play based on the action it has developed. Brainstorm possible rationales for the role-play. If the following ideas aren't mentioned, consider adding them.

> Role-plays allow us to experience some of the emotions that may be present on the day of the action, so that we can be better prepared to deal with them. They also allow us to see possible gaps in our planning, or spark our imaginations, enabling us to see a better way of executing our action.

The group should flesh out the scenario and brainstorm all the possible actors or roles. People should take different roles. Ensure that everyone has a role before the end of the session.

CONCLUSION — 15 MIN.

⊙ Nonviolence Journal

> *Suggested Question:*
> How important for you is the issue around which the group is creating a nonviolent action?

⊙ Nonviolent Action

1) Prepare for next session's role-play by reflecting on the character that you have agreed to play by way of her or his intentions, attitudes, desires, and passions (even if you find yourself opposed to the person's beliefs or actions in real life). If you don't know much about the character, talk to someone who might have a better idea. Reflect on one or two principles of nonviolence that you would like to act out, or oppose, in the role-play.

2) Work on the "action plan" for the item that you signed up for in preparing for the Group Action.

⊙ Next Session's Reading

Please read the material at the end of the next session.

⊙ Adding to the Wall of Learning and Growing

Please add your insights, learnings, or questions to the Wall.

⊙ Closing

Ask people to form a circle. Begin by presenting the following in your own words. Feel free to change the words that you will say to each other in this closing if other words seem more appropriate to your group.

> A significant dimension of nonviolence is acknowledging our own power and the power of others that is released when we act nonviolently.

In this exercise I invite us to go around the circle, one by one, and bow to each other in reverence and say "as you are powerful, so am I." I will begin by stepping into the circle, facing the person on my right, bowing, and saying, "as you are powerful, so am I." That person will then bow to me in return and say the same to me. Then I will go on to the next person in the circle.

When I am at the third person, the first person I bowed to will follow me in bowing to each of you in the circle, and so on until we have all gone around the circle and bowed to each other.

As you move to the fourth person, the first person is in front of the third person, and so forth. Continue around the circle until everyone has participated.

KEY ORGANIZATIONS

School of Americas Watch, PO Box 4566, Washington, DC 20017; (202) 234-3440; *info@soaw.org, www.soaw.org.* SOA Watch is an independent organization that seeks to close the U.S. Army School of the Americas, under whatever name it is called, through vigils and fasts, demonstrations and nonviolent protest, as well as media and legislative work.

War Resisters League (WRL), 339 Lafayette Street, New York, NY 10012; (212) 228-0450; *wrl@warresisters.org, www.warresisters.org.* WRL advocates Gandhian nonviolence as the method for creating a democratic society free of war, racism, sexism, and human exploitation through education and action.

Women's International League for Peace and Freedom (WILPF), 1213 Race Street, Philadelphia, PA 19107-1691; (215) 563 7110; *www.wilpf.org.* WILPF was founded in 1915 during World War I, with Jane Addams as its first president. WILPF works to achieve through peaceful means world disarmament, full rights for women, racial and economic justice, an end to all forms of violence, and to establish those political, social, and psychological conditions which can assure peace, freedom, and justice for all.

HOMEWORK

NONVIOLENCE JOURNAL

Suggested Question:

How important for you is the issue around which the group is creating a nonviolent action?

HOMEWORK

NONVIOLENT ACTION

1) Prepare for next session's role-play by reflecting on the character that you have agreed to play by way of her or his intentions, attitudes, desires, and passions (even if you find yourself opposed to the person's beliefs or actions in real life). If you don't know much about the character, talk to someone who might have a better idea. Reflect on one or two principles of nonviolence that you would like to act out, or oppose, in the role-play.

2) Work on the "action plan" for the item that you signed up for in preparing for the Group Action.

The Dynamics of Nonviolent Action
by Bob Irwin and Gordon Faison

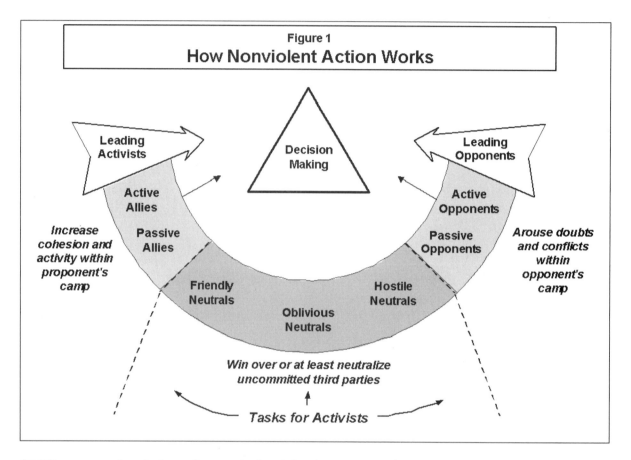

Figure 1
How Nonviolent Action Works

Decision Making

Leading Activists

Active Allies

Passive Allies

Increase cohesion and activity within proponent's camp

Friendly Neutrals

Oblivious Neutrals

Hostile Neutrals

Leading Opponents

Active Opponents

Passive Opponents

Arouse doubts and conflicts within opponent's camp

Win over or at least neutralize uncommitted third parties

Tasks for Activists

The conventional view of power is that it is something some people have and others don't. Power resides in soldiers, authority, ownership of wealth, and institutions. The nonviolent theory of power is essentially different: rather than seeing power as something possessed, it argues that power is a dynamic social relation. Power depends on continuing obedience. When people refuse to obey rulers, the rulers' power begins to crumble. This basic truth is in a sense obvious, yet it took the dramatic historical episodes of Gandhi's civil disobedience campaigns to begin to establish a new model of power. In routine social life this truth is obscured, but events like the overthrow of the former Shah of Iran or the oppressive regime in Bolivia in 1978 cannot be understood without it.

From the standpoint of the conventional view of power, heavily armed rulers hold all the cards. They can arrest protesters or, in more extreme instances, have them shot. But reality is more complex than that. Instead of merely two social actors being involved — rulers and opposition — a whole range of intermediary forces are potentially decisive. What if new protesters keep coming back? What if influential social groups or individuals begin to condemn acts of brutality? What if troops, or police, or their officers decide to disobey orders? The 1944 overthrows of dictators in both Guatemala and El Salvador (described by George Lakey in *Strategy for a Living Revolution*), and the overthrows of repressive regimes in Iran (1978-1979) and Bolivia (1978) show that such events are historically possible. [The successful use of nonviolent action to bring down repressive regimes in Poland, throughout Eastern Europe, and in the Philippines all occurred subsequent to the original writing of this essay in 1978; another cluster of regime changes occurred from 2000 onward in Serbia and several former Soviet republics.]

Sometimes nonviolent action is improvised in the heat of a crisis; other times it is carefully planned. Certain dynamics remain the same in either case. For help in understanding these dynamics, Gene Sharp's later chapter titles in *The Politics of Nonviolent Action* provide a convenient outline: laying the groundwork for nonviolent action; challenge brings repression; solidarity and discipline to fight repression; "political jujitsu"; and ways that success may be achieved.

Nonviolence is not magic; it is a way of mobilizing the strength we have for maximum effectiveness.

In a planned nonviolent campaign, laying the groundwork is fundamentally important. This means defining goals and objectives, choosing strategy and tactics, making contingency plans, training, etc. Nonviolence is not magic; it is a way of mobilizing the strength we have for maximum effectiveness.

Whether nonviolent action starts as a popular initiative to which authorities then react, or is an improvised public response to an event, the outline above shows that the initial "action and reaction" are only the beginning. Take the case of a nuclear power plant site occupation as an example. Along with the leading actors who clash with each other, there are also anti-nuclear activists who are not committing civil disobedience but playing active support roles; potential participants who didn't feel enough urgency or sense of being needed to take part in the particular action; people who would like to see an end to nuclear power but don't plan to do anything about it; people oblivious to the issue; people hostile to "environmentalists who delay needed progress;" people who say "lawbreakers should be punished," but will limit themselves to griping; on down to utility

executives, the governor's staff, bank presidents, etc. There are also police and perhaps National Guardspeople whose job it is to counter the demonstrators, but whose personal attitudes may lie anywhere on the spectrum. Figure 1 shows how activists seek to influence people with various viewpoints along this spectrum.

The actions of the main social actors potentially affect all these people. The outbreak of conflict draws attention to the issue. In an important respect the two sides are not just fighting each other directly, but also competing with each other for the allegiance and support of third parties or "the general public."

To gain their desired result, agents of repression must make the activists lose their solidarity and abandon their goals. If they maintain solidarity and discipline, repression becomes ineffective. But solidarity alone does not bring success. That may come through a kind of "political jujitsu," in which the repressive efforts themselves tend to shift the balance of power toward the nonviolent activists. People on the side of the activists increase their level of involvement, while those allied with the oppressive power may reduce their support or switch sides. Shifts of attitude are important as well as shifts of behavior, because both sides adjust their actions according to how they gauge their support.

Nonviolent action is not dependent on the opponent's being repressive or making mistakes. It is not stymied when the opponent is moderate and conciliatory. Most of the methods mobilize political strength regardless of the opponent's response.

This brings us to the question of how nonviolent action may attain its goals. Three main ways have been identified: conversion, accommodation, and nonviolent coercion. Conversion means that the opponent has a change of heart or mind and comes to agree with and work toward the activists' goal. At the top of the social structure, this is fairly unlikely, but significant instances may occur: for example, Daniel Ellsberg, who released the Pentagon Papers after being converted to opposition to the Vietnam War; Bob Aldridge, who left his job as chief missile designer for the Trident submarine in order to speak out against the growing threat of nuclear catastrophe.

At the other extreme is nonviolent coercion, where the activists have it directly in their power to frustrate the opponent's will. One example is the refusal by all workers to work on a construction project which a union has declared unecological (Australia's "green bans"); another was the invention of the

"search and avoid" missions by GIs in Vietnam who did not want to risk their lives in an unpopular war. Most commonly the outcome is determined by an intermediate process.

Accommodation means that the opponents give in, partly or completely, not because they have changed their minds, and not because they are completely powerless, but because it seems a lesser evil than any other alternative. It may be because continuing the struggle at that point would probably mean further erosion of support. Concessions may also be granted to halt the consciousness-raising process of struggle that would lead people to discover how much power they really have.

SESSION 11: READING 2

"Before a Drop of Blood Was Shed"
by Jonathan Schell

John Adams, who appointed the committee that wrote the Declaration of Independence, served as the first vice president and second president of the United States, and was called "the colossus of independence" by Thomas Jefferson, penned some reflections late in his life that form a perfect complement to those of Washington, Paine, and Burke. If these three had defined negatively what could not decide the outcome of the revolution—namely, force—Adams defined positively what it was that did decide it: the combination of noncooperation and a constructive program now familiar to us.

Adams, in his late seventies, lacked the time and strength, he said, to write a history of the revolution; and so he offered his reflections only in letters to friends. He was prompted to write by the news that one Major General Wilkinson was penning a "history of the revolution," which was to begin with the battle of Bunker Hill, in 1775. Wilkinson,

Adams wrote, would "confine himself to military transactions, with a reference to very few of the civil."

Such an account, Adams protested, would falsify history. "A history of the war of the United States is a very different thing," he claimed, "from a history of the first American Revolution." Not only was Wilkinson wrong to concentrate on military affairs; he had located the revolution in the wrong historical period. The revolution, Adams claimed, was over before the war began: General Wilkinson may have written the military history of the war that followed the Revolution; that was an effect of it, and was supported by the American citizens in defense of it against an invasion of it by the government of Great Britain and Ireland, and all her allies ... but this will by no means be a history of the American Revolution. The revolution was in the minds of the people, and in the union of the colonies, both of which were accomplished before hostilities commenced.

To his correspondent, Thomas Jefferson, a former political antagonist, he made the point emphatically: "As to the history of the revolution, my ideas may be peculiar, perhaps singular. What do we mean by the revolution? The war? That was no part of the revolution; it was only an effect and consequence of it. The revolution was in the minds of the people, and this was effected from 1760 to 1775, in the course of fifteen years, before a drop of blood was shed at Lexington."

Adams described an event that for him was a true turning point in the revolution. The English crown had decided to pay the judges of the Massachusetts Supreme Court directly. The colonists were indignant, and, at the suggestion of John Adams, voted to impeach the judges in the Massachusetts House of Representatives. The crown ignored the impeachment. Then came the decisive step. Jurors unanimously refused to serve under the embattled judges. Adams, who likes to use military metaphors to describe great deeds of peaceful noncooperation, remarks, "The cool, calm, sedate intrepidity with which these honest freeholders went through this fiery trial filled my eyes and my heart. That was the revolution—the decisive blow against England: In one word, the royal government was, that moment, laid prostrate in the dust, and has never since revived in substance, though a dark shadow of the hobgoblin haunts me at times to this day."

Adams's gallery of heroes are all civilians, his battles nonviolent ones. When he learns that Congress has appointed a national painter, he recommends paintings, to be executed in the grand style, of scenes of protest—a painting, for example, of Samuel Adams, his cousin and a sparkplug of the revolution, arguing with Lieutenant Governor Hutchinson against standing armies. "It will be as difficult," he remarks lightly, "to do justice as to paint an Apollo; and the transaction deserves to be painted as much as the surrender of Burgoyne. Whether any artist will ever attempt it, I know not."

Acts of noncooperation were one indispensable ingredient of what Adams calls "the real American revolution"; acts of association were another. At their center were the Committees of Correspondence, through which, beginning in the mid-1760s, the revolutionaries in the colonies mutually fostered and coordinated their activities. "What an engine!" Adams wrote of the Committees. "France imitated it, and produced a revolution. England and Scotland were upon the point of imitating it, in order to produce another revolution, and all Europe was inclined to imitate it for the same revolutionary purposes. The history of the world for the last thirty years is a sufficient commentary upon it. That history to convince all mankind that committees of secret correspondence are dangerous machines." Here, plainly, is another predecessor of the hierarchies parallels.

The revolution, Adams claimed, was over before the war began.

The decisive revolution, according to Adams, was thus the process by which ordinary people withdrew cooperation from the British government and then, well before even the Declaration of Independence, set up their own governments in all the colonies. The war that followed was the military defense of these already-existing governments against an attack by what was now a foreign power seeking to force the new country back into its empire. In his view, indeed, independence was nothing that could be won from the British; it had to be forged by the Americans. "Let me ask you, Mr. Rush," he wrote to his friend Richard Rush in April of 1815, in phrases that startlingly resemble Gandhi's later denial that Indian independence could be "given" her by England, "Is the sovereignty of this nation a gift? a grant? a concession? a conveyance? or a release and acquittance from Great Britain? Pause here and think. No! The people, in 1774, by the right which nature and nature's God had given them, confiding in original right, assumed powers of sovereignty. In 1775, they assumed greater power. In July 4th, 1776, they assumed absolute unlimited sovereignty in relation to other nations, in all cases whatsoever; no longer acknowledging any authority over them but that of God almighty, and the laws of nature and of nations."

In a recent description of the process Adams described, the historian Gordon Wood has written, "The royal governors stood helpless as they watched para-governments grown up around them, a rapid piecing together from the bottom up of a hierarchy of committees and congresses that reached from the counties and towns through the provincial conventions of the Continental Congress." On May 15, 1776, Adams notes, the Continental Congress declared that "every kind of authority under the . . . Crown should be totally suppressed," and authorized the states to found government sufficient to the exigencies of their affairs." "For if, Wood comments, "as Jefferson and others agreed, the formation of new governments was the whole object of the Revolution, then the May resolution authorizing the drafting of new constitutions was the most important act of the Continental Congress in its history. There in the May 15 resolution was the real

declaration of independence, from which the measures of early July could be but derivations." James Duane, a delegate to the first congress, called this process "a Machine for the fabrication of Independence." Adams responded, "It was independence itself."

It is interesting to observe that another very notable authority on American political history also located the foundation of the Republic before July 4, 1776. "The Union is much older than the Constitution," Abraham Lincoln said in his First Inaugural. "It was formed in fact by the Articles of Association of 1774."

If we accept Adams's view, then both the overthrow of the old regime, laid in the dust (as Adams said) through a series of acts of noncooperation, and the foundation of the new one, accomplished the moment the Americans set up governments to govern themselves, were, like the overthrow and the foundation in 1688-89, nonviolent events, and the war that followed could be seen as a war of self-defense. In that war, Adams wrote to Rush, "Heaven decided in our favor; and Britain was forced not to give, grant, concede, or release our independence, but to acknowledge it, in terms as clear as our language afforded, and under seal and under oath."

HOMEWORK

REFLECTIONS ON THE READINGS

Session 11:
Final Preparation

SESSION 11: **Final Preparation**

OBJECTIVES
- To perform and evaluate the group's nonviolent action role-play
- To practice and integrate nonviolent principles
- To review final plans and the details of the group's upcoming nonviolent action

AGENDA
- Welcome [1 min.]
- Opening [5 min.]
- Reflecting on Homework [10 min.]
- Final Planning for Group Nonviolent Action [45 min.]
- Break [10 min.]
- Group Nonviolent Action Role-Play [60 min.]
- Conclusion [15 min.]
    Nonviolence Journal
    Nonviolent Action
    Next Session's Reading
    Adding to the Wall of Learning and Growing
    Closing

READINGS
- Reading #1: Bob Irwin and Gordon Faison, "The Dynamics of Nonviolent Action"
- Reading #2: Jonathan Schell, "Before a Drop of Blood Was Shed"

NOTES FOR THE FACILITATOR

SESSION PREPARATION: BEFORE
- Review the entire session in depth. Role-play or practice setting up and facilitating the role-play beforehand. Wherever possible, put material into your own words. Feel free to make notes for this purpose on 3x5 cards or in the book next to the written instructions.
- Materials needed: masking tape or nametags for the role-play.
- Consider proposing that the group share a potluck meal before or after the last session.
- Write out on easel paper:
    - The debrief questions for the role-play (optional).

PREPARATION: ON THE DAY OF THE SESSION
- Play close attention to time in this session. You will need an hour for the role-play. Save about 5 minutes at the end for a discussion of the potluck, if that is something you want to do.

SESSION 11: **Final Preparation**

WELCOME — 1 MIN.

Welcome back for our eleventh session of the *Engage: Exploring Nonviolent Living* Study Program. In this session, we will review our action and do any last-minute planning and we will carry out a role-play of our nonviolent action (our political objective). As part of this we will examine the nonviolent principles we are putting into action.

If you would like to do the potluck, consider announcing the idea here, and finalizing it at the end.

OPENING — 5 MIN.

Feel free to use this opening or any other that you find inspirational:

To open our session, I'd like to read a prayer that Cesar Chavez of the United Farm Workers used to say:

Show me the suffering of the most miserable;
　　So I will know my people's plight.
Free me to pray for others;
　　For You are present in every person.
Help me take responsibility for my own life;
　　So that I can be free at last.
Grant me courage to serve others;
　　For in service there is true life.
Give me honesty and patience;
　　So that the Spirit will be alive among us.
Let the Spirit flourish and grow;
　　So that we will never tire of the struggle.
Let us remember those who have died for justice;
For they have given us life.
Help us love even those who hate us,
　　So we can change the world.

REFLECTING ON HOMEWORK — 10 MIN.

I again invite you to get together with your Nonviolence Partner to take a few minutes to reflect on your experiences or insights since the last session, as well as to reflect on the readings, journaling, or nonviolent action.

FINAL PLANNING FOR GROUP ACTIVITY — 45 MIN.

Share the following in your own words:

I would like to ask each individual or committee that was working on specific aspects of our upcoming nonviolent action (e.g., media, logistics) to present their planning work to the large group.

The group should deal with any issues that have arisen and then conclude its planning. If more time is needed, you can plan for an additional session, or plan outside the sessions. It is strongly recommended that you leave enough time in the session to fully carry out the role-play.

PERFORMING THE ACTION ROLE-PLAY — 60 MIN.

Convey the following:

We began to develop our action role-play in Session 10. Now let's finalize and carry out our role-play.

Ask the participants to write their role or character on a name tag and then put it on.

Think about your character's motivation. Try your best to go deeply into this motivation. I want to thank you ahead of time for being willing to assume roles that may be difficult to play!

While we're getting ready, please call to mind the nonviolent principles you have thought about since the last session. Think about how you might try to bring these into the scenario — or how you might try to thwart them.

Let's begin the role-play!

After a few minutes freeze the role-play. Then invite each person, while staying in role, to practice (or try to thwart) one of the nonviolence principles.

Resume the role-play. Let it continue for 5-10 minutes. Finally, call it to a close, applauding the group's effort. Ask the players to remain in their roles.

Debrief the role-players one at a time in the following manner, paying attention to time (if you have 10 actors, 3 minutes with each actor will be 30 minutes):

Set up three chairs facing the rest of the participants.

Invite a role-player to sit down in one of the chairs on the end. Sit next to the role-player in the middle.

Ask the role-player to stay in role. Ask the following questions:
- How did it feel to be in the situation you were in?
- How did it go?
- Do you have anything to say to any of the other characters?

Then ask the role-player if she or he is ready to let go of the role.

When she or he is, ask them to place their name badge on the chair where they were sitting and invite them to sit in the chair on the other side of you.

Ask them who they are now (they should say their own name). Ask the "real person" the following:

- How do you feel?
- What nonviolent principle(s) did you try to practice?
- How did it go, practicing that principle?
- Did anything shift in the process?
- Are there any other things you could have tried?
- Recalling your normal "script" of how you respond to conflict or violence (avoidance, accommodation, or counter-violence), how did your actions in the role-play differ, if they did?

Then ask the participant if she or he is ready to join the audience. If they are not yet ready, ask them what else they would like to say. Invite them to take a seat with the rest of the participants.

Debrief the other actors in the same way. After all the role-players have done this, debrief in the large group with the following questions:

- What did you learn in the role-play?
- Do we want to make any adjustments to our action based on what we've learned?

Thank everyone and lead another round of applause.

Sometimes deep emotions are expressed during role-plays. You may want to check in with the actors at the end of the role-play or at the end of the entire exercise to see if people need to let out their emotions. This can be done several ways. You can ask them to shake out body parts one at a time. You can have each person rub down the emotions off the different parts of her or his own body.

ON BEING COMMUNITY

Community. Somewhere, there are people to whom we can speak with passion without having the words catch in our throats. Somewhere a circle of hands will open to receive us, eyes will light up as we enter, voices will celebrate with us whenever we come into our own power. Community means strength that joins our strength to do the work that needs to be done. Arms to hold us when we falter. A circle of healing. A circle of friends. Someplace where we can be free.

— *Starhawk*

"LOVING THE POLICE OUT OF THE INTERSECTION"

In April 2000 eight members of the El Grupo Affinity Group traveled to Washington, D.C., to participate in economic justice movement demonstrations at the World Bank/International Monetary Fund meetings. This was the next major demonstration after the anti-globalization demonstrations at the World Trade Organization meeting held in Seattle in November-December 1999.

"El Grupo" ("The Group" in Spanish) was composed of people who had been at the events in Seattle who wanted to learn more about nonviolence. They had attended a *From Violence to Wholeness* (the precursor to *Engage*) training and this learning experience led them to form a support group or affinity group — that is, a group of people drawn together by shared affinity. El Grupo Affinity Group was born.

El Grupo then went through the *From Violence to Wholeness* Study Program. Group member Leila Salazar said, "Going through the FVTW process not only educated me more about the history of nonviolent struggles, but it also inspired me to use nonviolence as a method to struggle for social justice. It gave me examples of how nonviolence was used and tools for using it." The process also helped to strengthen the relationship between the members of the group. They really felt they could trust each other in the face of any challenging situation they might meet in Washington.

The demonstration scenario included having affinity groups occupy intersections near the building where the meetings were taking place. El Grupo was one of many affinity groups occupying a particular intersection. They sat in the intersection for hours. Finally, a group of police officers arrived. They began to push and shove the protesters. Another group of protesters (who were not committed to nonviolence or the specific nonviolence guidelines of the demonstration) started throwing trash at the police officers, who in turn became more agitated. They hit some protesters and broke one woman's nose. Other motorcycle police officers drove their bikes into the midst of the people sitting in the intersection.

The members of El Grupo sat in the intersection and started "toning": singing different vocal tones for an extended period of time. This began to change the atmosphere. Seeing El Grupo and others sitting in a non-threatening way and offering this soothing music that was non-confrontational and non-combative, the police found themselves relaxing. The contrast between their actions — and that of the many protesters sitting and "toning" in the street — led them to cool down. Finally, a police sergeant ordered the police out of the intersection and they left it entirely to the protesters.

As El Grupo member Bryan Neuberg later put it, "We loved the police out of the intersection."

CONCLUSION — 15 MIN.

⊙ **Nonviolence Journal**

Suggested Questions:
- How am I preparing spiritually (or how am I grounding myself and getting in touch with my deepest self) for our upcoming group nonviolent action?
- What nonviolent principles will I embody in the group nonviolent action?

⊙ **Nonviolent Action**

After the group nonviolent action there will be one more session. Think about what you may want to do as a follow-up to the twelve sessions. Please bring to the last session information about possible local or national movements and organizations to share with the group to help it decide what it might want to do next.

⊙ **Next Session's Reading**

Read the material located at the end of this session.

⊙ **Adding to the Wall of Learning and Growing**

Please add your insights, learnings, or questions to the "wall."

⊙ **Potluck Option**

If the group wants this option, decide when and where, and who will bring what.

⊙ **Closing**

Ask participants to take turns reading the Nonviolent Activity Guidelines aloud. You could invite the participants to read them aloud together as a group as a sign of their commitment to the Guidelines.

NONVIOLENT ACTIVITY GUIDELINES

When engaging in personal, interpersonal, or social-structural nonviolent action:
- Our attitude will be one of openness, friendliness, and respect towards all people we encounter;
- We will use no violence, verbal or physical, towards any person;
- We will protect opponents from insults or attack;
- We will not destroy property;
- We will not bring drugs or alcohol other than for medical purposes;
- We will not run — it creates panic;
- We will not carry weapons;
- We will behave in an exemplary manner; and
- We will not evade the consequences of our actions.

We will act in this spirit because we seek a win-win solution that contributes to a more just and peaceful situation and world. We commit to seek this solution guided by:
- The desire for the well-being of all;
- The awareness of the oneness and interdependence of all beings;
- The wisdom that this unity is strengthened and expressed through diversity and difference;
- The fact that everyone — including those with whom we struggle — has both a piece of the truth and a piece of the un-truth;
- The need to transform Us vs. Them thinking and doing; and
- The choice to transform fear, anger, and despair into empathy, compassion, and creative power.

We commit to take responsibility for our own actions guided by:

- The awareness of the sacredness and woundedness of ourselves and all others;
- Our truest self's longing for just and lasting peace;
- Our ability to actively challenge violence and injustice while acknowledging the humanity of those with whom we struggle;
- Our experiments in challenging the threat power or coercive power of violence through the unifying power or cooperative power of active nonviolence; and
- Our ability to transform fear and anger into compassion and empathy.

We pledge to ground our action in the power of nonviolence, including:

- The power to break the cycle of retaliatory violence through unilateral initiatives rooted in connectedness, cooperation, and compassion;
- The power to alert, educate, and mobilize a discontented and determined grassroots population that creates the conditions for change; and
- The power to resist violence and injustice and create a constructive alternative situation and world.

KEY ORGANIZATIONS

Global Peace Services, GPS/USA, P.O. Box 27922, Washington, DC 20038; (202) 216-9886; *john_eriksson@compuserve.com*. Movement to create a professional peace service by promoting education and skills-training for men and women based on a philosophy of active nonviolence.

Human Kindness Foundation, P.O. Box 61619, Durham, NC 27715; (919) 304-2220; *www.humankindness.org*. Besides its internationally respected Prison-Ashram Project, the Foundation sponsors a spiritual community and visitor's center called Kindness House.

Ruckus Society, 369 15th Street, Oakland, CA 94612; (510) 763-7078; *info@ruckus.org*; *www.ruckus.org*. The Ruckus Society provides environmental, human rights, and social justice organizers with the tools, training, and support needed to achieve their goals.

HOMEWORK

NONVIOLENCE JOURNAL

Suggested Questions:

- How am I preparing spiritually for our upcoming group nonviolent action?
- What nonviolent principles will I embody in the group nonviolent action?

HOMEWORK

NONVIOLENT ACTION

After the group nonviolent action there will be one more session. Think about what you may want to do as a follow-up to the ten sessions. Please bring to the last session information about possible local or national movements and organizations to share with the group to help it decide what it might want to do next.

The Story of Vedran Smailovic
by Robert Fulghum

It is the year 2050. In a large Eastern European city — one that has survived the vicissitudes of more than a thousand years of human activity — in an open square in the city center there is a rather odd civic monument. A bronze statue.

Not a solder or a politician.

Not a general on a horse or a king on a throne.

Instead, the figure of a somewhat common man, sitting in a chair.

Playing his cello.

Around the pedestal on which the statue sits, there are bouquets of flowers.

If you count, you will always find 22 flowers in each bunch.

The cellist is a national hero.

If you ask to hear the story of this statue, you will be told of a time of civil war in this city. Demagogues lit bonfires of hatred between citizens who belonged to different religions and ethnic groups. Everyone became an enemy of somebody else. None was exempt or safe. Men, women, children, babies, grandparents — old and young — strong and weak — partisan and innocent — all, all were victims in the end. Many were maimed. Many were killed. Those who did not die lived like animals in the ruins of the city.

Except one man. A musician. A cellist. He came to a certain street corner every day. Dressed in formal black evening clothes, sitting in a fire-charred chair, he played his cello. Knowing he might be shot or beaten, still he played. Day after day he came. To play the most beautiful music he knew.

For day after day after day. For twenty-two days.

His music was stronger than hate. His courage, stronger than fear.

And in time, other musicians were captured by his spirit, and they took their places in the street beside him. These acts of courage were contagious. Anyone who could play an instrument or sing found a place at a street intersection somewhere in the city and made music.

In time the fighting stopped.

The music and the city and the people lived on.

A nice fable. A lovely story. Something adults might make up to inspire children. A tale of the kind found in tourist guidebooks explaining and embellishing the myths behind civic statuary. A place to have your picture taken.

Is there any truth in such a parable other than the implied acknowledgement of the sentimentality of mythmaking? The real world does not work this way. We all know that. Cellists seldom become civic heroes — music doesn't affect wars.

Vedran Smailovic does not agree.

In the *New York Times Magazine*, July 1992, his photograph appeared.

Middle-aged, longish hair, great bushy moustache. He is dressed in formal evening clothes. Sitting in a cafe chair in the middle of the street. In front of a bakery where mortar fire struck a breadline in late May, killing 22 people. He is playing his cello. As a member of the Sarajevo Opera Orchestra, there is little he can do about hate and war — it has been going on in Sarajevo for centuries. Even so, every day for twenty-two days, he has braved sniper and artillery fire to play Albinoni's profoundly moving Adagio in G Minor.

I wonder if he chose this piece of music knowing it was constructed from a manuscript fragment found in the ruins of Dresden after the Second World War? The music survived the firebombing. Perhaps that is why he played it there in the scarred street in Sarajevo, where people died waiting in line for bread. Something must triumph over horror.

Is this man crazy? Maybe. Is his gesture futile? Yes, in a conventional sense, yes, of course. But what can a cellist do? What madness to go out alone in the streets and address the world with a wooden box and a hair-strung bow. What can a cellist do?

All he knows how to do. Speaking softly with his cello, one note at a time, like the Pied Piper of Hamelin, calling out the rats that infest the human spirit.

Vedran Smailovic is a real person.

What he did is true.

Neither the breadline nor the mortar shell nor the music is fiction.

For all the fairy tales, these acts do take place in the world in which we live.

Sometimes history knocks at the most ordinary door to see if anyone is at home.

Sometimes someone is.

Most everyone in Sarajevo knows now what a cellist can do — for the place where Vedran played has become an informal shrine, a place of honor. Croats, Serbs, Muslims, Christians alike — they all know his name and face.

They place flowers where he played. Commemorating the hope that must never die — that someday, somehow, the best of humanity shall overcome the worst, not through unexpected miracles but through the expected acts of the many.

Sarajevo is not the only place where Vedran Smailovic is known. An artist in Seattle, Washington, saw his picture and read his story. Her name is Beliz Brother. Real person — real name. What could an artist do?

She organized 22 cellists to play in 22 public places in Seattle for 22 days, and on the final day, all 22 played together in one place in front of a store window displaying burnt-out bread pans, twenty-two loaves of bread and twenty-two roses.

People came. Newspaper reporters and television cameras were there. The story and the pictures were fed into the news networks of the world. And passed back to Vedran Smailovic that he might know his music had been heard and passed on. Others have begun to play in many cities. In Washington, D.C., twenty-two cellists played the day our new president was sworn into office. Who knows who might hear? Who knows what might happen?

Millions of people saw Vedran's story in the *New York Times*. Millions have seen and heard the continuing story picked up by the media.

Now you, too, know.

Tell it to someone. This is urgent news. Keep it alive in the world.

As for the end of the story, who among us shall insist the rest of the story cannot come true? Who shall say the monument in the park in Sarajevo will never come to pass? The cynic who lives in a dark hole in my most secret mind says one cellist cannot stop a war, and music can ultimately be only a dirge played over the unimaginable.

But somewhere in my soul I know otherwise.

Listen.

Never, ever, regret or apologize for believing that when one man or one woman decides to risk addressing the world with truth, the world may stop what it is doing and hear.

There is too much evidence to the contrary.

When we cease believing this, the music will surely stop.

The myth of the impossible dream is more powerful than all the facts of history. In my imagination, I lay flowers at the statue memorializing Vedran Smailovic — a monument that has not yet been built, but may be.

Meanwhile, a cellist plays in the streets of Sarajevo.

> *Never, ever, regret or apologize for believing that when one man or one woman decides to risk addressing the world with truth, the world may stop what it is doing and hear. There is too much evidence to the contrary.*

SESSION 12: READING 2

Circles of Hope

Adapted from Bill Cane's "Universal Church: Circles of Faith, Circles of Hope"

The call to live a spirited life is not a call to self-satisfaction or self-complacency, but to self-transcendence. We are constantly being called out of our present existence, to form circles that do not yet exist.

Some years ago, I had a dream. I was standing alone in a small clearing amid trees and crags and gray boulders when I suddenly saw a large opening in the rocky hillside facing me. The wall of the opening was made of clear glass, as were the doors. Through the glass I could see a cavernous room with a number of people standing around talking excitedly to each other. Above the entrance, in red letters that could have been from San Francisco's Chinatown, hung a sign which said: "THE CHURCH OF THE TAI CHI."

A woman inside was beckoning to me through the glass doors. I did not recognize her, and looked around to see if perhaps she was waving to someone else, but no one else was there. I pointed to myself and motioned, "Me?" She nodded reassuringly, and again invited me in with a wave of her hand. I entered the group and felt immediately at home. At the time, I did not know the meaning of the words "tai chi," and I had no idea what the dream meant. I even took a course in tai chi movement at a local college to see if the course would enlighten me, but it did not.

Years later, I realized that the dream had been introducing me to a different sort of "church." Tai chi literally means "universal wholeness." ... The original meaning of the word "church" (*ekklesia* for the Christians and *kahal* for the Jews) was neither a building for worship nor a weekly gathering. It was a coming together of people who were being called out of slavery to a new life of freedom. They were asked to believe in a dream, in a story that had not yet happened and seemed at the time to have not even the slightest chance of becoming history! They dedicated their lives to making this new story happen, and this was their faith.

The words *kahal* and *ekklesia*, synagogue and church, originally meant "people called out" —people called to leave the ordinary existence around them and enter a new life. Following Moses or Jesus was no ordinary life. It meant leaving security behind and becoming part of shaky and radical movements. But these movements promised an abundance of spirit and life in the future . . . .

For [theologian] Eugene Rosenstock-Huessy, entering a new existence that did not yet exist meant turning his back on the prevailing institutions of his society. As a young soldier returning to Germany from World War I, he was offered a position in the government, a job as head of a major religious publishing house, and a chair at the university. He agonized over the decision he had to make and then, unexpectedly, he turned down all three offers! It was years before Hitler would come to power, yet Rosenstock already recognized the smell of death in the society . . . .

Only in retrospect did he fully realize what he had done. He later considered his refusal to enter these institutions his *metanoia*, his radical change of mind and heart. Turning his back on the major institutions of the society was for him the beginning of a new life in the spirit. "No social space or field exists outside the powers that be and the existing institutions are all that there is at the moment of one's metanoia, of one's giving up dead works."

"The words make no sense," he later wrote, "the atmosphere is stifled. One chokes. One has no choice but to leave. But one does not know what is going to happen, one has no blueprint for action. The 'decision' literally means . . . being cut off from one's own routines in a paid and honored position. And the trust that this sub-zero situation is bound to create new ways of life is our faith.

"I probably did not advance much in personal virtue by this about-face toward the future, away from any visible institution. I did not become a saint. All I received was life. From then on, I did not have to say anything which did not originate in my heart."

Institutions are good at preserving and passing on the steps humanity has already taken. But they cannot create new life. They cannot lead people into a different future. The Post Office preserves our right to communicate beyond national boundaries, which was originally a revolutionary step. The Post Office preserves that possibility for us, but if you try to get the Post Office to take any radical new steps, you will quickly find that such a massive and established bureaucracy will not easily budge.

People who move beyond the ordinary consciousness and conscience of religious institutions face very much the same problem. They can draw on the words and the symbols for support on their journeys. But they must not expect the institutions to create new life. The community that will support them can only be found along the way, as they themselves take steps into an unknown future.

The traditional spiritual symbols are valid . . . . We must acknowledge our illusions and lies and addictions. We must become part of the people if we are to be saved. We must live by faith and hope and love. We must, somewhere along the way, die to the world that systematically exploits the earth and its creatures. To be saved we must leave deadening power structures and be born again into a new community of life and hope.

People who have moved out of their ordinary existence and committed themselves to critical but shaky enterprises are part of a community still in the making. That community is being formed not around symbols or rituals, but around the life and death issues that the symbols have always

pointed to. Symbols can easily be made into realities unto themselves and get enshrined and worshipped as if they were complete. That is why Joseph Campbell insists that myth and symbol are not about something that happened way back then. Rather, they are a key to tell us what we can do now. We have keys to a possible future, but they are useless unless we act on them . . . .

In *Walking the Red Line* Deena Hurwitz introduces us to Israelis who are seeking justice for persecuted Palestinians (New Society Publishers, 1992). Rabbi Marshall Meyer marched with the women of the *Plaza de Mayo* in Argentina who were protesting the disappearance of their loved ones. He was threatened with death because he dared oppose the Argentine military government. From his roots, he knew that he was standing with the people against Pharaoh. He knew that the symbols exist only to lead us to the radical reality and call of our own time.

Brian Willson lost his legs trying to stop shipments of arms to Nicaragua. The women and children in India chained themselves to the trees so the loggers would not cut them down. Archbishop Romero told the Salvadoran soldiers they should not follow orders to shoot their peasant brothers and sisters. Chico Mendez was killed for trying to save part of the Amazon. Ninez Montenegro Garca risks her life for the families of the disappeared in Guatemala. These are people of extraordinary faith and courage who shake us out of our ordinary existence and face us with the life and death questions of our own moment in history. By entering an existence that does not yet exist, they open out for others the possibility of making changes in their own lives.

History is constantly providing us with opportunities for achieving enlightenment, for moving out of slavery into freedom, for being born again. We are constantly being called into a new existence, out of the lies and devastation and violence all around us. "With every breath of life," wrote Rosenstock-Huessy, "we either start afresh a time that we want to differ from the past, or we continue a time that we want to perpetuate one day more."

. . . [T]hat which gives life to the world is not confined to one place or to one group of people. It does not exist in one nationality or one religion or one economic system or one ideology. Rather, it is continually being called forth from people at the edges of different cultures and religions and nationalities and professions . . . .

We are now at a point in history where massive crisis is breaking in upon us, where people all over the earth are being called to give birth to a different future. They are being called to a new level of consciousness and conscience. They are taking parallel steps on local levels for survival, for peace, and for a sustainable way of living. They are challenging the structures that have been doing violence to the earth and violence to the poor. Some are highly organized; others are simply clusters of individuals trying to live their lives in a responsible fashion. But the questions they are asking and the steps they are taking bring them beyond the group consciousness and conscience of their backgrounds. For the first time in history, we are getting a glimpse of how our actions reverberate around the world, how they affect Gaia, how the future of life on earth hangs in the balance. For the first time, we can see that pledging allegiance to the Whole, not just to a particular nation or corporation or religious institution, is the way of patriotism and piety.

Who, then, will lead us from death into new life if the institutions will not do it? Who will bring us out of the ordinary existence we see all around us, out of the hypocrisy and hopelessness and pollution and hatred and war and weapons and greed? Only those who are listening to the call and making the difficult journey. Those journeys will affect

> *People all over the earth are being called to give birth to a different future. . . . They are taking parallel steps on local levels for survival, for peace, and for a sustainable way of living. They are challenging the structures that have been doing violence to the earth and violence to the poor.*

the institutions in time, but institutions seldom lead the way. Eventually, the institutions will benefit by the courage of the few—and will incorporate the values that they once felt so threatened by.

Page Smith, in his *A People's History of the United States*, describes the people who took part in the massive movement for the abolition of slavery in U.S. history. He describes how the movement arose and subsided, waxed and waned, and at times almost dropped out of existence. It was fueled by blacks and whites, by women and by runaway slaves, by people from the churches and synagogues, by humanists and by socialists, by artists and writers and politicians. When the gathering of believers reached its peak, and abolition finally became a reality, Smith says simply that the "church of the abolition" disbanded.

The community of people who are "called out" gathers itself together again, and again, and again, and is still gathering itself together at this moment. People from every culture and race and nationality are struggling and living heroically, fighting for human rights and justice and peace.

These are our brothers and sisters in faith. We do not know them, but we know that they are there. The people of spirit cannot be easily defined; there are no walls of separation, no "ins" and "outs." Whenever people put a fence around themselves and declare themselves a "spiritual people," they have fenced themselves in. They have made it harder to be called anywhere beyond their own enclosures.

The community of those who are called forth will always be acting from the future. They will see a new story and begin to live that story out now, before its time . . . .

HOMEWORK

REFLECTIONS ON THE READINGS

Session 12:
Going From Here

SESSION 12: **Going From Here**

OBJECTIVES
- To assess and learn from the group nonviolent action
- To explore future possibilities and plans: where do we go from here
- To honor the nonviolent journey we have been on together

AGENDA
- Opening [15 min.]
- Welcome [1 min.]
- Reflecting on Homework [10 min.]
- Assessing the Group Nonviolent Action [25 min.]
- Where Do We Go from Here? [45 min.]
- Break [10 min.]
- Conclusion [40 min.]
      Adding to the Wall of Learning and Growing
      Nonviolence Principles
      Evaluation
      Outcomes-Based Survey
      Closing

READINGS
- Reading #1: Robert Fulghum, "The Story of Vedran Smailovic"
- Reading #2: Bill Cane, "Circles of Hope"

NOTES FOR THE FACILITATOR

SESSION PREPARATION: BEFORE
- Review the entire session in depth. Role-play or practice setting up and facilitating exercises beforehand. Wherever possible, put material into your own words. Feel free to make notes for this purpose on 3x5 cards or in the book next to the written instructions.
- Materials needed: table, candles and matches for each person, small pots (1 for each person), flower seeds, soil, watering can, large container, newspaper, and singing bowl or bell for the closing.
- Write out on easel paper:
   - The 5 possible next steps listed in the sidebar "Next Steps."

PREPARATION: ON THE DAY OF THE SESSION
- Prepare a table with candles and matches for each person.
- Put the soil into the large container. Fill the watering can with water.

SESSION 12: **Going From Here**

WELCOME — 1 MIN.

Invite the participants to take their seats and say in your own words:

> Welcome back for our twelfth and final session of the *Engage: Exploring Nonviolent Living* Study Program. In this session, we will spend some time evaluating and learning from our group nonviolent action. Then we will reflect on the next steps we as individuals and perhaps as a group may want to take. Finally, we will take some time to mark the pilgrimage of nonviolence we have been on together.

OPENING — 15 MIN.

Prepare a table with candles and matches for each person.

> I invite you to relax and breathe deeply. Please close your eyes and bring to mind the name of a person from your personal life or from the history of active nonviolence whose example can strengthen and encourage you in your future nonviolent journey.

After a minute:

> Please come forward one at a time to light a candle and share the person's name out loud (if you choose to do so). Then, please stay standing at your chair, and after all have lighted a candle we will form a circle around the table.

After the last person has lit her or his candle, invite the participants to form a circle and hold hands. Offer a word honoring those that have been named. Then:

> I invite you to reflect on how those in this circle have offered us examples that can strengthen and encourage us in our future nonviolent journey.
> After two or three minutes of silence, gently squeeze your neighbors' hands, make eye contact, and invite people to take their seats.

REFLECTING ON HOMEWORK — 10 MIN.

> I again invite you to get together with your Nonviolence Partner to take a few minutes to reflect on your experiences or insights since the last session, as well as to reflect on the readings, journaling, or nonviolent action.

ASSESSING THE GROUP NONVIOLENT ACTION — 25 MIN.

Invite participants back to the large group and ask them to respond to each of the following questions, one at a time. Spend 5 or so minutes on each question. Write the responses down on easel paper.

- What were the positive aspects of this action?
- What were things that could be improved?
- Did our group action move toward our strategic goal of influencing the people we wanted to and encouraging them to act in the way that we wanted?
- How does the group's action fit into the larger human effort for a better world?

At the end of this process, lead the group in congratulating itself for the action they took with a round of applause.

> The day will come when, after harnessing space, the winds, the tides, and gravitation, we shall harness … the energies of love. And on that day, for the second time in the history of the world, we shall have discovered fire.
>
> — PIERRE TEILHARD DE CHARDIN

WHERE DO WE GO FROM HERE? — 45 MIN.

Share the following in your own words:

Now, I'd like to invite us to think about our possibilities for continuing to deepen the nonviolence journey.

We can do this as individuals and as part of a group. As we have discovered in many ways in this program, our nonviolent power multiplies as we join our energy, commitment, and creativity with that of others.

Let's look at this list of possible "Next Steps."

NEXT STEPS

Congratulations! By completing the *Engage: Exploring Nonviolent Living* Study Program, you've had an opportunity to explore active nonviolence in a variety of important ways. Now you have another opportunity: to build on what you have been able to experience here. This can be done in many ways. Key dimensions include: being part of a supportive and collaborative community; experimenting with nonviolence; taking part in movements and organizations working for nonviolent change; becoming familiar with the stories, history, and ideas of nonviolence; and being part of a growing global network of nonviolence practitioners. More specifically:

Form an Affinity Group or Nonviolence Circle

- Some or all of the members of the current study group may wish to continue as a group to offer one another support, to deepen your study of nonviolence, and to take nonviolent action together.
- Variously called small groups, affinity groups, or base communities, these Nonviolence Circles create an environment to support our work, to explore the depths of nonviolence, to take action, and to reflect on the meaning of the process of personal and social transformation.
- We suggest that you set a date for your first meeting and decide what you'd like to do. Many of the things listed below could be part of the activity of your group.
- Even if only a few of you want to start a group, that's fine — talk with other friends and colleagues about forming a group. If you have many new people in the group, you might want to lead the *Engage* Study Program for those who haven't gone through it yet.

- Whatever group emerges, we suggest two things. First, choose a name for your group (e.g., Spirit Affinity Group or The Two Hands Nonviolence Circle). Second, please let us know at Pace e Bene about your group.
- If you are in need of assistance in forming this group, you are welcome to contact the Pace e Bene *Engage* Program staff for consultation, advice, and support.

Participate in a Movement for Social Change
- Do research on local, regional, national, or international issues. Explore local movements or organizations who are committed to the nonviolent struggle for justice and peace.
- Think about the specific things you would like to do in these movements.
- Go talk with people involved in these movements, then go to a meeting or two to get a feel for them.
- Volunteer to be involved with some of the work of these efforts.
- Talk with people in your Nonviolence Circle about taking part in nonviolent activities of these movements and organizations.

Start a Nonviolence Book Club
- Drawing from the list of key books, participants could read and discuss a significant book on nonviolence once a month for a year. This would support your personal exploration and whatever choices you make about participating in nonviolent movements for justice and peace.

Host a Nonviolence Movie Club
- Organize a series of nonviolence videos for your group, friends, and family. These showings could be followed by a discussion period.
- Use the list for possible titles.
- We especially encourage all participants to watch the video series, *A Force More Powerful.* This series (shown on the Public Broadcasting System in the U.S.) features six half-hour segments on successful nonviolent struggles around the world. Additionally, we recommend *Bringing Down a Dictator,* a video about the nonviolent campaign that ended Serbian President Slobodan Milosevic's regime in 2000, created by the same film producers. Richard Attenborough's full-length motion picture *Gandhi* is also a powerful complement to the *Engage: Exploring Nonviolent Living* Study Program.

Deepen Your Engage: Exploring Nonviolent Living Experience
- Take an Engage Facilitator Training
- Host an Engage Workshop
- Facilitate an Engage Study Program in your community
- Stay in touch with Pace e Bene

For more information, see Staying Connected with Engage *at the end of the book.*

Explore each of the listed options with the group.
Then ask the group:

Are there issues you are interested in working together on? Are you interested in forming an ongoing reflection and action group or Nonviolence Circle?

Where would you like to go from here?

Write brainstorms on easel paper. If some or all of the people are interested in forming an ongoing reflection and action group, set a date and time for those who want to meet.

Now I would like to invite each person to spend five minutes to write her or his own Commitment to the Nonviolent Journey, at whatever level is comfortable for you. (This can be done on the page toward the end of the book.)

It may be as simple or as comprehensive as you like. It can include your exploration of the vision or orientation of active nonviolence. It can include a specific direction you want to take.

We will use these as part of the closing of this session.

> *"Hitlers will come and go. Those who believe that when Hitler dies or is defeated his spirit will die, err grievously. What matters is how we react to such a spirit, violently or nonviolently. If we react violently, we feed that evil spirit. If we act nonviolently, we sterilize it."*
>
> — MOHANDAS GANDHI

BREAK — 10 MIN.

CONCLUSION — 60 MIN.

The Wall of Learning and Growing [10 min.]

Add ideas from this session. Then review the entire wall.

> *"If the method of violence takes plenty of training, the method of nonviolence takes even more training, and that training is much more difficult than the training for violence."*
>
> — MOHANDAS GANDHI

Oral Evaluation [15 min.]

Make two columns on the easel paper.
Ask the participants what they thought worked well.
List these on the left.
Then ask them to share the things that could have been improved. List these on the right.

Questionnaire [10 min.]

Ask people to fill out the Engage: Exploring Nonviolent Living *Outcomes-Based survey at the end of the book. Please send these forms to Pace e Bene as soon as possible: 1420 W. Bartlett Street, Las Vegas, NV 89106.*

Closing Ritual — Planting Seeds of Peace [15 min.]

This closing ritual permits participants to reflect on and publicly articulate (at whatever level they feel comfortable) their nonviolence journey, and to receive support from the community for living out this commitment in whatever way they choose. It marks this moment of both ending and beginning and whatever decisions people have made about peace and justice. It seeks to send people forth strengthened and renewed so as to better meet the challenges they will encounter in their everyday lives and in the effort to make the world a better place.

Spread the newspaper on the ground in the middle of the space and place the large container with soil onto it. Place one pot next to each participant's chair.

Play some appropriate instrumental music and invite the participants to get grounded in their chairs. Invite them to breathe in the breath of life and breathe life out into the world. Repeat this four or five times. Sound the singing bowl. Then say the following in your own words:

> I invite you to come up one at a time to the center, bringing your small pot, and fill it with soil from the large container. As you fill your pot, please share with the group what seeds of nonviolence you would like to commit to planting in your own life or in the world. Then, as you plant the seeds in your soil, please share how you want to nurture those seeds for nonviolence, as we all bear witness and hold you in the circle we are.

> "There is nothing wrong with a traffic law which says you have to stop for a red light. But when a fire is raging, the fire truck goes right through that red light, and normal traffic had better get out of its way. Or, when a man is bleeding to death, the ambulance goes through those red lights at top speed. There is a fire raging now ... Disinherited people all over the world are bleeding to death from deep social and economic wounds. They need brigades of ambulance drivers who will have to ignore the red lights of the present system until the emergency is solved."
>
> — MARTIN LUTHER KING, JR.

As facilitator, model this by starting with your own pot and seed as an example. As each person returns to her or his seat, the whole group might also be instructed to say only, "May it come to life." or "May it be so." Or you may simply sound the singing bowl. When the last person has finished filling pots and setting seeds, say the following in your own words:

> Let's take a moment to hold in our hearts all we have heard within the circle we are. Honoring our need for each other as co-creators in nurturing a culture of nonviolence, please come to the center of the circle now, one at a time as you are moved to do, and carry the watering can to someone else's pot to water their seeds of nonviolence. As you water another's seeds, find words to offer the vision of that participant's seeds. You might say in your own way, "With this water, I champion, or bless, or give courage to, the seeds of your vision." Then replace the watering can back in the center of the circle and be seated. After your pot has been watered, please pick it up and hold it while others have their seeds watered.

When you believe all the pots have been watered, ask:

> Are there any seeds that still need watering?

Then invite participants to close their eyes again for a closing meditation and say,

> Let us take this moment in silence to locate, in the rich soil of our hearts, our commitment to being courageous, loving stewards of our shared visions for a culture of nonviolence.

Wait a few seconds, then say,

> Let us be mindful of how we are all also stewards for the gifts of creation, like water, that we need to sustain us and our visions.

Wait a few seconds, then say,

> Let us honor in our beings, that just as we are nourished by our differences, we also all draw our lives from the same source (however we understand or name it), from the one sacred well of life.

Then invite the participants to stand and hold hands and say the following in your own words:

> You have made your commitment. You have been affirmed by this community. Go now to be a healer for your community and our world. Pace e Bene!

KEY ORGANIZATIONS

Department of Peace Campaign. P.O. Box 3259, Center Line, MI 48015; (586) 754-8105; *peace@renaissancealliance.org*. An historic citizen lobbying effort to create a U.S. Department of Peace (HR 1673), sponsored in the House of Representatives by Congressman Dennis Kucinich. This bill establishes nonviolence as an organizing principle of American society, providing the U.S. president with an array of peace-building policy options for domestic and international use.

Eastern Mennonite University Conflict Transformation Program. 1200 Park Road, Harrisonburg, VA 22802-2462; (540) 432-4000; *www.emu.edu/ctp*. EMU educates students to live in a global context. Its peace church tradition invites students to pursue their life calling through scholarly inquiry, artistic creation, guided practice, and life-changing cross-cultural encounter. EMU's Summer Peacebuilding Institute offers graduate courses in conflict transformation to students from around the world.

COMMITMENT TO THE NONVIOLENT JOURNEY

You are invited to describe as fully as possible your current understanding of, and commitment to, your nonviolent journey:

PART FOUR:
Resources

ORGANIZING AN ENGAGE STUDY GROUP

The *Engage* curriculum is best experienced by a group of 8-12 people interested in exploring the power of nonviolence for use in their own lives and in making a difference in the world. Assembling such a group often depends on well-organized planning, outreach, and follow-up. The following ideas are offered as suggestions for meeting this goal. Feel free to contact the *Engage* staff for additional consultation and support *(info@EngageNonviolence.org)*.

Forming an Organizing Committee

To organize an *Engage* study group, it is strongly recommended that an Organizing Committee of 3 or more people be formed.

Once the committee is established, its members should first discuss their own hopes for this process, as well as their own commitment of time and energy to it.

The committee should be clear about its goals. Is this study program being organized to introduce new ideas? Used as the basis of forming a long-term nonviolence group? Strengthening an existing group? Getting clear on objectives and expectations will help guide the rest of the organizing.

The committee should then develop an organizing plan (including a checklist and a timeline). This plan should include the following tasks.

Identifying Participants

While The *Engage* Study Program can be used with fewer or more participants, its exercises and process are ideally designed for groups of 8-12 people. To achieve this number, consider pre-registering 12-15 people, because one or more individuals often decides to drop out beforehand for a variety of reasons.

To meet this goal, plan to outreach to at least three or four times that number.

Consider who to outreach to as potential participants. Here are some basic approaches.

Outreaching to an already existing group
- Do members of the committee belong to any existing groups? Would any of them be interested in going through the *Engage* program? Consider exploring this at the next meeting of one or more of these groups.
- What are some of the other groups in the community? Make a list. Do committee members have any connections to them? Explore whether or not one or more of these groups are open to a presentation about the program.
- It could be that an entire group would want to participate. Then again, some members of the group might be interested. If that is the case, they could be invited to join a group with people from several different settings.

Forming a new group
- This group can be formed from among friends, family-members, people at work, community groups, civic organizations, business organizations, political groups, religious congregations, groups working against violence, and peace and justice groups.

Setting the Time

Plan the *Engage* Study Program far enough in advance to successfully identify and pre-register participants. Decide the time and day of the week the program will be held. (Usually a weekday evening, 6:30 – 9 pm or 7:00 – 9:30 pm works best.) Decide whether you will meet once a week, once every two weeks, or once a month. (Ideally, groups meet once a week or once every two weeks. This allows time for people to reflect on the material between sessions, but not so much time that group continuity is lost.)

You may decide to wait until participants are identified to ask them what dates and times work for them.

Setting the Location

Possible venues include homes, community centers, or congregational settings (synagogues, mosques, churches, etc.). Consider the following when choosing a space for the sessions:

- *Atmosphere:* Choose a place that offers an environment suitable for this study program;
- *Convenience:* Choose a place near public transportation;
- *Size:* Choose a room location that provides enough space to move around but not so much space that one loses the intimacy of the setting;
- *Noise:* Choose a space that will not be disturbed by outside noise; and
- *Wall space:* Choose a space that has enough wall space to hang easel paper.

Deciding About Finances

The one fundamental expense of the *Engage* Study Program is the *Engage* Book, which each participant must purchase. The facilitators may decide that the rest of the program is free, or they may decide to charge a small amount of money ($5.00-$10.00) for refreshments, additional copying, etc.

In some cases, a fee may be charged to provide the facilitators with a stipend to cover the time she or he spends organizing and preparing the process. (For example, $25.00 could be charged per participant.) If an individual or organization decides to use this curriculum and program on an on-going basis (for nonprofit purposes only), please contact Pace e Bene and consider donating a percentage of the fees to Pace e Bene for the continuance of our work. In any case, financial terms should be settled and advertised *before* the Study Program begins.

Publicity

The following are a number of ways to promote the *Engage* Study Program:

- Talking Points. Use and adapt the following Engage "talking points" for all printed materials and to talk with prospective participants.

    #### Engage Talking Points:
    Engage offers participants the opportunity to:

    - Learn how to respond to violence
    - Find ways to live a more just and peaceful life
    - Deepen their relationship with themselves and others
    - Experience the power of nonviolence

    Also use the Engage FAQs (Frequently Asked Questions) located at: *www.EngageNonviolence.org*.

- Create a Flier. Effective outreach materials are critical to attract participants. A one-page flyer is ideal. Adapt the *Engage* sample flier for your publicity. (See sample flier at: *www.EngageNonviolence.org*.)

- Send e-mail notices to friends, family, colleagues and affiliated organizations.

- Send postcards announcing this program to friends, family, colleagues and affiliated organizations.

- Place ads in relevant publications (newsletters, etc.). (For sample ads, see: *www.EngageNonviolence.org*.)

- Attend local community events to pass out fliers.

- Send press releases announcing this event to local media and try to get on a local radio program to talk about the upcoming study program.

Engage Introductory Presentation

Some people may be reluctant to commit to a 12-week study program immediately. Consider organizing a one-hour *Engage* introductory presentation (with refreshments) to provide more information about the program.

This informational gathering could be held at one of the committee member's home (or at another suitable location). The presentation could be designed for the communities noted above: friends, family-members, people at work, community groups, civic organizations, business organizations, religious congregations, etc. (For agenda, see: *www.EngageNonviolence.org*.)

Responding to Inquiries

When someone calls or e-mails about more information, it is important to respond to them as soon as possible (preferably within one business day). This will instill confidence in the process. Follow up immediately by responding to any questions they have or needs for more information. Refer them to the Pace e Bene website.

Advance Registration

Pre-register people ahead of the start date of the study program — the earlier the better! For example, if the announcement of the study program is made two months before it begins, consider having a "pre-registration deadline" two to four weeks before it begins. This will allow the facilitators to gauge whether the program will meet its required number of participants. (Setting this deadline, of course, does not preclude adding people after it has passed.) (See *www.EngageNonviolence.org* for sample pre-registration sheet.)

After people have pre-registered, send them a confirmation by mail or e-mail.

Logistics

Identify any logistical requirements and develop a plan to meet them (transportation; refreshments; etc.). See each session for its material requirements.

Program Planning

Choose session facilitators (preferably two). Prepare for sessions. (For in-depth guidance on facilitation, see the "*Engage* Study Program Facilitation Guidelines" that follow.)

First Meeting

At the first meeting, make sure that co-facilitators are prepared ahead of time and welcome people as they arrive. It's also important to provide refreshments so people feel welcome.

Getting Copies of The *Engage* Book

Order copies of The *Engage* Book from:

Pace e Bene
1420 W. Bartlett Ave.,
Las Vegas, NV 89106
Email: *paceebene@paceebene.org;*
Phone: 702-648-2281

Price: $22.00. Five or more copies: $18.00 per copy.
Plus shipping and handling: $4.00 for first copy; $1.00 for each additional copy.

Finally, Please Contact *Engage!*

Please let *Engage* staff know about your study program plans! We are exited to learn about what you are organizing, and we will be happy to share your news with our growing *Engage* network.

We are available for consultation and support at any point through the process. Contact us at *info@EngageNonviolence.org*. Thank you!

ENGAGE STUDY PROGRAM FACILITATION GUIDELINES

The *Engage* Study Program is a small-group learning process in personal and social transformation designed for a wide range of contexts and settings. It can be led either by people with a minimum of facilitation experience or by those with significant background in leading group process.

The more experienced a facilitator is, the more effective she or he will likely be, and it is for this reason Pace e Bene leads the three-day *Engage* Facilitation Training. For those who wish to gain more in-depth skill in facilitation, we encourage you to take this training.

At the same time, however, the *Engage* curriculum has been organized so that people with little formal facilitation training can facilitate it. The facilitator is provided with the objectives for each session and clear directions for every element and exercise. Many stories draw out the key insights of each session and there are directions for the participant's "home work": journaling, action, and reading for the next session.

All *Engage* facilitators, no matter the degree of their facilitation experience, are asked to do two important things:

- First: be diligent. This means reading the session text and readings carefully ahead of time; taking the time to grasp the intent and flow of the content; and following the instructions for the "Session Preparations" found at the beginning of each session.
- Second: do one's best to create a safe and productive environment where the program participants can explore the vision and tools of nonviolent power for use in their lives and the world.

The following facilitation guidelines – which have emerged from the experience of hundreds of trainings, workshops, and small group study programs led by Pace e Bene since 1997 — are designed to help the facilitator accomplish these two objectives.

The Structure and Content of the Engage Study Program

Co-Facilitation

Though not absolutely necessary, it is best to have two co-facilitators lead the *Engage* series. Not only will this share the responsibilities between two people, it will also allow the person not immediately facilitating to be a "vibes watcher": to gauge the mood of the group and its needs and to intervene if necessary. The person not facilitating is available to:

- Add pieces that the facilitator may miss
- Provide support in challenging situations (for example, broken agreements)
- Carry out logistical tasks (for example, take notes), and
- Be available to take over if necessary

When there are two facilitators, the process is shaped by the wisdom and experiences of two people, it keeps both people fresh, and it models nonviolence collaboration for the group.

Generally speaking, gender balance and cultural diversity strengthen *Engage* co-facilitation.

Twelve Sessions

The *Engage* Study Program is comprised of 12 sessions. The value and impact of the program comes from the cumulative momentum of the entire dozen sessions that integrate the power and dynamics of personal and social change. We highly recommend scheduling and completing the entire program. The sessions can be once a week, once every two weeks, or once a month.

For some groups, however, it will not be possible to complete 12 consecutive sessions for various reasons.

Under these circumstances, one possible adjustment could be to group a series of the sessions and space them throughout the year. (For example, Sessions 1-4 in the fall; Sessions 5-8 in the spring; and Sessions 9-12 in the summer.)

Or consider doing half one year, and the second half the next year.

Our recommendation is that one begins the series and works through it sequentially (even if a group decides that it can do no more than four or five or six sessions). The most important thing is to begin — as people participate, they may discover the importance of scheduling the entire study program.

The Structure of Each Session

Each session is 2.5 hours in length. In general, each session has the following structure:

- Each session begins with a short welcome where the facilitator welcomes everyone back to the group and gives an overview of the session.
- This is followed by an opening process that offers centering and focus. Sometimes this includes music, reading poetry, candle lighting, silence or ritualistic movement.
- Then, after the opening, participants (beginning with Session 2), discuss with their "Nonviolence Partners" insights or relevant issues since the previous session.
- Each session then offers multiple styles of learning and being: large group exercises, nonviolence story-telling, small group reflections, times of creative expression (using various art media), role-plays, and de-briefing. In all of these segments, we often encourage participants to reflect on, and honor, their own life experience.
- The last part of each session focuses on closure and preparation for the next session. Each participant is asked to do "nonviolence journaling," and a "nonviolent action" before the next session. They are also asked to read the required material for the next gathering (found in the Readings Section of the next session). At the back of each session pages are provided to keep one's journal, to write about the action one has taken, and to write one's responses to the readings.
- This is also the time when participants are asked to add any thoughts or insights they have had during the immediate session to "The Wall of Learning and Growing," several pieces of easel paper taped to the wall which you are asked to re-hang for each session. By the end of the 12th session, "The Wall" should have quite a few entries.
- Finally, every session has a closing that, like the opening, may include any number of different meditative elements.

Preparing Each Session

- Each session has an agenda that outlines the elements of the gathering, each with suggested times. Certain topics, reflections, or role-plays, however, may lead to long but valuable group discussion. Please feel free to adjust the agenda if this happens.
- Review the agenda beforehand and read through the entire session (including the readings). Prepare any necessary logistics as suggested in the "Session Preparation" section at the bottom of the agenda (art supplies, candles, easel, felt markers, a bell, etc.).
- Have the room set up (and any logistics, etc.) before people arrive.
- For all sessions, you will need an easel with easel paper and non-toxic felt markers. If an easel is not available, tape large pieces of paper on the wall.
- Consider using appropriate music between exercises.
- Throughout this study program there are activities encouraging participants to creatively express their feelings or thoughts. Art supplies (crayons, colored pencils, clay, pastels, wire, drawing paper, etc) are helpful to this process. Perhaps they can be bought with fees collected for the course or from a special collection during the first session.

- In addition to this study program, it is highly beneficial for participants to also watch nonviolence videos (see video list in Part IV). You might do some research on the availability of a number of these videos locally so that people can have access to them during this process.

Personal Preparation for Each Session

In addition to session preparation, being an *Engage* facilitator requires personal preparation.

It is best to be centered and grounded when facilitating *Engage*. If a facilitator typically practices a particular spiritual discipline or regimen (for example, meditation, art-work, singing, writing, or mindful walking) she or he is encouraged to partake in this practice prior to facilitating the *Engage* program.

While facilitating she or he may wish to re-center and re-ground him or herself as necessary during the break.

If a facilitator is dealing with personal issues that prevent her or him from being fully present to the group, seek the personal and professional support before facilitating *Engage*.

Specific Elements of Facilitating Engage

Creating a Centered Environment

Create a tone and atmosphere in the room where the group will meet by using meaningful objects, artworks, colorful cloth, and so forth. Set a "nonviolence table" with meaningful objects. Invite participants to bring objects that embody justice, peace or nonviolence to them (pictures, items from nature, etc.) that can be put on the table throughout the study program. Invite participants to add to the " nonviolence table" at any point during the series.

Putting Instructions and Comments into Your Own Words

In each session there are:

- Instructions for the facilitator, and
- Instructions, presentations, and comments that the facilitator is to convey to the participants

The instructions for the facilitator are un-indented italicized text. The facilitator's instructions, presentations and comments to be conveyed to the participants are indented unitalicized (plain) text. Each time, the facilitator is prompted to put the comments or instructions IN HER OR HIS OWN WORDS. This will be indicted by the phrase:

Convey the following in your own words:

Here is an example from Session 4:

WELCOME – 1 MIN.

Convey the following in your own words:

> Welcome back for our fourth session of the *Engage: Exploring Nonviolent Living* Study Program. In this session, we will begin to reflect on nonviolent power. One of the sources we will draw on for this is the vision and practice of Mohandas Gandhi. For almost sixty years, Gandhi experimented with unlocking and unleashing this power in the pursuit of justice and the well being of all. One of the things we will do in this session is focus on one of Gandhi's key principles: that each of us possesses a piece of the truth.

"Convey the following in your own words," means literally that. The more you can present the comments or instructions to the participants naturally and in your own way, the better the flow will be.

It is a very good idea to read these instructions, presentations or comments over several times ahead of time.

Opening and Closing Each Exercise

The facilitator should open every exercise with a one-sentence description of the exercise and its purpose. This provides the participants with a framework for what they should get out of the exercise. At the end of the exercise, conclude by briefly summing up the learnings from the exercise. This reinforces what the participants just learned.

Creating Flow by Building Bridges Between the Segments

One way to prepare one's facilitation is to notice the flow from one agenda item to the next and to build bridges between them. Flow helps participants to move smoothly on the journey and not to feel disjointed or jarred when a new agenda item is introduced. One way to do this is to reiterate previous material and connect it to the new exercise or issue. This provides an anchor for participants to build on as new material is added.

Debriefing the Content

Debriefing is the process of reflecting on the experience of an exercise or segment. It gives participants the opportunity to articulate and integrate their learnings from an exercise. Debriefs should be allotted as much time as the original exercise or segment.

In general, *Engage* uses a three-part process for debriefs. If possible, position three easels with paper next to each other with the following headings: Feelings/Noticings, Learnings, and Applications. Debrief the exercise according to these three categories:

- *First: Noticings.* These are observations without judgment. They are the sensory experiences of the exercise: what participants felt, saw, and heard.
- *Second: Learnings.* Where did participants grow? What were their new discoveries? The *Engage* process often asks more specific learning questions.
- *Third: Applications.* How can participants apply what they learned to their life and work? This gives time for them to reflect on how to make the material more immediately relevant.

Take at least 5 minutes for each section of the debrief. Sometimes a participant will make a response that belongs in a different section. Check with the participant if she or he thinks it belongs in the other section, and then ask the group to continue to give input on the section you are still in.

When a participant shares something that is unclear during the debrief, don't respond by making an interpretation of what the participant said. Use a question to gather more information. For example, ask the participant, "Can you say more about that?"

Balancing "Experiential Learning" with Presentations

Much of the *Engage* process focuses on reflecting on the experience of its participants. The *Engage* debrief process found above, for example, draws information from the experiences of the participants. This method is called *experiential learning*. "Popular education," developed by Paulo Friere in Brazil, is an example of the experiential learning method.

At the same time, in the *Engage* process the book and the facilitator provide input to the participants. This input is important because there is a rich history of nonviolence contained in the stories and principles that participants can learn from and apply to their lives. Some examples of presentation include:

- Bringing out key principles of nonviolence related to an exercise
- Telling a nonviolence story to illustrate a nonviolence principle

- Teaching a way to practice a nonviolence skill

Engage integrates these two learning methods.

Sharing Personal Stories

It is helpful for the facilitator to share personal stories illustrating principles of nonviolence whenever possible. This models the importance of connecting the *Engage* material to one's life and encourages the participants to do the same.

Stories don't need to be very elaborate or intense examples of nonviolent power. In fact, basic, simple stories from ordinary, everyday life are powerful because they show how creative nonviolence is ordinary and can be part of everything we do.

Using Humor

Humor is important for several reasons. Since discussions of violence and nonviolence are serious and heavy issues, humor helps to lighten things and keep people from getting overwhelmed. Ways of incorporating humor include using funny stories, jokes, short and simple games, or nurturing an atmosphere where participants can be humorous. It is important to be careful not to use humor violently (for example, put-down humor).

Using the Diversity of Learning Channels

There are four primary learning channels: visual, auditory, kinesthetic (or learning through body movement), and emotional (or heart learning). Learning happens through all of these channels, but each person tends to process primarily through one or two of the channels. Vary the channels as much as possible in order to make the process more inclusive. Also, try to attend to multiple channels at one time. For example, write notes on easel paper during debriefs to attend to the visual along with auditory channels.

Creating a Productive and Safe Environment

The *Engage* Study Program explores the power of nonviolence through stories, readings, group discussion, exercises, and journaling. These activities encourage participants to come to a deeper understanding of violence and nonviolence by reflecting on their own experience, learning from the other participants, and taking action at whatever level they feel comfortable. Each session is structured to create a space conducive to attentive learning and contemplative reflection.

The facilitator creates this environment through the structure and rhythm of each of the 12 sessions and the sensitivity and respect they display and cultivate.

Facilitating, Not Dictating

In the *Engage* Study Program we want to honor everyone's contribution. Discussions should not turn into debates. If differences of opinion arise in the group, the facilitator should encourage everyone to listen to each of the opinions and to take a long view, waiting to see how it might all unfold over the course of the 12 sessions.

This program is most successful when the facilitator *facilitates*, literally "helps to make things go easily." As facilitator, you should not dominate the conversation nor jump into a discussion or dispute with the *right* answer. Instead, help all the participants to participate and keep the rhythm of the process moving. The facilitator should avoid lecturing and/or spending a very long time explaining something. The assumption is not that you have all the answers, but that you are a co-learner and explorer who supports the growth of the group. Facilitators should not pressure themselves to be perfect.

Creating Safe Space

A key dimension of the *Engage* process is the sharing of stories, feelings, and other personal information that often requires trust and safety. The *Engage* facilitator therefore must create an environment where all the members of the group feel comfortable and safe to share in this way. There are several components in creating this environment. The first is a set of Group Agreements.

Making Agreements

One important way to establish this safety is through the "Shared Agreements" presented in Session 1 and reproduced here:

During our time together I agree to share and participate at whatever level I feel safe and comfortable.

- I will share what I want to share. If I choose not to share, that's fine. If I want to share a little, that's fine. If I want to share more, that's fine. Together we will create an environment where our feelings and thoughts are respected.
- While I have the opportunity to always share at whatever level I feel safe and comfortable, I may be open to voluntarily take opportunities as they arise to feel uncomfortable when that might help facilitate my growth. In every case, this is up to me.
- The facilitators are not acting in the capacity of professional psychotherapists or counselors. They are ordinary people helping us explore alternatives to the violence in our lives and the larger world. If something comes up for me during our time together that would warrant or benefit from consulting with an appropriate health professional, I am encouraged to do so.

During our time together I agree to maintain confidentiality about personal stories or experiences shared in my small group or in the large group, unless I have been given permission to share them with others.

- In the *Engage* process we work in small and large groups. I will not share a story or experience that someone else has shared in either small or large groups unless she or he has given their permission. When in doubt I will err on the side of caution and not share the story or experience. I will feel free, however, to share any insights that this story or experience may have stimulated.

During our time together I will strive to appreciate and honor our differences.

- Diversity is an opportunity for me to grow and learn in a new way. I will try to nurture openness to, and celebration of, persons, approaches, and ways of being that are different from mine.
- As part of this, I recognize the fact that there are power dynamics in every group, including this one. I will do my best to be sensitive to the use of power based on race, gender, sexual preference, money or class. If someone uses power over someone else like this in this group, I will try to respond to this situation in a clear and loving way.

These agreements serve as a container for the group process, in the way a bowl of water contains water and prevents it from spilling. The agreements act as a container that creates boundaries and safety beyond which one's sharing will not be "spilled."

The agreements are made at the beginning of the study program. They are written on easel paper and posted on the wall throughout the sessions. When exercises require more personal sharing, it can be helpful to restate the agreements.

Reestablishing Safety When an Agreement is Broken

A broken agreement provides the facilitator and the participants with an opportunity to practice nonviolence in a real-life scenario. When an agreement is broken, raise the issue with the group and share what you are feeling. (If a participant notices the broken agreement, ask that person to share her/his feelings.) In either case, get some feedback from the rest of the group by asking what they are feeling or noticing. After receiving feedback, if you have an idea what to do next, suggest it to the group for feedback. If you are not sure what to do, ask the group for ideas.

Here is an example. When someone shares an experience and another participant says, "No, it's not like that. It's this way…" The second person is denying the experience of the first person. The facilitator response may be something like, "I am feeling uncomfortable with what just happened. Alicia shared her story and Martin denied that person's experience." Then follow the process outlined above. Try to re-fashion the agreement in light of the current situation.

Paying Attention to The Comfort Zone, The Discomfort Zone, and The Alarm Zone

Please read the section in Session 2 on the *Comfort Zone, The Discomfort Zone,* and *The Alarm Zone.*

It is important to support participants in the growing process while ensuring that participants don't feel overwhelmed and end up shutting down. Encourage sharing within the group at whatever level feels comfortable. At the same time, encourage participants to be voluntarily and freely open to potentially experiencing discomfort when the opportunity for stretching and growth may create those feelings. If it appears that a participant is going into their alarm zone, check in with that person as soon as possible. If it happens in the middle of a session, check-in with the person on the spot by giving the person the opportunity to share or not share what's happening. Or stop the process by taking a break. Then do a one-on-one follow-up with that person immediately.

Facilitation Challenges

Facilitating *Engage* can be both rewarding and challenging. The following is a list of challenges that facilitators often have to negotiate.

Keeping on Schedule

One of the most difficult facilitator challenges is adhering to the times scheduled on the Session Agenda. The facilitator must balance adhering to the schedule with allowing time for a variety of learning styles *and* for the deep reflection and sharing that the *Engage* material often inspires.

The *Engage* process integrates different elements, such as stories, exercises, and small group reflections because people learn in multiple ways and because learning is enhanced when multiple methods are used. The drawback of using multiple methods is that it can take longer.

Even more challenging is the deep reflection and sharing some topics can provoke. The temptation is to spend significantly more time than is allotted for that segment. What do you do?

The times allotted for exercises are the best estimates based on our experience. Try to remain within the time frame suggested. If an exercise is going over time, decide whether or not to continue with the exercise. If an exercise is continued, a later exercise may need to be reduced or eliminated altogether. Either decision is acceptable. In general, it is better to complete fewer exercises well than to rush through the session in order to cover every exercise. Depth is better than superficial understanding. However, if the group continually feels like it is getting bogged down and not getting to all of the material, this may have a negative impact on the group. If you stay relatively close to the times allotted, facilitators should be able to avoid this dilemma. The following are some ways to help the group stay on time.

First, in Session 1 the group is asked to make an agreement about keeping to allotted times. The facilitator explains the reasons given above and asks participants to agree to this principle. This will build in sensitivity to time throughout the study program.

Second, gauge the energy or sharing in the group. If participants maintain a great deal of energy in an exercise, or they continue deep sharing, consider continuing an exercise that is exceeding its time limit.

Third, while it is good to maximize participation, this doesn't mean taking every hand during an exercise. Acknowledge the raised hand(s) and ask if it's okay to move on since time is running over. Encourage participants to continue to reflect on the material in their journals between sessions.

As time in an exercise is running down, it can be helpful to announce, "I'll take one or two more hands." This lets people know time is running out and will help prepare the participants for the transition to the next exercise. If you're really stuck (people are wanting to continue to share and you'd like to move to the next exercise), ask the group by saying something like, "This is really important sharing AND we are going over time. If we continue with this sharing, some parts of the agenda will be cut out. What would you like to do?"

This empowers the group to make the decision. If it is at the end of the workshop, contract with the group to go over time. If people are going off the topic on hand, bring them back on task. This often signals that it's time to move on.

Balancing time requirements with growth opportunities is a skill that is learned over time with the experience of doing it.

Balancing Individual Growth and the Growth of the Group

A facilitator must consider whether one individual's processing of an experience or insight is helping or hindering the rest of the group's process. If a discussion seems to be benefiting only one person and frustrating the others, try to move the process along. One way to deal with this challenge is to acknowledge and appreciate that one person's contribution, say "It's time to move on," and offer to check-in more with that person after the session.

Being Transparent

Facilitators should not be considered experts on the subject, but co-learners along with the participants. A good facilitator does not need to be the expert on every problem or issue that arises. A good rule of thumb is, "When is doubt, ask the group for assistance and decide what to do next together."

Situations sometimes arise where it is unclear how to handle a situation. A good strategy is to consult with one's co-facilitator. Instead of talking with her or him in private, though, discuss the issue with the co-facilitator in front of the whole group so that everyone can hear the exchange. This models nonviolent teamwork by embodying openness and transparency in co-facilitation. It dispels the myth that the facilitator is supposed to have the solution to every situation.

Varying Interaction Modes

Although *Engage* is a group process, it also incorporates individual reflection time in order to pursue deeper introspection. This is especially important for more introverted individuals who may be more comfortable processing the material in this way.

In *Engage* there is a movement between individual, small group, and large group activities. If there are too many consecutive large group activities, the group may need to do a small group or individual activity. For example, if during a large group debrief no one is responding to a question and the energy is very low, consider asking each participant to turn to the person sitting next to them and respond to the question. Usually, the energy will increase dramatically. Likewise, too many individual and/or small group activities may diffuse the energy of the group and require a large group activity.

Getting Support

Thanks for your willingness to facilitate the *Engage* process. The *Engage* staff and associates are available to consult with you about the *Engage* material before a session and to assist if you have any problems.

Feel free to give Pace e Bene staff any feedback based on your experience of facilitating the *Engage* Study Program.

Please don't hesitate to contact us. Pace e Bene!

NONVIOLENCE ORGANIZATIONS

Alternatives to Violence Project (AVP). AVP/USA: 1050 Selby Ave., St. Paul, MN 55104, 877-926-8287, *avp@avpusa.org*, *www.avpusa.org*. AVP empowers people to lead nonviolent lives through affirmation, respect for all, community building, cooperation, and trust. AVP/USA is an association of community based groups and prison based groups offering experiential workshops in personal growth and creative conflict management. The national organization provides support for the work of these local groups.

American Friends Service Committee (AFSC). AFSC National Office. 1501 Cherry Street, Philadelphia, PA 19102, (215) 241-7000, *afscinfo@afsc.org*, *www.afsc.org*. AFSC is a practical expression of the faith of the Religious Society of Friends (Quakers). Committed to the principles of nonviolence and justice, it seeks in its work and witness to draw on the transforming power of love, human and divine.

Blue Mountain Center of Meditation, P.O. Box 256, Tomales, CA 94971 USA; (800) 475-2369; *www.easwaran.org*. For a tried-and-true method of meditation available to all, religious or not, we highly recommend this center with its many retreats, books, tapes and courses. Everything you need, including inspiring passages to begin meditating on, will be found.

Capacitar International, Inc. 23 East Beach Street, Suite 206, Watsonville, CA 95076, 831-722-7590, *www.capacitar.org*. *Capacitar* — meaning, in Spanish, to empower, to encourage, to bring each other to life — is an international network of empowerment and solidarity connecting people from grassroots groups. Capacitar uses simple practices of healing, team-building and self-development to awaken people to their own source of strength and wisdom so they can reach out to heal injustice and create a more peaceful world.

Center for Nonviolent Communication. 2428 Foothill Boulevard, Suite E, La Crescenta, CA 91214, 818-957-9393, *www.cnvc.org*. CNC is a global organization whose vision is a world where all people are getting their needs met and resolving their conflicts peacefully. In this vision, people are using Nonviolent Communication (NVC) to create and participate in networks of worldwide life-serving systems in economics, education, justice, healthcare, and peace-keeping.

Department of Peace Campaign. PO Box 3259, Center Line, MI 48015, (586) 754-8105, *peace@renaissancealliance.org* . An historic citizen lobbying effort to create a U.S. Department of Peace (HR 1673), sponsored in the House of Representatives by Congressman Dennis Kucinich. This bill establishes nonviolence as an organizing principle of American society, providing the U.S. President with an array of peace-building policy options for domestic and international use.

Dolores Huerta Foundation. Post Office Box 9189, Bakersfield, California 93309, (661) 322-3033, *www.doloreshuerta.org*. The non-profit organization's mission is to build active communities working for fair and equal access to healthcare, housing, education, jobs, civic participation and economic resources for disadvantaged communities with an emphasis on women and youth.

Eastern Mennonite University Conflict Transformation Program. 1200 Park Road, Harrisonburg, VA 22802 – 2462, 540-432-4000, *www.emu.edu/ctp*. EMU educates students to live in a global context. Our Anabaptist Christian community challenges students to pursue their life calling through scholarly inquiry, artistic creation, guided practice, and life-changing cross-cultural encounter. We invite each person to experience Christ and follow His call to: witness faithfully, serve compassionately, and walk boldly in the way of nonviolence and peace. Teaches graduate courses in conflict transformation primarily through its Summer Peacebuilding Institute. Has students from all around the world.

Fellowship of Reconciliation. 521 N. Broadway, Nyack, NY 10960, 845-358-4601, *www.forusa.org*. FOR seeks to replace violence, war, racism, and economic injustice with nonviolence, peace, and justice. It is an interfaith organization committed to active nonviolence as a transforming way of life and as a means of radical change. They educate, train, build coalitions, and engage in nonviolent and compassionate actions locally, nationally, and globally.

M.K. Gandhi Institute for Nonviolence. C/O Christian Brothers University, 650 East Parkway, South Memphis, TN 38104, 901-452-2824, *www.gandhiinstitute.org*. Led by Mahatma Gandhi's grandson, Arun Gandhi, the Institute promotes and applies the principles of nonviolence locally, nationally, and globally, to prevent violence and resolve personal and public conflicts through research, education, and programming.

Global Peace Services. 202-216-9886, *john_eriksson@compuserve.com*. GPS/USA, P.O. Box 27922, Washington, DC 20038. Movement to create a professional peace service by promoting education and skills-training for men and women based on a philosophy of active nonviolence. Human Kindness Foundation. PO Box 61619, Durham, NC 27715, (919) 304-2220, *www.humankindness.org*. Besides its internationally respected Prison-Ashram Project, the Foundation sponsors a spiritual community and visitor's center called Kindness House, plus Bo Lozoff's free talks and workshops. Since 1973, Bo has spoken in hundreds of prisons, hospitals, churches, universities and spiritual centers around the globe.

Institute for Peace and Justice (IPJ)/Families Against Violence Advocacy Network (FAVAN). 4144 Lindell Boulevard #408, St. Louis, MO 63108, 314-533-4445, *ppjn@aol.com*, *www.ipj-ppj.org*. IPJ is an independent, interfaith, not-for-profit organization that creates resources, provides learning experiences, and advocates publicly for alternatives to violence and injustice at the individual, family, community, institutional and global levels.

The Martin Luther King, Jr. Center. 449 Auburn Avenue, NE, Atlanta, GA 30312, 404-526-8900, *information@thekingcenter.org*, *www.thekingcenter.org*. Established in 1968 by Mrs. Coretta Scott King, the King Center is the living memorial and institutional guardian of Dr. Martin Luther King, Jr.'s legacy. The King Center accomplishes this through programming, building a network of organizations, providing a clearinghouse for Dr. King's writings, and managing visitor services.

METTA Center for Nonviolence. 236 West Portal Avenue #47, San Francisco, CA 94127, 650-270-6966, *codirectors@mettacenter.org*, *www.mettacenter.org*. The METTA Center works to inspire and support the study and practice of nonviolence. By providing resources and other educational activities, we empower ourselves and others to enliven the legacy of Mahatma Gandhi, Dr. Martin Luther King Jr., and all those who have blazed a trail to the "beloved community" and a nonviolent future for humanity.

Michigan Peace Team (MPT). 1516 Jerome Street, Lansing, MI 48912, 517-484-3178, *michpeaceteam@peacenet.org, www.michiganpeaceteam.org.* MPT empowers people to engage in active nonviolent peacemaking. It was started in 1993, in response to the growing need for civilian peacemakers both in the U.S. and abroad. MPT seeks a just world grounded in nonviolence and respect for the sacred interconnectedness of all life.

Nevada Desert Experience. PO Box 46645, Las Vegas, NV 89114- 6645, 702-646-4814, *nde@peacenet.org, www.nevadadesertexperience.org.* NDE works to stop nuclear weapons testing through a campaign of prayer, education, dialogue, and nonviolent direct action. NDE mobilizes people of faith to work toward nuclear abolition.

Nonviolence International (NI). 4545 42nd Street N.W., Washington, D.C., (202) 393-3616, *nonviolence@igc.org, www.nonviolenceinternational.net.* NI assists individuals, organizations, and governments striving to utilize nonviolent methods to bring about changes reflecting the values of justice and human development on personal, social, economic, and political levels. NI is committed to educating the public about nonviolent action and to reducing the use of violence worldwide.

Nonviolence Peaceforce (NPF). NPF Bay Area, 721 Shrader Street, San Francisco, CA 94117, *peaceworkers at igc.org,* 415-751-0302, *www.nonviolentpeaceforce.org.* NPF is building a trained, international civilian peaceforce committed to third-party nonviolent intervention.

Pace e Bene Nonviolence Service. *www.paceebene.org;* Engage: *www.EngageNonviolence.org;* 1420 W. Bartlett Ave., Las Vegas, NV 89106; 702-648-2281; *paceebene@paceebene.org.* Launched in 1989, Pace e Bene cultivates nonviolent living and the emergence of nonviolent cultures through training, publishing, advocacy, and spiritual practice. Pace e Bene has led hundreds of nonviolence trainings, workshops, retreats and classes for thousands of people throughout the world.

Peace Brigades International. (PBI)/USA, 428 8th St. SE, 2nd fl., Washington DC 20003 202-544-3765, *info@pbiusa.org, www.peacebrigades.org.* PBI provides nonviolent international peacekeeping in areas of violent conflict and repression, offering unarmed protective accompaniment to individuals, organizations, and communities threatened with political violence and human rights violations.

Peace Justice Studies Association (PJSA). 5th Floor University Center, 2130 Fulton Street, San Francisco, CA 94117-1080, Phone: 415-422-5238, *www.peacejusticestudies.org.* PJSA works to create a just and peaceful world through: the promotion of peace studies within universities, colleges and K-12 grade levels; the forging of alliances among educators, students, activists, and other peace practitioners in order to enhance each other's work on peace, conflict and non-violence; the creation and nurturing of alternatives to structures of inequality and injustice, war and violence through education, research and action.

Resources Advancing Initiatives in Nonviolence (RAIN). 1545 Farwell, Chicago, IL USA; 773-338-8445; *www.RainOnline.org.* RAIN is a nonprofit organization dedicated to developing resources that explore the creativity and spirituality of active nonviolence to promote the well-being of all. These resources include media that tell the stories of active nonviolence through video, print and web formats.

Ruckus Society. 369 15th Street, Oakland, CA 94612, 510 763-7078, *info@ruckus.org*, *www.ruckus.org*. The Ruckus Society provides environmental, human rights, and social justice organizers with the tools, training, and support needed to achieve their goals.

School of Americas Watch. PO Box 4566, Washington DC 20017, 202-234-3440, *info@soaw.org*, *www.soaw.org*. SOA Watch is an independent organization that seeks to close the US Army School of the Americas, under whatever name it is called, through vigils and fasts, demonstrations and nonviolent protest, as well as media and legislative work.

Season for Nonviolence (SNV). 1815 Garden Street, Santa Barbara, CA 93101, 805-563-7343, *snv@agnt.org*, *www.agnt.org/snv02.htm*. Convened by the Association for Global New Thought, SNV runs from January 30 - April 4, a national 64-day educational, media, and grassroots campaign dedicated to demonstrating that nonviolence is a powerful way to heal, transform, and empower our lives and our communities. Inspired by the 50th and 30th memorial anniversaries of Mahatma Gandhi and Dr. Martin Luther King, Jr., this international event honors their vision for an empowered, nonviolent world.

Soulforce, Inc. PO Box 3195, Lynchburg, VA 24503-0195, 877-705-6393, *info@soulforce.org*, *www.soulforce.org*. Soulforce is an interfaith movement committed to ending spiritual violence perpetuated by religious policies and teachings against gay, lesbian, bisexual, and transgender (GLBT) people.

Training for Change. 1501 Cherry St, Philadelphia, PA 19102, 215-241-7035, *peacelearn@igc.org*, *www.trainingforchange.org*. Training for Change offers workshops teaching skills and tools to individuals and groups working for nonviolent social change.

United States Institute for Peace. 202-457-1700, *www.usip.org*. 1200 17th Street NW, Washington, DC 20036. USIP's Religion and Peacemaking initiative helps US faith-based organizations to become more active and effective as international peacebuilders.

University of Rhode Island Nonviolence Institute, Center for Nonviolence and Peace Studies. Multicultural Center, University of Rhode Island, 74 Lower College Road, Kingston, RI 02881, 401-874-2875, *www.uri.edu/nonviolence*. The program helps build a world of mutual understanding among people, in which nonviolent processes are used to reconcile conflicts and build community. We seek to study and apply approaches which will foster more harmonious relationships at every level. The Center will accomplish this mission by providing educational and research opportunities, and leadership development at the University of Rhode Island, and help facilitate such programs throughout the state.

Victim-Offender Reconciliation Program (VORP). 1007 NE 118th Avenue, Portland, OR 97220, 503-255-8677, *martyprice@vorp.com*, *www.vorp.com*. VORP works to bring restorative justice reform to our criminal and juvenile justice systems, to empower victims, offenders and communities to heal the effects of crime, to curb recidivism and to offer our society a more effective and humanistic alternative to the growing outcry for more prisons and more punishment.

War Resisters League. 339 Lafayette Street, New York, NY 10012, 212-228-0450, *wrl@warresisters.org*, *www.warresisters.org*. WRL advocates Gandhian nonviolence as the method for creating a democratic society free of war, racism, sexism, and human exploitation through education and action.

Women's International League for Peace and Freedom (WILPF). 1213 Race Street, Philadelphia PA - 19107 1691, 215-563 7110, *www.wilpf.org.* WILPF was founded in 1915 during World War I, with Jane Addams as its first president. WILPF works to achieve through peaceful means world disarmament, full rights for women, racial and economic justice, an end to all forms of violence, and to establish those political, social, and psychological conditions which can assure peace, freedom, and justice for all.

NONVIOLENCE BIBLIOGRAPHY

Ackerman, Peter and Jack Duvall, *A Force More Powerful: A Century of Nonviolent Conflict* (New York: St. Martin's Press, 2000).

Anders, Gunther and Claude Eatherly, *Burning Conscience: The Guilt of Hiroshima* (New York: Paragon House, 1989).

Ansbro, John J., *Martin Luther King, Jr.: The Making of a Mind* (Maryknoll NY: Orbis Books, 1982).

Barbe, Domingos, *Theological Roots of Nonviolence* (Las Vegas: Pace e Bene, 1989).

_____, *A Theology of Conflict and Other Writings on Nonviolence* (Maryknoll NY: Orbis, 1989).

Bedlau, Hugo Adam, *Civil Disobedience: Theory and Practice* (Indianapolis: Bobbs-Merrill, 1969).

Berrigan, Daniel, *To Dwell in Peace* (San Francisco: Harper & Row, 1987).

Bobo, Kim, Jackie Kendall, and Steve Max, *A Manual for Activists in the 1990s* (Seven Locks Press, 1991).

Bondurant, Joan, *Conquest of Violence* (University of California Press, 1958).

Borman, William, *Gandhi and Nonviolence* (Albany NY: State University of New York Press, 1986).

Butigan, Ken, Mary Litell, and Louis Vitale, *Franciscan Nonviolence: Stories, Reflections, Principles, Practices and Resources* (Berkeley, CA: Pace e Bene Press, 2003).

Butigan, Ken, *Pilgrimage Through a Burning World: Spiritual Practice and Nonviolent Protest at the Nevada Test Site* ((Albany NY: State University of New York Press, 2003).

Camara, Dom Helder, *The Spiral of Violence* (Sheed and Ward, 1975).

Cooney, Robert and Helen Michalowski, *The Power of the People: Active Nonviolence in the United States* (Philadelphia: New Society Publishers, 1987).

Coover, Deacon, Esser and Moore, eds., *Resource Manual for a Living Revolution* (Philadelphia: New Society Publishers 1977).

Dear, John, *Disarming the Heart: Toward a Vow of Nonviolence* (New York: Paulist Press, 1987).

_____, *Our God is Nonviolent: Witnesses in the Struggle for Peace and Justice,* (New York: Pilgrim Press, 1990).

_____, *The God of Peace: Toward a Theology of Nonviolence* (Maryknoll, NY: Orbis Books, 1994).

_____, *Seeds of Non-Violence* (Baltimore: Fortkamp Publishing Co., 1992).

Deming, Barbara, *We Cannot Live Without Our Lives* (Grossman Publishers, 1974).

_____, *Revolution and Equilibrium* (Grossman Publishers, 1971).

Desroches, Leonard, *Allow the Water: Anger, Fear, Power, Work, Sexuality, and the Spirituality and Practice of Active Nonviolence* (Toronto, Ontario: Dunamis Publishers). Contact: 407 Bleeker St., Toronto, Ontario, Canada M4X 1W2.

Desai, Narayan, *Toward a Nonviolent Revolution* (Sarva Seva Sangh Prakashan).

Douglass, James W. *Lightning East to West* (New York: Crossroad, 1983).

_____, *The Nonviolent Coming of God* (Maryknoll NY: Orbis, 1991).

_____, *The Nonviolent Cross: A Theology of Revolution and Peace* (New York: Macmillan, 1966).

_____, *Resistance and Contemplation* (Garden City NY: Doubleday, 1972).

Easwaran, Eknath, *Nonviolent Soldier of Islam: Badshah Khan, A Man To Match His Mountains.* (Tomales, CA: Nilgiri Press, 1984, 1999).

Egan, Eileen, *Peace Be With You: Justified Warfare or the Way of Nonviolence* (Maryknoll, NY: Orbis Books, 1999).

Erickson, Erik, *Gandhi's Truth* (New York: W.W. Norton, 1969).

Fischer, Louis, *The Life of Mahatma Gandhi*, Louis Fischer (New York: Harper & Row, 1954).

Ford, J. Massyngbaerde, *My Enemy is My Guest: Jesus and Violence in Luke* (Maryknoll NY: Orbis Books, 1984).

Fromm, Erich, *The Anatomy of Human Destructiveness* (Holt).

Gandhi, Arun, *Legacy of Love: My Education in the Path of Nonviolence* (El Sobrante, CA: North Bay Books, 2003).

Gandhi, Mohandas K., *My Experiments with Truth* [also published as *Gandhi: An Autobiography*] (Boston: Beacon Press, 1957).

_____, *Nonviolence in Peace and War* (New York: Garland Press, 1972).

_____, *Nonviolent Resistance* (Schoken Books, 1962).

_____, *Pathway to God* (Ahmedabad, India: Navajivan Publishing House).

_____, *Satyagraha in South Africa* (New York, 1954).

_____, K. Kripalani, ed., *All Men Are Brothers: Autobiographical Reflections* (New York, Continuum, 1980).

The Garland Library of War and Peace (New York: Garland Publishing Inc., 1970). A collection of 360 titles reprinted in 328 volumes.

Glassman, Bernie, *Bearing Witness* (New York: Bell Tower, 1998).

Gregg, Richard, *The Power of Nonviolence* (London: James Clark, 1960 and Schoken Books, 1970).

Hare, A. Paul and Herbert H. Blumberg, eds., *Nonviolent Direct Action* (Washington and Cleveland: Corpus Books, 1968).

Harding, Vincent, *Hope and History: Why We Must Share the Story of the Movement* (Maryknoll, NY: Orbis Books, 1990).

Haring, Bernard, *The Healing Power of Peace and Nonviolence* (Paulist Press, 1986).

Holmes, Robert L., *Nonviolence in Theory and Practice* (Belmont CA: Wadsworth, 1990).

Holst, Johan, *Civilian-Based Defense in a New Era* (Boston: Albert Einstein Institution for Nonviolent Sanctions, 1990).

Houver, Gerard A, *Nonviolent Lifestyle: Conversations with Jean and Hildegard Goss-Mayr* (1981).

Ingram, Catherine, *In the Footsteps of Gandhi: Conversations with Spiritual Social Activists* (Parallax Press, 1990).

Jayaprakash, Narayan, *Total Revolution* (Sarva Seva Sangh Prakashan, 1975).

Jesudasan, Ignatius, *A Gandhian Theology of Liberation* (Maryknoll, NY: Orbis Books, 1984).

Juergensmeyer, Mark, *Gandhi's Way: A Handbook of Conflict Resolution* (Berkeley: University of California, 1984 [2002]).

King, Mary, *Mahatma Gandhi and Martin Luther King, Jr.: The Power of Nonviolent Action* (Paris, France: UNESCO Publishing, 1999).

Kyi, Aung San Suu, *Freedom from Fear* (New Delhi ; New York, NY : Penguin Books, 1995).

King, Jr., Martin Luther, *Loving Your Enemies* [pamphlet], M.L. King, Jr., A.J. Muste Foundation, n.d.

_____, *Strive Toward Freedom* (Harper & Row, 1958).

_____, *Trumpet of Conscience* (New York: Harper & Row, 1967).

_____, *Why We Can't Wait* (Harper and Row, 1964).

Kownacki, Mary Lou and Gerard Vanderhaar, *Way of Peace: A Guide to Nonviolence* (Pax Christi, 1987).

Lakey, George et al., *Powerful Peacemaking: A Strategy for a Living Revolution* (New Society Publishers,1987).

Laffin, Arthur J. and Anne Montgomery, *Swords into Plowshares* (San Francisco: Harper & Row, 1987).

Lewis, John with Michael D'Orso, *Walking with the Wind: A Memoir of the Movement* (San Diego, CA : Harcourt Brace, 1999).

Lynd, Staughton ed., *Nonviolence in America: A Documentary History* (New York: Bobbs-Merrill Co., 1966.

McAllister, Pam, ed., *Reweaving the Web of Life: Feminism and Nonviolence* (Philadelphia: New Society Publishers, 1982).

_____, *You Can't Kill the Spirit: Stories of Women and Nonviolent Action* (Philadelphia: New Society Publishers, 1991).

McGinnis, Jim with Thelma Burgonio-Watson et al., *A Call to Peace: 52 Meditations on the Family Pledge of Nonviolence* (Liguori, MO : Liguori, 1998).

McManus, Philip and Gerald Schlabach, eds., *Relentless Persistence: Nonviolent Action in Latin America* (Philadelphia: New Society Publishers, 1991).

Macgregor, G.H.C. *The New Testament Basis of Pacifism* (Nyack NY: Fellowship Publications, 1936).

Merton, Thomas, *Faith and Violence* (South Bend: Notre Dame Press, 1968).

Moyer, Bill, *Doing Democracy: The MAP Model for Organizing Social Movements* (Gabriola Island, BC: New Society Pub., 2001).

Myers, Ched, *Binding the Strong Man: A Political Reading of Mark's Story of Jesus* (Maryknoll NY: Orbis Books, 1988).

Nagler, Michael, *America Without Violence: Why Violence Persists and How You Can Stop It* (Covelo, CA: Island Press, 1982).

_____, *Is There No Other Way? The Search for a Nonviolent Future* (Berkeley, CA: Berkeley Hills Books, 2001).

Nhat Hanh, Thich. *Love in Action: Writings on Nonviolent Social Change* (Berkeley, CA : Parallax Press, 1993).

O'Gorman, Angie, ed., *The Universe Bends Toward Justice: A Reader on Christian Nonviolence* (Philadelphia: New Society Publishers, 1991).

Powers, Roger S. and William B. Vogele, eds., *Protest, Power, and Change: An Encyclopedia of Nonviolent Action from ACT-UP to Women's Suffrage* (New York, London: Garland Publishing Co., 1997).

Ross, Fred, *Conquering Goliath: Cesar Chavez at the Beginning* (Keen, CA).

Schell, Jonathan, *The Unconquerable World: Power, Nonviolence and the Will of the People* (New York: Metropolitan Books, Henry Holt & Co., 2003).

Shepard, Mark, *Gandhi Today* (Seven Locks Press, 1981).

Sharp, Gene, *Gandhi as a Political Strategist* (Boston: Porter Sargent, 1979).

_____, *The Politics of Nonviolent Action.* Three volumes. (Boston: Porter Sargent, 1973).

Sulak Sivaraksa, *Global Healing : Essays and Interviews on Structural Violence, Social Development, and Spiritual Transformation* (Bangkok : Thai Inter-Religious Commission for Development, Sathirakoses-Nagapradipa Foundation, 1999).

Thoreau, Henry David, "Civil Disobedience ," in *Modern Essays* (Boston, International Pocket Library, 1964).

Thurman, Howard, *Jesus and the Disinherited* (New York, Abingdon-Cokesbury Press, 1949).

Tolstoi, Leo *Writings On Civil Disobedience and Nonviolence* (Philadelphia: New Society Publishers, 1987).

Trocme, Andre, *Jesus and the Nonviolent Revolution* (Scottsdale, PA: Herald Press, 1973).

True, Michael, *Justice Seekers, Peace Makers: 32 Portraits in Courage* (Mystic CT: Twenty-third Publications, 1987).

Vanderhaar, Gerard A. *Enemies and How to Love Them* (Twenty-Third Publications, 1985).

_____, *Nonviolence in Christian Tradition* (Pax Christi USA, 1983).

_____, *Nonviolence Theory and Practice* (Mid-South Peace and Justice Center, 1985).

Washington, James, *A Testament of Hope: The Essential Writings and Speeches of Martin Luther King, Jr.* (Hayes-Collins, 1986).

Welch, Sharon, *Communities of Resistance and Solidarity: A Feminist Theology of Liberation* (Maryknoll, NY: Orbis Books, 1985).

Wink, Walter, *Engaging the Powers: Discernment and Resistance in a World of Domination* (Minneapolis: Fortress, 1992).

_____, ed. *Peace is the Way: Writings on Nonviolence from the Fellowship of Reconciliation* (Maryknoll, NY: Orbis, 2000).

_____, *Violence and Nonviolence in South Africa: Jesus' Third Way* (Philadelphia: New Society Publishers, 1987).

Yoder, J.H., *The Politics of Jesus* (Grand Rapids MI: Wm. B. Eerdmans, 1972).

Zahn, Franklin, *Deserter from Violence: Experiments with Gandhi's Truth* (New York: Philosophical Library, 1984).

Zahn, Gordon, *Solitary Witness: The Life and Death of Franz Jaggerstatter* (Philadelphia: Templegate, 1986).

Howard Zinn, *A People's History of the United States: 1492-Present* [New ed.].
(New York : HarperCollins, 2003).

_____, ed. *The Power of Nonviolence: Writings by Advocates of Peace* (Boston: Beacon Press, 2002).

RECOMMENDED NONVIOLENCE VIDEOS

TITLE	DESCRIPTION	CONTACT INFORMATION	TIME	YR
An Unlikely Friendship	An Unlikely Friendship is a film about a surprising friendship which emerged between an embittered Ku Klux Klan leader and an outspoken black woman activist.	Filmakers Library: 212-808-4980 *info@filmakers.com*	43 min.	—
Baynard Rustin — Brother Outsider	Winner of numerous awards, "Brother Outsider" presents a feature-length documentary portrait, focusing on Bayard Rustin's activism for peace, racial equality, economic justice and human rights.	Calif. Newsreel, *www.newsreel.org* *http://www.pbs.org/pov/pov2002/ brotheroutsider/*	90 min.	—
Beyond Rangoon	Laura goes on vacation to Burma and falls in with students fighting for democracy using nonviolence. She and their leader, U Aung Ko, travel through Burma, whilst witnessing many bloody acts of repression by the dictatorship, in an attempt to escape to Thailand. Based on a true story.	A Hollywood movie, this is available at most movie stores or through *www.amazon.com*	100 min.	1995
Born on the 4th of July	The biography of Ron Kovic. Paralyzed in the Vietnam war, he becomes an anti-war and pro-human rights political activist after feeling betrayed by the country he fought for.	A Hollywood movie, this is available at most movie stores or through *www.amazon.com*	145 min.	1989
Bringing Down the Dictator, Unarmed Commitment	The extraordinary story of the overthrow of the "Butcher of the Balkans" by an avowedly nonviolent group of student revolutionaries whose weapons included humor, ridicule, and the Internet.	Contact Films For the Humanities at 1-800-257-5126, or visit *http://www.films.com.*	120 min.	
Citizen King	A 2-hour documentary on the last 5 years of Dr. Martin Luther King, Jr's life.	*http://www.pbs.org/wgbh/amex/ mlk/index.html*	120 min.	2004
Eyes on the Prize Series	A 6-part series, EYES ON THE PRIZE is the most comprehensive television documentary ever produced on the American civil rights movement. It focuses on the events, issues, triumphs and tragedies of ordinary people during a period termed "the Second American Revolution".	Order from PBS: *pbsvideodb.pbs.org*		
Friendship Village	The film documents an international group of veterans who are building a village in Vietnam for children with Agent Orange-related deformities.	*www.vietnamfriendship.org*	50 min.	1999
From Montgomery to Memphis	Compiled from newsreel footage and interspersed with celebrity commentary, this film has a heavy impact, showing Rev. King, not as a saint, but as a compassionate man of God with great goals for all people.	*www.imdb.com*	185 min.	1970
Gandhi (starring Ben Kingsley; Dir. Attenborough)	This film describes the life and times of Mahatma Gandhi, Indian political leader who managed to free his country from the British rule using nonviolent means and thus giving hope and inspiration for generations to come.	A Hollywood movie, this is available at most movie stores or through *www.amazon.com*	180 min.	1982
Greenpeace's Greatest Hits	These are Greenpeace's major campaigns from 1971 through 1988, including efforts to preserve Antarctica, and to halt seal hunting, nuclear testing, toxic waste dumping, and commercial whaling.	*www.amazon.com*	60 min.	1995

Improbable Pairs/ So. Africa	The film is about pairs of people who have made peace with each other against truly extraordinary odds, notably a Palestinian father and an Israeli father who have both lost sons.		18 min.	1999
In Remembrance of Martin	Personal comments from family members, friends, former classmates and advisors are chronicled in this moving documentary honoring Dr. Martin Luther King, Jr. Coretta Scott King is joined by Rev. Ralph Abernathy, Julian Bond, former President Jimmy Carter, Bill Cosby, Bishop Desmond Tutu and others, who remember highlights in Dr. King's career.	*http://teacher.shop.pbs.org/ product/index.jsp?product Id=1403951*	60 min.	
In the Company of Fear (Peace Brigades Int'l)	A documentary on the work within Colombia of Peace Brigades International, an organization using nonviolent accompaniment to protect threatened human rights workers.	Jill Sharpe, 604-251-1307, *jdsharpe@istar.ca,* see also *www.peacebrigades.org*	60 min.	1999
Life and Debt in Jamaica	Utilizing excerpts from the award-winning non-fiction text "A Small Place" by Jamaica Kincaid, Life & Debt is a woven tapestry of sequences focusing on the stories of individual Jamaicans whose strategies for survival and parameters of day-to-day existence are determined by the U.S. and other foreign economic agendas.	*www.lifeanddebt.org*	90 min.	2001
Long Night's Journey into Day: South Africa's Search for Truth and Reconciliation	This film reveals a South Africa trying to forge a lasting peace after 40 years of government by the most notorious system of racial segregation since Nazi Germany. The documentary studies South Africa's Truth and Reconciliation Commission (TRC).	*www.irisfilms.org*	94 min.	2000
Martin Luther King: I Have a Dream	On August 28, 1963, Martin Luther King spoke these words as he addressed a crowd of more than 200,000 civil rights protesters gathered at The Lincoln Memorial in Washington, DC.	*www.mpihomevideo.com*	25 min.	1986
Not in Our Town	The inspiring documentary film about the residents of Billings, Montana who responded to an upsurge in hate violence by standing together for a hate-free community.	*www.theworkinggroup.org*		1996
Peace by Peace: Women on the Frontlines	Filmed in Afghanistan, Bosnia-Herzegovina, Burundi, Argentina and the US, this documentary, narrated by Academy Award-winner Jessica Lange, takes viewers into the lives of courageous women working to build peace out of conflict and crisis.	*www.peacexpeace.org*	86 min.	2003
Revolution Will Not Be Televised	With dramatic, on-scene coverage, this documentary covers the shortest-lived coup d'etat in history, the removal of the democratically-elected Venezuelan President Hugo Chavez.	*www.chavezthefilm.com*	70 min.	2004
Romero	Chronicles the life of Catholic Archbishop Oscar Romero, a champion for the oppressed poor in El Salvador (starring Raul Julia).	A Hollywood movie, this is available at most movie stores or through *www.amazon.com*	102 min.	1989

Samaritan: The Mitch Synder Story	Fact-based story about Mitch Snyder (Martin Sheen), a Washington crusader for the homeless, who took their case to Congress. Working for the Community for Creative Nonviolence, Snyder became outraged at the number of homeless people who had been dumped on the Washington streets.	Made for TV movie, 1986		
Seniors for Peace: A Portrait of Extraordinary Senior Peace Activists	An inspiring 26-minute documentary on a group of remarkably articulate and passionate senior peace activists (average age 85) from The Redwoods Retirement Community in Mill Valley, California	*www.dlbfilms.com*	26 min.	2004
SOA: Guns and Greed	Rarely seen footage in this documentary shows how the combat-ready SOA graduates use their guns to protect the greed of large corporations and world financial institutions. Acting on their own or under orders from their governments, the soldiers target labor organizers, human rights advocates, educators, religious leaders and others who speak out against exploitation.	*www.soaw.org*	20 min.	2000
Desmond Tutu with Bill Moyers	Moyer interviews Archbishop Desmond Tutu who talks about the South Africa struggle against apartheid and the Truth and Reconciliation Commissions.	*kenan.ethics.duke.edu*		1999
Steps to Peace — The Journey of Sept. 11th	This documentary includes interviews with people who lost loved ones on 9/11, their decision to speak out as a voice for peace, the formation of the group Peaceful Tomorrows and highlights of major activities.	*www.peacefultomorrows.org*	13 min.	
The Democracy University Tapes	Hundreds of video and audio tapes of speeches by many leading authors, speakers, artists, etc. in peace and justice. $5 for 5 hrs.	*www.justicevision.org*		
The Good War & Those Who Refused to Fight It	This film sheds light on a previously ignored part of the World War II saga — the story of American conscientious objectors who refused to fight "the good war." It is a story of personal courage, idealism and nonconformity based on both ethical and religious beliefs — about men whose love of country could not extend to killing their fellow man.	*www.pbs.org/itvs/thegoodwar*	57 min.	2000
The Meeting	A fictitious 1965 confrontation between Martin Luther King, Jr., Baptist minister and champion of nonviolence, and Malcolm X, advocate of self-defense by any means and himself the center of factional warring within his own Muslim faith.	*www.synapseproductions.com*, 216-932-9475, *editpro@n2net.net*	80 min.	
The Scarlet and the Black	Based on a true story, Fr. Hugh O'Flaherty is a Vatican official in 1943-45 who has been hiding downed pilots, escaped prisoners of war, and Italian resistance families in the midst of the Nazi occupation of Italy.	A Hollywood movie, this is available at most movie stores or through *www.amazon.com*		1983

Weapons of the Spirit

Le Chambon-sur-Lignon was a tiny Protestant farming village in the mountains of south-central France. Defying the Nazis and the French government that was collaborating with the Nazis, the villagers of the area of Le Chambon provided a safe haven throughout the war for whoever knocked on their door.

www.chambon.org

STEPS OF A NONVIOLENT STRATEGY

We need a carefully developed strategy in order to transform social injustice and its underlying cultural assumptions. The following six steps are key phases of a nonviolent strategy.

1) *Information Gathering and Analysis*

- In approaching any injustice that we want to transform, we need to know the facts and factors of the situation. We need to understand the policy or condition "in the round" — from every angle.
- First, this means carefully describing this policy and its consequences.
- Second, this means identifying the power relations: who holds the power? We have to understand the position of the opponent and her or his interests that underlie this position. Who are the allies of the opponent? What are the cultural attitudes or assumption that keep this policy in place? In other words, how is this policy sustained?
- But this also means analyzing the power of those opposing the policy. As Gene Sharp writes in *The Politics of Nonviolent Action* (Boston: Porter Sargent, 1973), political power ultimately rests with the general population. Power is not a magical substance invested in policy-makers; in fact, policy-makers rely on the consent of the people. We need to analyze the ways the population has given its tacit or overt support to this policy.
- These steps, then, are part of the Gandhian process of identifying the truth of the situation: the truth and untruth of our position, and the truth and untruth of the opponent's position.

2) *Choosing a Concrete Objective*

- This is based on our analysis and must address an injustice that violates central human and cultural values.

3) *Dialogue*

- Using intelligence and persistence, communicate to the other party the list of injustices and your concrete plan for addressing and resolving these injustices. Look for what is positive in the actions and statements the opposition makes. Do not seek to humiliate the opponent but find creative ways to call forth the good in the opponent. Look for ways in which the opponent can also win.

4) *Securing Public Support*

- If change does not occur, we must next secure public support for change. This involves a broad effort to educate the public, and at the same time, to build alliances with key organizations. This phase includes the development of "public participation events" (interfaith services, marches, petitions, phone-in campaigns, etc.).

5) *Action*

- Nonviolent direct action is taken to move the opponent to work with you to resolve the injustices when the other means of persuasion have not reached the objective. These actions need to reveal with the greatest clarity the injustice being denounced. Such actions should be designed to give the largest number of people possible the opportunity to participate.

- Direct action introduces a "creative tension" into the conflict. It is most effective when it illustrates the injustice it seeks to correct.

6) *Resolution and Reconciliation*

- Education, dialogue and action can create the conditions for a humane alternative to the identified injustice.
- This alternative addresses the specific issue at hand, and changes the dynamics between the opponents. Nonviolence seeks friendship and understanding with the opponent. Nonviolence is directed against evil systems, forces, oppressive policies, and unjust acts, not against persons.
- Reconciliation includes the opponent being able to "save face." Each act of genuine reconciliation is one step closer to the goal of human life, which Martin Luther King, Jr. called the "Beloved Community."
- Both the individuals and the entire community are empowered. With this comes new struggles for justice and a new beginning.

Sources: Alvaro Diaz, Lines of Strategy in the Nonviolent Struggle *by (an essay published by Pace e Bene) and on the work of Dr. Martin Luther King, Jr., summarized in "M.L. King: A Way of Nonviolence" (available from Fellowship of Reconciliation USA).*

SEVEN STRATEGIC ASSUMPTIONS OF SUCCESSFUL SOCIAL MOVEMENTS

By Bill Moyer

1) *Social Movements Are Proven To Be Powerful*

Social movements have been a powerful means for ordinary people to participate directly in creating positive social change, particularly when formal channels for democratic political participation do not work. Social movements helped end slavery, create labor unions and child labor laws, attain women's suffrage, end atmospheric nuclear testing, achieve many civil rights for blacks, women, gays and lesbians, end the Vietnam War, oust dictators, challenge South African Apartheid, curb the cold war, and move Eastern Bloc nations toward democracy. Almost every positive aspect of American society has been influenced by successful people's movements. Social movements are more numerous and powerful than ever. Much acclaim is given to the social movements of the 1960s, but those of the 1970s, 1980s, and 1990s were bigger and more numerous.

2) *Movements Are At The Center of Society*

Most social movements are not exceptional [or] rare protest events on society's fringe, and activists are not anti-social rebels. Quite the contrary, progressive nonviolent social movements are at the center of society's "historicity," the ongoing process of society evolving and redefining itself. In the words of Dr. Martin Luther King, a chief purpose of social movements is "to fulfill the American Dream, not to destroy it." Social movements are deeply grounded in our founding values of justice, democracy, civil right, security, and freedom. In contrast, they oppose vested interests that use public offices and corporate institutions in ways that violate these principles. Implication: Social movements, therefore, must consciously articulate society's central value and sensibilities. Almost all ordinary citizens consider themselves patriots; that is, they strongly believe in the positive values of their country. Movement activists will be successful only to the extent that they can convince the great majority of people that the movement, and not the powerholders, truly represent society's values and sensibilities. In contrast, movements are self-destructive to the extent that they define themselves as being rebels on the fringes of society who oppose the majority and are trying to overthrow core social values and structures.

3) *The Real Issue Is Social Justice vs. Vested Interest*

The experience of social movements is consistent with Arnold Toynbee's dictum that the real struggle in the world is between vested interests and social justice. An elite minority holds enormous political, economic, and social power and influence, which they use to benefit a minority of elites at the expense of society's majority. In their attempt to promote democracy, justice, peace, ecological sustainability, and the general social welfare, social movements must oppose the excessive power and influence of the elite powerholders. The consequence of such opposition is, inevitably, conflict with the political, economic, and corporate powerholders — whether they be military contractors wanting to increase the military budget and prolong the nuclear arms race, doctors wanting to undermine guaranteed health care, or logging companies wanting to destroy the remaining old-growth forests. The struggle between vested interests and social welfare will be intensified with the growing crises during in the 1990s. Implication: In the face of this inevitable struggle, movement activists must neither become discouraged nor believe their movement is losing when powerholders do not change their minds or policies. Even though a social movement may be supported by a majority who opposes current policies and condition, powerholders will fight until it becomes in their interest to change.

4) The Grand Strategy Is To Promote Participatory Democracy

The grand strategy of social movements is to promote participatory democracy through people power, in which an ever-increasing majority of ordinary citizen is alerted, won over, and becomes involved in addressing critical social problems and achieving progressive change.

The lack of democracy is a major source of social problems. The American system increasingly exemplifies that power corrupts and absolute power corrupts absolutely. When a society functions to support the self-serving interests of its privileged few, lack of concern for the welfare of all people helps to engender environmental destruction, massive poverty, reduced social programs, vast military expenditures, support of Third World dictators, and global military intervention.

Political power ultimately rests with the general population. The official power-holders in any society can only rule as long as they have the consent of the people. Ultimately, the general population will give this consent only as long as those who govern are perceived to be upholding the public trust and the basic morals, values, and interests of the whole society. (That is why all governments — including those of the democratic West as well as the harshest dictatorships — spend enormous money and effort trying to justify their power and policies to the ordinary public, wrapping them in terms of widely-accepted values and traditions.) There have been remarkable examples of the power of ordinary citizens to overthrow even brutal Stalinist dictatorships in the Eastern Bloc nations. Participatory democracy, led by social movement people-power, therefore, is a key to facing the awesome problems that confront us today and to establishing a more humane world. The resolution of today's problems require an informed, empowered and politicized population that assertively demands democracy, justice, security, equality, human welfare, peace, and ecological preservation.

5) Social Movements Focus on Winning Over Ordinary Citizens, not Powerholders

Social change happens only when the majority of citizens are alerted, educated, and motivated to be concerned about a problem. Social movements are only as powerful as the power of their grassroots support. The chief task of the activist, therefore, is to focus on and to win over the public, not to change the minds and policies of official powerholders. Implication: The formal powerholders will not change their policies until there is overwhelming pressure from the general population. Ignoring this reality is a chief source of activists' feelings of powerlessness and movement failure. When powerholders fail to respond to initial movement demands, many activists become depressed and angry. This can lead to burnout, dropout, unnecessary compromises, or aimless rebelliousness. This creates a cycle of increased failure, because rebellious acts alienate the general public, the true source of movement power.

6) Success is a Long-Term Process, Not An Event

The process of putting a social problem on society's agenda, winning a large majority, and subsequently achieving long-range movement goals (such as cutting the military budget in half and curbing the cold war) occurs over many years. This lengthy process includes reaching many sub-goals along the way.

Implications: Activists should evaluate their movement by how well it is moving along the road of success, not by whether it has achieved its long-term goals. And activists should develop strategies and tactics that advance their movement along the next segment of the road, instead of trying to achieve the long-range goals directly—and feeling they have failed because those long-range goals have not yet been reached.

7) *Social Movements Must Be Nonviolent*

Following Gandhi and King, the ideology and method of nonviolence provides social movements with the optimum opportunity to win over and involve the general citizenry in people power because:

- Nonviolence is based on timeless national, cultural, human, and religious values and principles such as equality, security, preservation, justice, democracy, love, forgiveness, caring, compassion, and understanding.
- Nonviolence appeals to these values and principles held by people and nations
- Nonviolence is less threatening to ordinary citizens.
- Nonviolence (unlike militaristic or violent methods) allows everyone to participate: women men, elderly, youth and even children; people from all traditional levels of strength and weakness.
- In nonviolence, the means are consistent with the ends—they are the ends in the making.
- Nonviolence has the capacity to reduce the effectiveness of police and state violence—the powerholder's ultimate weapon — and to turn it to the movement's advantage.
- A clear policy of nonviolence makes it difficult for agent provocateurs to disrupt or discredit movements by promoting internal violence, hostility, dissension, dishonesty and confusion.
- Successful social movements need participants and organizations that effectively play four different roles: citizen, rebel, social change agent, and reformer.

PREPARING FOR NONVIOLENCE

by Servicio Paz y Justicia

The following document from the Brazilian branch of the international Servicio Paz y Justicia (SERPAJ) nonviolence network explores the principles of *firmeza permanente* [literally "relentless persistence"] from the perspective of the popular movements there and discusses the need for and the content of training for nonviolent action. While it reflects the time (the mid-1970s) and the setting (Brazil) in which it was written, it nevertheless offers us critical insights which can be used to guide our contemporary efforts to organize nonviolent activity in a wide variety of contexts.

Convictions and Consequences of Active Nonviolence

Active nonviolence offers to both the oppressed and the oppressor the possibility of safeguarding their honor and their person. In the unjust, it attempts to nurture understanding, transformation, and even collaboration toward the good of all. It does not seek the humiliation of the enemy, nor his or her destruction...

This struggle enriches the adversaries — both aggressor and victim. Even if in the first stage of the struggle the victims are not able to achieve their objectives or to emerge victorious, they should not allow apparent failure to discourage them or diminish their struggle. Even without immediate positive or visible results, our conviction — and the guarantee of nonviolent action — is that truth and loving action have within them an all-encompassing, redeeming, and life-giving value: "To wish to save all humankind, including the oppressor."

This "universality" of the act of liberating nonviolence has infinite repercussions in the lives of men and women. Active nonviolence seeks to be the expression of authentic love at the core of political combat.

Some Principles of Nonviolence

1. In order to attain a just society, we need means that are better than intrigue, plotting, coups d'état, torture, murder, and terrorism. To achieve justice and peace it is necessary to find just and peaceful means. Since such means are consistent with the ends we desire in the long run, they will be simpler and more effective.

2. *Firmeza permanente* or "relentless persistence," a term sometimes used in place of active nonviolence, is in no way cowardly submission to the oppressors. On the contrary, it opposes the tyrants and the violent ones with all its strength. The practitioner of nonviolence continually attempts to overcome bad with good, lies with truth, hatred with love.

3. The struggle of *firmeza permanente* draws all of its strength from truth. To withdraw from truth is to withdraw from the source of our strength. Therefore the struggle cannot be clandestine. If you act in secret, you end up lying in order to disguise your efforts.

4. Violence may be impressive at first sight if it is part of a courageous search for justice. With time, however, we find that the way of violence does not deliver the hoped for result.

5. Courage in isolation is not enough. The struggle must be collective and organized...

6. If the people do not want to use the very weapons that dehumanize the oppressor, the only

solution is to accept, without retreating, the blows and the brutality of the adversary. There is no such thing as a human being who wishes to be inhuman until the end. Such is our hope.

7. Those who use violence attempt to provoke the practitioner of nonviolence in order to get them to abandon their principal weapon: the use of *firmeza permanente*.

8. In a situation of weakness, *firmeza permanente* is more effective than violence.

9. By overcoming the oppressor through violence, one achieves only a partial victory. The roots of injustice remain within the oppressor who was defeated and within the victor who is liberated from the oppressor, since both used violence and so kept within themselves the evil that they fought.

10. We cannot offer any guarantees to anybody that they will not be imprisoned. We can only guarantee that we will go together and nobody will skip out on the others.

11. Since its first commitment is to truth and justice, *firmeza permanente* is not limited to strictly legal actions.

12. Violence comes from aggressive impulses that are not channeled constructively. Since it is irrational it leads to hatred. The practitioner of nonviolence, fed by the conviction that we are all brothers and sisters, aspires to act for justice through the control of reason over instinct.

13. Violence is often impatient. *Firmeza permanente* endeavors to wait and to respect the necessary stages, recognizing that the conservatives know how to compromise or to change when they need to.

14. In the face of the practitioner of nonviolence, the anger and the might of the oppressor are useless. He [or she] loses his [or her] sense of self-assurance because of the attitude of the victim and the appeals to reason that the victim makes. The transformation and the defeat that he [or she]suffers then are moral. Instead of humiliating him, they enrich him.

15. The important thing is not to be brave once in a while, but rather persistent all of the time. "We may die, but we are not going to run," pledged the workers of PERUS in the strike of 1967.

16. If you cannot commit yourself to be nonviolent, be violent. What you cannot be is submissive.

17. When somebody attacks another in an act of physical violence and the victim replies in kind or flees, the response of the victim gives the aggressor a great security and moral support, since it shows that the moral values of the victim are the same as those of the attacker. Any attitude of fight or flight on the part of the victim reinforces the morale of the aggressor. But if the attitude of the victim is calm and firm, the fruit of self-discipline and self-control, the aggressor is disarmed by the show of love and the respect for him or her as a person. This only happens because the victim does not respond to the violence of the aggressor either with cowardice or with counter-violence. Instead the victim attacks the aggressor at the level of thought, of intelligence, of reason, using the weapons of truth, justice, and love.

Training for Nonviolent Action

Firmeza permanente is not improvised. We must take training for nonviolent action seriously. *Firmeza permanente* requires training that is as much spiritual as practical, as much in the inspiration as in the tactics of nonviolence.

Analysis and Method

We do not propose to elaborate an overall strategy to resolve [for example] the land tenure problem nor to offer complete solutions... This is necessary, but we must be more modest. What we want to do is simply to offer some ideas that perhaps will help us to resist and attack in the way of active nonviolence when violent conflicts like these emerge. Let us consider a specific example.

In a factory, three workers file a complaint against the company. In accordance with the law, they are seeking salaries equal to those of other workers who are doing the same work. After various unsuccessful attempts to reach an agreement, they ask for a meeting with the manager. How should they prepare for this conversation/conflict, knowing that the company has a number of lawyers backing it, while they only have the assistance of the one union lawyer who has to handle many other cases besides? One method of preparation is to play out a "socio-drama."

Socio-Drama

Socio-drama is one of the best known and undoubtedly one of the most emotionally engaging training methods. It is a preview, in the form of theater, of a conflict that the participants are actually going to encounter. For example:

The case of the workers: Role play the conversation between the workers and the manager. Each one should give careful attention to preparing his or her role. Who will play the part of the manager and how? Of the workers? Of the lawyer from the union who accompanies them? Of the boss's secretary? Imagine the content of the conversation, the ambiance, the arguments each side will use. Anticipate the emotional reactions of the manager, the feelings of the workers. Divide up the tasks: During the conversation, who is going to speak? When? What tactic will you use?

The organizer who will train the others in this socio-drama should define with great care the theme (the principal problem which will be confronted), the setting (what will the environment be like?) and the place (where?) of the action. The roles of the other persons who are present should also be explained in detail. The actors assume their roles while the other members of the group constitute the public. Each person takes a few moments to get into his or her role and then the simulation begins. When the coordinator gives a signal, the simulation is stopped and the group critiques the actors. Did they represent, or better said, really express the feelings of the boss? Of the workers? Of the union representative? Was it realistic? Were there mistakes? Insights? Would the tactic they used work? Did the arguments carry weight? Are there other approaches?

Evaluation of the Socio-Drama

The goal of *firmeza permanente* is the efficacy of nonviolence. We want to achieve the objective without anyone dying, either morally or physically. A socio-drama permits us to evaluate realistically the resources that we actually have to carry an action through to the end.... Among the innumerable advantages that the socio-drama offers, we would single out the following:

1. It situates the action in its actual setting: the place (where will it be?); the time (exactly when? for how long?).

2. It familiarizes the participants with the situations in which they are engaged. Through the

physical and emotional reactions that surface in the training, they are able to develop more appropriate responses to various situations, such as contact with the adversary, prison, shooting, negotiations with the authorities, surprise developments. This practical preparation for nonviolent action is very important because the diverse exercises enable one to take into account the psychological factors (critical to the course of an action), the rational factors (cool analysis of what should in fact be done), and the practical factors (which a simple theoretical study of the situation would not allow one to foresee). As such, the goal of a socio-drama goes far beyond traditional, superficial preparation, sitting around a table.

3. It attempts to comprehend the position of the adversary. This is an important step in nonviolence. It is necessary to put oneself in the place of the adversary in order to know why s/he acts in that manner. In this way, it is possible to prevent irresponsible actions in which the only result is to uselessly provoke the adversary and reinforce his or her error. There is no point in humiliating one's opponent. Rather, through truth and justice, we must find an honorable way out for everyone. Experiencing the difficulties that the adversary must overcome enables us to discover the adversary's strong points and, as a result, makes our action more effective, because we will know when and where to act to maximize the chances of success.

4. It reinforces and nurtures the unity of the group. How? It develops the confidence of each individual in the group, stretches the bonds of friendship, and familiarizes the group with tense situations. Often the training enables the discharge of internal tensions, allowing each individual to regain a sense of calm at the time of the action.

5. It reinforces and nurtures self-confidence in each individual. This is a crucial aspect. This trust in oneself develops if the person comprehends that she or he has the power to react in certain situations, that she or he is a member of a group that offers support, and finally, that she or he can take part in the unfolding of a situation in which the phases are known and understood. She or he is no longer a pawn.

6. It teaches the group to do self-evaluation. Evaluation is the essential phase of the training. It gives an opportunity to judge the success or failure of the exercise and, above all, to see whether or not adequate resources actually exist to undertake an action. New and original ideas come up to overcome obstacles. There is no training without evaluation...

Spiritual Training

Finally, we cannot forget this fundamental aspect of training. ... Before any action that is likely to awaken the strongest passions, everyone should do such things as increase their vigils of prayer, ask the pardon of their brothers and sisters, purify themselves of evil, do justice in their own life, and fast.

Why all of this? Because we believe in the power of truth. It is truth that is going to triumph in the social, political, and other realms of human endeavor. Gandhi wrote: "By its very nature, truth gives evidence of itself. From the moment we leave behind all the stubborn webs of ignorance, the truth shines in splendor.... The way of truth is full of unimaginable obstacles. But in the faithful lover of truth there is neither deception nor defeat. For the truth is all-powerful, and the disciple of truth can never be overcome."

Translated from the Portuguese by Philip McManus.

SOME OF THE PRINCIPLES OF ACTIVE NONVIOLENCE

Gandhian Principles
- Nonviolence holds that all life is one.
- Nonviolence asserts that we each have a piece of the truth and the un-truth.
- Nonviolence is rooted in the idea that human beings are not reducible to the evil they commit.
- For nonviolence, the means must be consistent with the ends.
- Nonviolence underscores "difference without division": we become our truest selves the more we celebrate both our differences and our fundamental unity.
- Nonviolence maintains that we become our truest selves by transforming "us" versus "them" thought and action.
- Nonviolence is a process of becoming increasingly free from fear.
- Nonviolence is the desire for, and action on behalf of, the well-being of all.

Kingian Principles
- Nonviolence is a way of life for courageous people.
- Nonviolence seeks to win friendship and understanding.
- Nonviolence seeks to defeat injustice, not people.
- Nonviolence holds that voluntary suffering can educate and transform.
- Nonviolence chooses love instead of hate.
- Nonviolence believes that the universe is on the side of justice.

Additional Engage: Exploring Nonviolent Living *Principles*
- Nonviolence is active, constructive, cooperative and creative power for justice, equality, reconciliation and the well-being of all that employs neither passivity nor violence.
- Nonviolence unifies rather than threatens; integrates rather than fragments and destroys; and seeks the truth rather than the conquest of one side over another.
- Nonviolence is a process that refrains from violence to break the cycle of escalating and retaliatory violence; to reach out to the opponent and to potential allies; to focus on the issue at hand; and to seek to reveal more clearly the truth and justice of the situation.
- Nonviolence is organized love that includes loving one's opponent. That is, it acknowledges, safeguards and engages with the humanness, woundedness, and sacredness of the other, while actively challenging and resisting her or his violence and injustice.

The Principles Of Attitudinal Healing
- The essence of our being is love.
- Health is inner peace. Healing is letting go of fear.
- Giving and receiving are the same.
- We can let go of the past and the future.
- Now is the only time there is and each instant is for giving
- We can learn to love ourselves and others by forgiving rather than judging.
- We can become love finders rather than fault finders.
- We can choose and direct ourselves to be peaceful inside regardless of what is happening outside.
- We are students and teachers to each other.
- We can focus on the whole of life rather than the fragments.
- Since love is eternal death need not be viewed as fearful.

- We can always perceive ourselves and others as either extending love or giving a call for help.

Principles of Successful Social Movements (Bill Moyer)
- Social movements are proven to be powerful
- Movements are at the center of society
- The real issue is social justice vs. Vested interest
- The grand strategy is to promote participatory democracy
- Social movements focus on winning over ordinary citizens, not powerholders
- Social movements must be nonviolent to most effectively alert, win and mobilize ordinary citizens
- Success is a long-term process, not an event

UNIVERSAL DECLARATION OF HUMAN RIGHTS

On December 10, 1948 the General Assembly of the United Nations adopted and proclaimed the Universal Declaration of Human Rights the full text of which appears in the following pages. Following this historic act the Assembly called upon all Member countries to publicize the text of the Declaration and "to cause it to be disseminated, displayed, read and expounded principally in schools and other educational institutions, without distinction based on the political status of countries or territories."

PREAMBLE

- Whereas recognition of the inherent dignity and of the equal and inalienable rights of all members of the human family is the foundation of freedom, justice and peace in the world,
- Whereas disregard and contempt for human rights have resulted in barbarous acts which have outraged the conscience of mankind, and the advent of a world in which human beings shall enjoy freedom of speech and belief and freedom from fear and want has been proclaimed as the highest aspiration of the common people,
- Whereas it is essential, if man is not to be compelled to have recourse, as a last resort, to rebellion against tyranny and oppression, that human rights should be protected by the rule of law,
- Whereas it is essential to promote the development of friendly relations between nations,
- Whereas the peoples of the United Nations have in the Charter reaffirmed their faith in fundamental human rights, in the dignity and worth of the human person and in the equal rights of men and women and have determined to promote social progress and better standards of life in larger freedom,
- Whereas Member States have pledged themselves to achieve, in co-operation with the United Nations, the promotion of universal respect for and observance of human rights and fundamental freedoms,
- Whereas a common understanding of these rights and freedoms is of the greatest importance for the full realization of this pledge,

Now, Therefore THE GENERAL ASSEMBLY proclaims THIS UNIVERSAL DECLARATION OF HUMAN RIGHTS as a common standard of achievement for all peoples and all nations, to the end that every individual and every organ of society, keeping this Declaration constantly in mind, shall strive by teaching and education to promote respect for these rights and freedoms and by progressive measures, national and international, to secure their universal and effective recognition and observance, both among the peoples of Member States themselves and among the peoples of territories under their jurisdiction.

Article 1. All human beings are born free and equal in dignity and rights. They are endowed with reason and conscience and should act towards one another in a spirit of brotherhood.

Article 2. Everyone is entitled to all the rights and freedoms set forth in this Declaration, without distinction of any kind, such as race, colour, sex, language, religion, political or other opinion, national or social origin, property, birth or other status. Furthermore, no distinction shall be made on the basis of the political, jurisdictional or international status of the country or territory to which a person belongs, whether it be independent, trust, non-self-governing or under any other limitation of sovereignty.

Article 3. Everyone has the right to life, liberty and security of person.

Article 4. No one shall be held in slavery or servitude; slavery and the slave trade shall be prohibited in all their forms.

Article 5. No one shall be subjected to torture or to cruel, inhuman or degrading treatment or punishment.

Article 6. Everyone has the right to recognition everywhere as a person before the law.

Article 7. All are equal before the law and are entitled without any discrimination to equal protection of the law. All are entitled to equal protection against any discrimination in violation of this Declaration and against any incitement to such discrimination.

Article 8. Everyone has the right to an effective remedy by the competent national tribunals for acts violating the fundamental rights granted him by the constitution or by law.

Article 9. No one shall be subjected to arbitrary arrest, detention or exile.

Article 10. Everyone is entitled in full equality to a fair and public hearing by an independent and impartial tribunal, in the determination of his rights and obligations and of any criminal charge against him.

Article 11. (1) Everyone charged with a penal offence has the right to be presumed innocent until proved guilty according to law in a public trial at which he has had all the guarantees necessary for his defence.

(2) No one shall be held guilty of any penal offence on account of any act or omission which did not constitute a penal offence, under national or international law, at the time when it was committed. Nor shall a heavier penalty be imposed than the one that was applicable at the time the penal offence was committed.

Article 12. No one shall be subjected to arbitrary interference with his privacy, family, home or correspondence, nor to attacks upon his honour and reputation. Everyone has the right to the protection of the law against such interference or attacks.

Article 13. (1) Everyone has the right to freedom of movement and residence within the borders of each state.

(2) Everyone has the right to leave any country, including his own, and to return to his country.

Article 14. (1) Everyone has the right to seek and to enjoy in other countries asylum from persecution.

(2) This right may not be invoked in the case of prosecutions genuinely arising from non-political crimes or from acts contrary to the purposes and principles of the United Nations.

Article 15. (1) Everyone has the right to a nationality.

(2) No one shall be arbitrarily deprived of his nationality nor denied the right to change his nationality.

Article 16. (1) Men and women of full age, without any limitation due to race, nationality or religion, have the right to marry and to found a family. They are entitled to equal rights as to marriage, during marriage and at its dissolution.

(2) Marriage shall be entered into only with the free and full consent of the intending spouses.

(3) The family is the natural and fundamental group unit of society and is entitled to protection by society and the State.

Article 17. (1) Everyone has the right to own property alone as well as in association with others.

(2) No one shall be arbitrarily deprived of his property.

Article 18. Everyone has the right to freedom of thought, conscience and religion; this right includes freedom to change his religion or belief, and freedom, either alone or in community with others and in public or private, to manifest his religion or belief in teaching, practice, worship and observance.

Article 19. Everyone has the right to freedom of opinion and expression; this right includes freedom to hold opinions without interference and to seek, receive and impart information and ideas through any media and regardless of frontiers.

Article 20. (1) Everyone has the right to freedom of peaceful assembly and association.

(2) No one may be compelled to belong to an association.

Article 21. (1) Everyone has the right to take part in the government of his country, directly or through freely chosen representatives.

(2) Everyone has the right of equal access to public service in his country.

(3) The will of the people shall be the basis of the authority of government; this will shall be expressed in periodic and genuine elections which shall be by universal and equal suffrage and shall be held by secret vote or by equivalent free voting procedures.

Article 22. Everyone, as a member of society, has the right to social security and is entitled to realization, through national effort and international co-operation and in accordance with the organization and resources of each State, of the economic, social and cultural rights indispensable for his dignity and the free development of his personality.

Article 23. (1) Everyone has the right to work, to free choice of employment, to just and favourable conditions of work and to protection against unemployment.

(2) Everyone, without any discrimination, has the right to equal pay for equal work.

(3) Everyone who works has the right to just and favourable remuneration ensuring for himself and his family an existence worthy of human dignity, and supplemented, if necessary, by other means of social protection.

(4) Everyone has the right to form and to join trade unions for the protection of his interests.

Article 24. Everyone has the right to rest and leisure, including reasonable limitation of working hours and periodic holidays with pay.

Article 25. (1) Everyone has the right to a standard of living adequate for the health and well-being of himself and of his family, including food, clothing, housing and medical care and necessary social services, and the right to security in the event of unemployment, sickness, disability, widowhood, old age or other lack of livelihood in circumstances beyond his control.

(2) Motherhood and childhood are entitled to special care and assistance. All children, whether born in or out of wedlock, shall enjoy the same social protection.

Article 26. (1) Everyone has the right to education. Education shall be free, at least in the elementary and fundamental stages. Elementary education shall be compulsory. Technical and professional education shall be made generally available and higher education shall be equally accessible to all on the basis of merit.

(2) Education shall be directed to the full development of the human personality and to the strengthening of respect for human rights and fundamental freedoms. It shall promote understanding, tolerance and friendship among all nations, racial or religious groups, and shall further the activities of the United Nations for the maintenance of peace.

(3) Parents have a prior right to choose the kind of education that shall be given to their children.

Article 27. (1) Everyone has the right freely to participate in the cultural life of the community, to enjoy the arts and to share in scientific advancement and its benefits.

(2) Everyone has the right to the protection of the moral and material interests resulting from any scientific, literary or artistic production of which he is the author.

Article 28. Everyone is entitled to a social and international order in which the rights and freedoms set forth in this Declaration can be fully realized.

Article 29. (1) Everyone has duties to the community in which alone the free and full development of his personality is possible.

(2) In the exercise of his rights and freedoms, everyone shall be subject only to such limitations as are determined by law solely for the purpose of securing due recognition and respect for the rights and freedoms of others and of meeting the just requirements of morality, public order and the general welfare in a democratic society.

(3) These rights and freedoms may in no case be exercised contrary to the purposes and principles of the United Nations.

Article 30. Nothing in this Declaration may be interpreted as implying for any State, group or person any right to engage in any activity or to perform any act aimed at the destruction of any of the rights and freedoms set forth herein.

CREDITS AND CITATIONS

We are very grateful to all those from whom we have learned and borrowed and adapted. If you see something improperly credited, please contact us.

SESSION 1

pg: 6   "A human being is part of the whole…" by Albert Einstein,1954.

pg: 11   "Shine on in Montana" by Jo Clare Hartsig — *Nonviolence Today (Fellowship of Reconcilation)* and in *Peace is the Way: Writings on Nonviolence* (NY: Orbis, 2000), pp 255-6.

pg: 12   "If only it were so simple…" by Alexandr Solzhenitzyn — *The Gulag Archipelago 1918-1956*, Abridged (NY: HarperCollins, 1985).

pg: 15   "Now is the Time" poem by Mzwakhe Mbuli, a performance artist and activist in South Africa — from an album "Change is Pain" released in 1987 (Rounder Select).

pg: 18   "Brother Grab my Hand" by Usman Farman — original posting located at *http://e46fanatics.com/phorum/read.php?f=1&i=45274&t=45274.*

pg: 20   "That's How I Like to See a Woman" by Sue Monk Kidd — excerpted from *The Dance of the Dissident Daughter* (New York: HarperCollins, 1996), pp 7-10.

pg: 22   "The Costs of a Violent Society" by Jerry Large — *Seattle Times.* (Thu, 15 April, 2004 – Fourth edition ROP Northwest Life — page C1).

SESSION 2

pg: 28   "Zones of Learning." This exercise has been adapted from a handout "Using Discomfort Zones For Learning," by *Future Now: A Training Collective* which incorporated ideas first developed by *Training for Change.* For more info see *futurenow@igc.org; www.trainingforchange.org*

pg: 29   "Violence Spectrum Exercise." This exercise has been developed and used by many organizations, including the *American Friends Service Committee* and *Peace Brigade International.*

pg: 31   "I believe war is a weapon of persons..." by Alice Walker — excerpt from *Sent by Earth: A Message from the Grandmother Spirit After the Bombing of the World Trade Center and the Pentagon* (Open Media, 2001), p 17.

pg: 32   "Engage in Action." The story has been adapted by the authors of this study guide. The author of the original piece is a social worker who wishes to remain anonymous to protect the identity of her clients.

pg: 33   "There is so much focus on the distinction …" by Thich Nhat Hanh — *In the Footsteps of Gandhi: Conversations with Spiritual Social Activists.* Catherine Ingram. (Berkeley: Parallax Press, 1990).

pg: 34   Definition of Violence — by Miki Kashtan of *Bay Area Nonviolent Communication, www.baynvc.org.*

pg: 34   Definition of Violence by John Dear — from "Forgetting Who We Are," in *Disarming the Heart: Toward a Vow of Nonviolence.*(Scottsdale, PA: Herald Press, 1993).

pg: 34   Definition of Violence by Johan Galtung — adapted from *www.transcend.org.*

pg: 41   "Soul Force" by Cynthia Stateman. She can be contacted at *cynjay@prodigy.net.*

pg: 43   "The Seville Statement" — UNESCO Culture of Peace: Programme 7, Place de Fontenoy, 75352 PARIS 07 SP FRANCE.

SESSION 3

pg: 51   "Popeye and the Violence System" by Walter Wink—excerpted from *Engaging the Powers: Discernment and Resistance in a World of Domination* (Minneapolis, MN: Fortress Press, 1992), pp 18-19.

pg: 53   "Think of what a world we…" Albert Einstein from an interview in 1929.

pg: 54   "The Enemy Maker" poem by Sam Keen, from *Faces of the Enemy* (Olympic Marketing Corporation, 1986). Note that his book and the PBS documentary can be ordered from *www.samkeen.com.*

pg: 57   "Rice Bags Defeat Nukes" by David Albert — *People Power: Applying Nonviolence Theory*, p 43, from War

Resisters League 2002 calendar (end of Apr, May).

pg: 58 "Two Hands" by Barbara Deming. *On Revolution and Equilibrium* (NY: AJ Muste Memorial Institute), p 16.

pg: 62 "My Faith in Nonviolence" by Mohandas Gandhi, can be found in *Nonviolent Resistance* (New York: Schocken Books, 1961.)

pg: 63 "The Power of Noncooperation" by Shelley Douglass. The essay was written in 1983 when she was part of the Ground Zero Center for Nonviolent Action in Washington.

SESSION 4

pg: 71 "Story of Karen Ridd" by Michael Nagler. *The Search for a Nonviolent Future: A Promise of Peace for Ourselves, Our Families, and Our World* (Maui: Inner Ocean, 2004).

pg: 73 "The stick, the carrot, and the hug may…." by Kenneth Boulding. *Three Faces of Power*, (Newbury Park: Sage, 1989).

pg: 74 "We are constantly being astonished these days by the…" by Mohandas Gandhi — *The Collected Works of Mohandas Gandhi*, (Vol. 72, August 19, 1940).

pg: 80 "Love Walks" by Ken Butigan. He can be contacted at *kenbutigan@paceebene.org*.

pg: 81 "Communication: An Introduction to a Historical Model and to the New Powerful, Non-Defensive Communication Model" by Sharon Ellison. Excepted from her website, *www.pndc.com*, and her book *Taking the War Out of Our Words: The Art of Powerful Non-Defensive Communication* (Berkeley, CA: Bay Tree, 2002), pp. 82, 126-7, 165-6.

SESSION 5

pg: 89 Circle of Truths Exercise. Thanks to Janet Chisolm who helped to further develop this exercise that originally appeared in *From Violence To Wholeness*.

pg: 90 CARA process — CARA is based on a four part process developed by the late Bill Moyer. Elements used in Steps Two through Four are drawn from Sharon Ellison's process called Powerful, Non-Defensive Communication. See her book, *Taking the War Out of Our Words: The Art of Powerful, Non-Defensive Communication* (Berkeley, CA: Bay Tree, 2002). For more information, see *www.pndc.com*.

pg: 91 "Nonviolence is the greatest force…" by Mohandas Gandhi — *The Collected Works of Mohandas Gandhi*, (Vol. 61, July 20, 1931).

pg: 91 "… can put more pressure on the antagonist for whom we show human concern…." Barbara Deming. *On Revolution and Equilibrium* (NY: AJ Muste Memorial Institute, 1985), p 16.

pg: 91 "The nonviolent approach does not immediately change the heart of the oppressor…" by Martin Luther King, Jr. *Stride Toward Freedom* (NY and Evanston, IL: Harper & Row, 1964).

pg: 91 "Nonviolence is the power…." by Michael Nagler, class notes, PACS 164A, University of California, Berkeley, 2002.

pg: 91 "Love your enemies…wanting wholeness and well-being for those who may be broken…" by Angie O'Gorman. Excerpted from "Defense Through Disarmament" in *The Universe Bends Toward Justice: A Reader on Christian Nonviolence in the U.S.* (Philadelphia: New Society Publishers, 1990), p 242.

pg: 91 "The essence of nonviolence is understanding and compassion, so when you cultivate understanding and compassion…" by Thich Nhat Hanh as quoted in an article by Pierre Marchand, "Cultivating the Flower of Nonviolence: An Interview with Thich Nhat Hanh" for *Fellowship Magazine* (Jan/Feb. 1999).

pg: 91 "Nonviolence is the unfinished democratic revolution…." by Ken Butigan. He can be contacted at *kenbutigan@paceebene.org*.

pg: 92 "Q: Why are we violent but not illiterate?" by Colman McCarthy. Excerpted from "I'd Rather Teach Peace: Bringing Pacifism to Schools."

pg: 94 "If you really want to cultivate nonviolence, you should take a pledge that come what may…" Mohandas Gandhi. *The Collected Works of Mohandas Gandhi*, (Vol. 67, Jan.7, 1939).

pg: 95 "Compassion" by Thich Nhat Hanh — Excerpted from: *Peace is Every Step* (New York: Bantam Books, 1991).

pg: 100 "Learning a New Dance — A story from Venezuela" by Veronica Pelicaric, a trainer with Pace e Bene, and Leonor Andrade, a participant in a workshop. You can contact Veronica at *veronicapelicaric@paceebene.org*.

pg: 101 "Romaine Patterson's Angel's Wings" by Askari Mohammad for Time Classroom; *http://www.time.com/time/classroom/laramie/qa_patterson.html*; *The Bear Facts*, Alief-Hastings High School, Alief, Texas.

pg: 104 "Anti-Oppression Glossary." Many excerpts and adaptations from: Heidi Kiran Mehta's "Anti-Racist Glossary." "Internalized Privilege" by Bahia Asante Cabral, Margo Adair, and William Aal, *Tools for Change*; *www.toolsforchange.org*. "Rank" by Arnold Mindell, Ph.D., *Sitting in the Fire: Large Group Transformation Using Conflict and Diversity* (Portland, OR: Lao Tse Press, 1995). "Dominant Culture" by Antonia Darder, excerpted from *Culture and Power in the Classroom: A Critical Foundation for Bicultural Education*, 1991. "Power" by Ron Chisom & Michad Washington, in *Undoing Racism: A Philosophy of International Social Change* (People's Institute Press, 2nd ed, 1997). "Privileges" by *The Exchange Project, Peace Development Fund*, *www.peacedevelopmentfund.org*.

SESSION 6

pg: 112 "Be the change…" by Mohandas Gandhi.

pg: 112 "What's in the Bag" Exercise is an adaptation of an exercise created by Karen Ridd, which was itself a shorter version of an exercise entitled "Star Power: A Simulation Game" by R. Garry Shirts.

pg: 114 "Working Women" excerpted from *www.amazoncastle.com/feminism/myths.shtml*.

pg: 114 "Structural violence exits when…" adaptation of Johan Galtung's definition of structural violence. *www.transcend.com*.

pg: 115 "Three Forms of Power" by Starhawk. Excerpted from *Truth or Dare: Encounters with Power, Authority and Mystery* (HarperSanFrancisco, 1989), pp 14-15.

pg: 116 "What's a Doll to You." An excerpt from Cynthia Kaufman's book entitled *Ideas for Action — Relevant Theory for Radical Change* (South End Press, 2003) pp 121,129.

pg: 122 "The Journey from Indifference to Heart-Unity in the Struggle Against Structural Violence" by Ken Butigan. Adapted and expanded from the work of Leticia Nieto, Ph.D., "Stages of Allyship Skills," unpublished mss., Saint Martin's College, Lacey, WA. Also: Kenneth Boulding, *The Three Faces of Power* (Newbury Park: Sage, 1989), and Michael Nagler, Ph.D., "Peace Studies" lecture at Northwestern University, April, 2005.

pg: 124 "Why I quit the Clan: An Interview with CP Ellis" by Studs Terkel. Excerpted from *American Dreams: Lost and Found* (New York: New Press, 1999).

pg: 127 "Letter from Delano" by Cesar Chavez. *Christian Century* (Chicago: April 23, 1969).

SESSION 7

pg: 134 Opening by Lilla Watson, an Australian Aboriginal educator and activist based in Brisbane. Can be found at *home.vicnet.net.au/~aar/*

pg: 134 "Not everything that is faced can be changed, but nothing can be changed until it is faced." James Baldwin, author.

pg: 136 "The Townies vs. Outsiders." Based on an experience of Cynthia Stateman. She can be contacted at *cynjay@prodigy.net*.

pg: 138 Closing from Pam McAllister. Excerpted from *You Can't Kill the Spirit: Stories of Women and Nonviolence* (Phil: New Society Publishers, 1988).

pg: 142 "The Milgram Experiment" found in the wikipedia — free encyclopedia. *http://en.wikipedia.org/wiki/Stanley_Milgram*.

pg: 146 "The Spirit of the Redwoods" by Julia Butterfly Hill — Excerpted from "Spirit of the Redwoods:An Interview with Julia 'Butterfly' Hill" by Sara Marand, with thanks to Maerian Morris and Luna Media Services.

pg: 149 "Stages of Community Building" by Scott Peck, excerpted from *A Different Drum: Community Making and Peace* (New York: Adult Publishing Group, 1978), pp 86-106.

SESSION 8

pg: 156 Opening on "Obedience" adapted from an excerpt from Leonard Desroches', *Allow the Water: Anger, Fear, Power, Work, Sexuality, Community and the Spirituality and Practice of Nonviolence* (Canada: Trafford Publishing, 2004).

pg: 157 "Nonviolent Community Exercise" was adapted from Pom (a Thai grassroots environmental activist) and Karen Ridd (a Canadian activist).

Faison; edited by David H. Albert in 1978; Revised December 1983 by Bob Irwin; Scanned and adapted in 2001 by Peter Woodrow; Prepared for and posted on the Web by Randy Schutt, September 2002. *http://www.vernalproject.org/OPapers/WhyNV/WhyNonviolence1.html*

pg: 214   "Before a Drop of Blood Was Shed," excerpted from Jonathan Schell, *The Unconquerable World: Power, Nonviolence, and the Will of the People* (Metropolitan Books, 2003).

SESSION 11

pg: 221   "Farmer Workers' Prayer" by Cesar Chavez.

pg: 222   "Performing the Action Roleplay." Adapted from the Alternatives to Violence Project — *http://www.avpusa.org/*

pg: 223   "On Being Community" by Starhawk, excerpted from *Dreaming the Dark: Magic, Sex, and Politics* (Boston: Beacon Press, 1997).

pg: 224   "Loving the Police Out of the Intersection" by El Grupo. Written by Ken Preston-Pile as told to him by Leila Salazar and Bryan Neuberg.

pg: 229   "The Story of Vedran Smailovic" by Robert Fulghum. Excerpted from *Maybe (Maybe Not): Second Thoughts From a Secret Life* (New York: Villard Books, 1993).

pg: 231   "Circles" by Bill Cane — adapted from *Universal Church: Circles of Faith, Circles of Hope* (Maryknoll, NY: Orbis Books). Available at IF, 160 Sunflower Lane, Watsonville, CA 95076.

SESSION 12

pg: 238   "The day will come when..." by Pierre Teilhard de Chardin, excerpted from *The Evolution of Chastity*.

pg: 240   "Hitlers will come and go" from *The Collected Works of Mohandas Gandhi* (Vol;. 73, February 15, 1940).

pg: 240   "If the method of violence takes plenty of training ..." *The Collected Works of Mohandas Gandhi* (Vol. 67, May 4 and 14, 1938).

pg: 241   "There is nothing wrong with a traffic law that says ..." by Martin Luther King, Jr. *The Trumpet of Conscience* (New York: Harper & Row, 1967).

APPENDICES

pg: 272   "Steps of a Nonviolent Strategy." Adapted from Alvaro Diaz, *Lines of Strategy in the Nonviolent Struggle* (an essay published by Pace e Bene) and the work of Dr. Martin Luther King, Jr., summarized in "M.L. King: A Way of Nonviolence."

pg: 274   "Seven Strategic Assumptions of Successful Social Movements" by Bill Moyer. See *Doing Democracy* (Philadelphia: New Society Publishers, 2001).

pg: 277   "Essay on Preparing for Nonviolence" by Servicio Paz y Justicia. Reprinted from *Relentless Persistence: Nonviolent Action in Latin America* (New Society Publishers, 1991) — translated from the Portuguese by Phil McManus.

pg: 283   "The Universal Declaration of Human Rights." Adopted and proclaimed by the United Nation's General Assembly resolution 217 A (III) of 10 December 1948.

STAYING CONNECTED WITH ENGAGE

Engage: Exploring Nonviolent Living is developing a growing network of individuals and groups in the United States and around the world committed to creating a more nonviolent world. We invite you to be part of this network by staying connected with Pace e Bene and *Engage: Exploring Nonviolent Living*. To do so, please fill out the following form:

❏ Yes! Send me Pace e Bene's free quarterly newsletter!

❏ Yes! Send me free online updates and Pace e Bene's e-newsletter!

❏ I am interested in facilitating an *Engage* study program!

❏ I am interested in helping to host an *Engage* workshop!

❏ I am interested in becoming an *Engage* promoter. A promoter encourages individuals and groups in their community to use the *Engage* Study Program or to host *Engage* workshops. They also network and connect local people with *Engage* staff. *Engage* is developing a regional network of facilitators and promoters.

❏ I am interested in becoming an *Engage* workshop facilitator. The Engage Facilitator Training prepares people to lead this Study Program.

❏ I want to offer my skills/volunteer to help *Engage* staff develop this program. Areas of expertise needed include: marketing, graphic design, fundraising, web site development, etc.

❏ I want to make a tax-deductible donation to help this program thrive!

❏ $25 ❏ $50 ❏ $100 ❏ $250 ❏ $500 Other:

NAME:

ADDRESS:

CITY/STATE/ZIP:

ORGANIZATION OR AFFILIATION:

PHONE:

E-MAIL:

Please send this form to:
Pace e Bene
California Office
2501 Harrison Street, Oakland, CA 94612
510-535-2143
pbcal@paceebene.org
www.engagenonviolence.org

For additional book sales, contact the Pace e Bene Nevada Office:
1420 W. Bartlett, Las Vegas, NV 89106, 702-648-2281, *paceebene@paceebene.org*.

PACE E BENE RESOURCES

Franciscan Nonviolence: Stories, Reflections, Principles, Practices and Resources by Ken Butigan, Mary Litell, OSF and Louis Vitale, OFM

A collection of reflections on the stories of St. Francis and St. Clare that illuminate nonviolence as a relevant spiritual practice in today's world.
Available in English and Spanish, Paperback, 124 pages

Engage: Exploring Nonviolent Living by Laura Slattery, Ken Butigan, Veronica Pelicaric and Ken Preston-Pile

A twelve-part curriculum for group study in the spirituality and practice of active nonviolence. Paperback, 300+ pages

From Violence to Wholeness
by Ken Butigan with Patricia Bruno, OP

A ten-part curriculum for group study in the spirituality and practice of active nonviolence. Available in English and Spanish, Paperback, 170 pages

Roots of Violence in the U.S. Culture: A Diagnosis Toward Healing by Alain Richard, OFM

A groundbreaking book exploring the origins and current causes violence in US culture today. Paperback, 156 pages

Pilgrimage Through a Burning World
by Ken Butigan

A compelling and insightful account of the Nevada Desert Experience and its spiritually grounded nonviolent challenge to nuclear testing. Paperback, 234 pages

Peace Grows! by Rosemary Lynch, OSF and Mary Litell, OSF

This packet of materials developed as part of Pace e Bene's **Nurturing a Culture of Peace** program for use in workshops and retreats. Includes a curriculum, music CD, and a video (VHS or DVD). May be ordered separately or as a package.

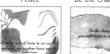

Peace | Be the Change... | Poppies | Leaves | Flowers/Pottery

Peace Cards Cards featuring ten different quotations from key visionaries of peace. Example: *"Every act of love is an act of peace, no matter how small"* — Mother Teresa.

Pace e Bene T-Shirts
FRONT: Pace e Bene logo BACK: *"For all those interested in nonviolence, let them join the experiment."* Mahatma Gandhi
100% cotton, white, union-made, pre-shrunk

ORDER FORM

Franciscan Nonviolence	_____ @ $12.95	_____
Engage: Exploring Nonviolent Living	_____ @ $22.00	_____
Ordering 5 or more:	_____ @ $18.00	_____
From Violence to Wholeness	_____ @ $19.95	_____
Ordering 5 or more:	_____ @ $15.95	_____
Roots of Violence	_____ @ $14.95	_____
Pilgrimage Through a Burning World	_____ @ $21.95	_____
Peace Grows!		
Curriculum only:	_____ @ $17.95	_____
Ordering 5 or more:	_____ @ $14.95	_____
Curriculum w/ CD and DVD:	_____ @ $49.95	_____
Curriculum w/ CD and VHS:	_____ @ $44.95	_____
Peace Grows! CD	_____ @ $12.95	_____
Peace Grows! DVD	_____ @ $24.95	_____
Peace Grows! VHS	_____ @ $19.95	_____
Packet of ten identical **Peace Cards**	_____ @ $12.00	_____

Please select one: ❑ Mahatma Gandhi ❑ Mother Teresa ❑ Nelson Mandela ❑ Albert Camus ❑ Wendell Berry ❑ Gregory Bateson ❑ Thich Nhat Hanh ❑ Dorothy Thompson

Packet of six assorted **Peace Cards**	_____ @ $8.00	_____

Peace Cards created by Sister Sharon Havelak, OSF, of the Sisters of St. Francis of Sylvania, Ohio

New! Packet of six **"Be the Change..."** Cards (Blank inside)	_____ @ $12.00	_____
New! Packet of six **"Be the Change..."** Cards (Christmas quote inside)	_____ @ $12.00	_____
New! Packet of six **Poppies** Cards	_____ @ $12.00	_____
New! Packet of six **Leaves** Cards	_____ @ $12.00	_____
New! Packet of six *Flowers/Pottery* Cards	_____ @ $12.00	_____
Pace e Bene T-Shirts	_____ @ $15.00	_____

Sizes (select one): ❑ S ❑ M ❑ L ❑ XL ❑ XXL
(Shipping and handling $3.00 first shirt; $1.00 each additional shirt.)

Shipping/Handling *(see top of next column)* ____   _____

TOTAL *(prepayment is required)* _____   _____

Yes! I want to support Pace e Bene with a donation of:

❑ $35 ❑ $25 ❑ $50 ❑ $100 ❑ $250 ❑ Other:_____

Shipping and handling:
All books: Add $4.00 for first copy, $1 for each additional copy
Nurturing a Culture of Peace: Curriculum only: $4 each
    Curriculum w/ CD and DVD or VHS: $6 each
Peace Grows: CD or DVD only: $2 each; VHS: $4 each

Prices subject to change without notice.

Name _____

Organization _____

Address _____

_____

City _____

State _____ Zip _____

Phone _____

E-mail _____

Enclosed: ❑ Check **(payable to Pace e Bene)**

Charge my: ❑ Visa ❑ Mastercard

Account # _____

Expiration Date _____

Signature _____

(MAIL ORDER) **Pace e Bene Nonviolence Service**
1420 W. Bartlett Ave.,
Las Vegas, NV 89106

(PHONE AND FAX ORDER) **(702) 648-2281**

(E-MAIL ORDER) **paceebene@paceebene.org**

www.paceebene.org
www.engagenonviolence.org

Engage Questionnaire

STUDY PROGRAM *(Before)*

Location/Group: _____ Date: _____ Number: _____

Thanks so much for taking a couple of minutes to fill out this survey. Your responses will help us to improve our trainings. All responses are strictly confidential.

Instructions: Please answer the following questions about violence and nonviolence according to the rating scales on the right. Circle only one of the numbers from 0-6 for each question. Please answer each question as honestly as possible. The whole questionnaire should take less than ten minutes, so you don't need to take too much time on any question. At the end, please offer any reactions to taking this survey, and ideas to help us improve it.

In your view, is violence more …	physical			equally both			psychological
	0	1	2	3	4	5	6

In your view, is violence more …	personal			equally both			social
	0	1	2	3	4	5	6

In your view, is violence more about …	attitudes			equally both			behaviors
	0	1	2	3	4	5	6

How often do you believe that …	Never			Sometimes			Always
… nonviolence works	0	1	2	3	4	5	6
… nonviolence is powerful	0	1	2	3	4	5	6
… nonviolence is strong and active	0	1	2	3	4	5	6
… nonviolence is transformative	0	1	2	3	4	5	6
… nonviolence is creative	0	1	2	3	4	5	6

To what degree do you know about …	None			Some			A Lot
… nonviolence in general	0	1	2	3	4	5	6
… the principles of nonviolence	0	1	2	3	4	5	6
… the history of nonviolence	0	1	2	3	4	5	6
… nonviolent social movements	0	1	2	3	4	5	6

How often are you willing to …	Never			Sometimes			Always
… talk about your experiences of violence	0	1	2	3	4	5	6
… talk about your experiences of nonviolence	0	1	2	3	4	5	6
… express your emotions of sadness, fear, and/or anger resulting from your experiences of violence	0	1	2	3	4	5	6

To what degree does nonviolence …	None			Some			A lot
… give you hope for the future	0	1	2	3	4	5	6
… offer you new options for your life	0	1	2	3	4	5	6
… help you see yourself in a more positive way	0	1	2	3	4	5	6
… help you recognize your need for change	0	1	2	3	4	5	6
… make you more willing and motivated to change	0	1	2	3	4	5	6

(CONTINUED ON REVERSE)

How often are you able to …	Never			Sometimes			Always
… resolve conflict nonviolently	0	1	2	3	4	5	6
… use ritual and spiritual expression to practice nonviolence	0	1	2	3	4	5	6
… practice nonviolence in your community	0	1	2	3	4	5	6

How much do you value …	None			Some			A Lot
… nonviolence (kind of obscure question)	0	1	2	3	4	5	6
… the well-being of all	0	1	2	3	4	5	6
… other peoples' truth	0	1	2	3	4	5	6
… the sacredness of all life	0	1	2	3	4	5	6

How often do you …	Never			Sometimes			Always
… act nonviolently toward others in everyday life	0	1	2	3	4	5	6
… act to ensure the well-being of your family	0	1	2	3	4	5	6
… act to ensure the well-being of your friends	0	1	2	3	4	5	6
… act to ensure the well-being of strangers	0	1	2	3	4	5	6
… act to ensure the well-being of your enemies	0	1	2	3	4	5	6
… intervene in conflicts to bring peaceful resolution	0	1	2	3	4	5	6
… cooperate with injustice	0	1	2	3	4	5	6

Please add any additional comments that you have below:

_____

_____

_____

_____

_____

_____

_____

_____

_____

_____

_____

_____

_____

_____

_____

**This questionnaire will be administered before you experience the *Engage* training and at the very end of the training. We will be measuring the differences in your responses between the beginning and the end to determine the change you have experienced as a result of this process. This information will help us to determine the effectiveness of the *Engage* training, and to improve the training as necessary. The data will be coded according to the number assigned at the top right corner, not your name. Also, the data will be analyzed collectively, not individually.

STUDY PROGRAM (*After*)